PACEMAKER®

United States History

Fourth Edition

TEACHER'S PLANNING GUIDE

GLOBE FEARON

Pearson Learning Group

REVIEWERS

We thank the following educators, who provided valuable comments
and suggestions during the development of this book:

Lawrence Broughton, North Chicago Community High School, North Chicago, Illinois
Dr. Dorothy Fields, Miami Dade Public Schools, Miami, Florida
Nadine Liebow, Indio High School, Indio, California
Paula Young, Orange County Public Schools, Orlando, Florida

Subject Area Consultant: Peter Myers, Department of History, Palo Alto College, San Antonio, Texas
Pacemaker® Curriculum Advisor: Stephen C. Larsen, formerly of The University of Texas at Austin
Writers: Becky Manfredini and Jenny Reznick, Kids at Heart

The following people have contributed to the development of this product:

Art & Design: Patricia Battipede, Evelyn Bauer, Susan Brorein, Jenifer Hixson, Angel Weyant
Editorial: Elaine Fay, Jane Petlinski, Jennie Rakos
Manufacturing: Mark Cirillo
Marketing: Katie Erezuma
Production: Irene Belinsky, Karen Edmonds, Suellen Leavy, Jennifer Murphy
Publishing Operations: Travis Bailey, Thomas Daning, Kate Matracia

ISBN 0-13-024425-2
Printed in the United States of America
1 2 3 4 5 6 7 8 9 10   07 06 05 04 03

1-800-321-3106
www.pearsonlearning.com

Contents

About the Teacher's Planning Guide   vi
More About Cooperative Group Activities   ix
More About Customizing for Individual Needs
        More About Assessment   xi
Individual Activity Rubric   xii
Group Activity Rubric   xiii

UNIT 1: SETTLING THE AMERICAS   **xiv**
Chapter 1: Early America (Prehistory–1492)   **1**
        Opening the Chapter   2
Section 1 The First Americans   3
        Building Your Skills: Reading a Timeline   4
Section 2 Europeans Explore New Routes   4
Section 3 Europeans Search For Wealth   5
        Closing the Chapter   6
        Assessing the Chapter   7

Chapter 2: Colonies Are Settled (1519–1733)   **8**
        Opening the Chapter   9
Section 1 Spain and France Begin Colonies   10
Section 2 The First English Colonies   11
        Connecting History and Science:
        Colonial Medicine   12
Section 3 The Growth of the Thirteen Colonies   12
        Closing the Chapter   13
        Assessing the Chapter   14

Chapter 3: Growth of Colonial Society
(1630–1760)   **15**
        Opening the Chapter   17
Section 1 Economies of the Colonies   17
Section 2 The Growth of Towns and Cities   18
        Voices From the Past: Anna Green Winslow   19
Section 3 New Ideas in the Colonies   19
        Closing the Chapter   20
        Assessing the Chapter   21

Chapter 4: The Struggle for Freedom
(1754–1783)   **22**
        Opening the Chapter   24
Section 1 The French and Indian War   24
Section 2 The Colonists Unite   25
Section 3 The War for Independence   26
        Voices From the Past: Thomas Jefferson   27
        Closing the Chapter   27
        Assessing the Chapter   28

UNIT 2: GROWTH OF A NEW NATION   **29**
Chapter 5: Building a New Government
(1780–1800)   **30**
        Opening the Chapter   31
Section 1 The Articles of Confederation   32
        Building Your Skills: Reading a Chart   33
Section 2 The Constitution and the Bill of Rights   33
Section 3 The New Government Begins   34
        Closing the Chapter   35
        Assessing the Chapter   36

Chapter 6: Economy and Expansion
(1789–1830)   **37**
        Opening the Chapter   38
Section 1 Growth and Conflict   39
Section 2 Northern Manufacturing   40
Section 3 Southern Agriculture   41
        Connecting History and Economics:
        The Cotton Gin   42
        Closing the Chapter   42
        Assessing the Chapter   43

Chapter 7: The Changing United States
(1820–1850)   **44**
        Opening the Chapter   45
Section 1 The Policies of Monroe and Jackson   46
        Voices From the Past: George M. Harkins   47
Section 2 Moving West   47
Section 3 Gold and California   48
        Closing the Chapter   49
        Assessing the Chapter   50

Chapter 8: Newcomers and New Ideas
(1820–1860)   **51**
        Opening the Chapter   52
Section 1 New Ways and New People   53
Section 2 Women and Political Rights   54
        Voices From the Past: Elizabeth Cady Stanton   55
Section 3 Working for Reform   55
        Closing the Chapter   56
        Assessing the Chapter   57

UNIT 3: A NATION DIVIDED   **58**
Chapter 9: North and South Disagree
(1820–1861)   **59**
    Opening the Chapter   60
Section 1 Expansion and Compromise   61
    Building Your Skills: Reading a Map   62
Section 2 Northerners Change Their Thinking   63
Section 3 Troubles Build   63
    Closing the Chapter   64
    Assessing the Chapter   65

Chapter 10: The Civil War (1861–1865)   **66**
    Opening the Chapter   67
Section 1 Preparing for War   68
Section 2 The Early Years of War   69
Section 3 Life at Home   70
    Connecting History and Technology:
    The Technology of War   70
Section 4 The End of the War   71
    Closing the Chapter   72
    Assessing the Chapter   73

Chapter 11: Rebuilding a Divided Nation
(1865–1877)   **74**
    Opening the Chapter   75
Section 1 Reconstruction Begins   76
Section 2 Congress Takes Charge   77
Section 3 African Americans Work
    to Build New Lives   78
    Voices From the Past: Tempie Cummins   79
    Closing the Chapter   79
    Assessing the Chapter   80

UNIT 4: A GROWING NATION   **81**
Chapter 12: Americans Move West (1860–1900)   **82**
    Opening the Chapter   83
Section 1 Joining the Nation Together   84
    Building Your Skills: Distinguishing
    Fact From Opinion   85
Section 2 Problems on the Great Plains   85
Section 3 Life on the Great Plains   86
    Closing the Chapter   87
    Assessing the Chapter   88

Chapter 13: The Growth of Industry (1860-1890)   **89**
    Opening the Chapter   90
Section 1 The Machine Age   91
Section 2 The Rise of Big Business   92
    Voices From the Past: Andrew Carnegie   93
Section 3 The Work Force   93
    Closing the Chapter   94
    Assessing the Chapter   95

Chapter 14: Cities and Immigration
(1880–1920)   **96**
    Opening the Chapter   97
Section 1 Immigrants From Southern
    and Eastern Europe   98
    Connecting History and Technology:
    Skyscrapers, Streetcars, and Bridges   99
Section 2 Immigrants From Asia and Latin America   99
Section 3 African Americans Move North   100
    Closing the Chapter   101
    Assessing the Chapter   102

UNIT 5: BECOMING A WORLD LEADER   **103**
Chapter 15: The Reformers (1870–1920)   **104**
    Opening the Chapter   105
Section 1 Early Reforms   106
    Building Your Skills:
    Identifying Cause and Effect   107
Section 2 The Progressives   108
Section 3 Reform Continues   108
    Closing the Chapter   109
    Assessing the Chapter   110

Chapter 16: Expansion Overseas (1890–1914)   **111**
    Opening the Chapter   112
Section 1 Looking Toward Asia   113
Section 2 The Spanish-American War   114
    Voices From the Past: José Martí   115
Section 3 The "Big Stick" and the Panama Canal   116
    Closing the Chapter   116
    Assessing the Chapter   117

Chapter 17: World War I (1914–1920)   **118**
    Opening the Chapter   120
Section 1 A World War Begins   121
Section 2 From Neutral to Declaration of War   121
    Connecting History and Language: Propaganda   122
Section 3 The Home Front   123
Section 4 The War to End All Wars   123
    Closing the Chapter   124
    Assessing the Chapter   125

UNIT 6: YEARS OF UNCERTAINTY   **126**
Chapter 18: The Roaring Twenties (1919–1929)   **127**
    Opening the Chapter   128
Section 1 A Time of Prosperity   129
    Building Your Skills: Comparing on a Chart   130
Section 2 Good Times For Many   130
Section 3 A Time of Change   131
    Closing the Chapter   132
    Assessing the Chapter   133

Chapter 19: The Great Depression (1929–1934) 134
Opening the Chapter 135
Section 1 The Nation's Troubled Economy 136
Section 2 Hard Times For Americans 137
Connecting History and the Environment:
The Dust Bowl 138
Section 3 The U.S. Government and the
Great Depression 138
Closing the Chapter 139
Assessing the Chapter 140

Chapter 20: The New Deal (1933–1941) 141
Opening the Chapter 142
Section 1 The New Deal Begins 143
Voices From the Past: Franklin D. Roosevelt 144
Section 2 Social Reform and the New Deal 144
Section 3 Americans at Leisure 145
Closing the Chapter 146
Assessing the Chapter 147

UNIT 7: THE UNITED STATES IN CRISIS 148
Chapter 21: Leading Up to War (1922–1941) 149
Opening the Chapter 150
Section 1 Dictators in Europe 151
Building Your Skills:
Recognizing a Point of View 152
Section 2 Japan Rises to Power 153
Section 3 From Isolation to Pearl Harbor 153
Closing the Chapter 154
Assessing the Chapter 155

Chapter 22: A World at War (1941–1945) 156
Opening the Chapter 157
Section 1 A World at War Again 158
Section 2 The Allies Strike Back 159
Section 3 The War at Home 160
Voices From the Past: Yuri Tateshi 161
Section 4 Winning the War 161
Closing the Chapter 162
Assessing the Chapter 163

Chapter 23: The Cold War (1945–1960) 164
Opening the Chapter 165
Section 1 The Cold War Begins 166
Connecting History and Government:
The United Nations 167
Section 2 Communism in Asia 168
Section 3 The Cold War at Home 168
Closing the Chapter 169
Assessing the Chapter 170

UNIT 8: A CHANGING SOCIETY 171
**Chapter 24: Changing Ways of Life
(1945–1960) 172**
Opening the Chapter 173
Section 1 Progress and Change 174
Building Your Skills: Reading a Graph 175
Section 2 The Growth of Popular Culture 175
Section 3 Eisenhower as President 176
Closing the Chapter 177
Assessing the Chapter 178

**Chapter 25: The Struggle For Equality
(1947–1965) 179**
Opening the Chapter 180
Section 1 Early Gains for Equal Rights 181
Section 2 Fighting for an Equal Education 182
Section 3 Protests and Marches for Equality 183
Voices From the Past:
Dr. Martin Luther King, Jr. 184
Closing the Chapter 184
Assessing the Chapter 185

**Chapter 26: A New Frontier and a Great Society
(1960–1968) 186**
Opening the Chapter 187
Section 1 The New Frontier 188
Connecting History and Science:
The Space Race 189
Section 2 Kennedy's Foreign Policy 189
Section 3 President Johnson and the Great Society 190
Closing the Chapter 191
Assessing the Chapter 192

UNIT 9: YEARS OF CHANGE 193
Chapter 27: Working for Change (1960–1975) 194
Opening the Chapter 195
Section 1 African American Protests 196
Building Your Skills: Writing an Essay 197
Section 2 Women Demand Equality 197
Section 3 Rights for All Americans 198
Closing the Chapter 199
Assessing the Chapter 200

Chapter 28: The Vietnam War (1960–1973) 201
Opening the Chapter 202
Section 1 A Distant War Divides a Nation 203
Voices From the Past: Protest Songs 204
Section 2 The Conflict Grows 204
Section 3 The War Ends 205
Closing the Chapter 206
Assessing the Chapter 207

Chapter 29: Entering a New Decade
(1970–1975)   **208**
    Opening the Chapter   209
Section 1 Ending the Cold War   210
Section 2 Changes at Home   211
Section 3 Watergate   212
    Connecting History and Economics: Inflation   212
    Closing the Chapter   213
    Assessing the Chapter   214

UNIT 10: FORWARD TO THE FUTURE   **215**
Chapter 30: Changes at Home
and Abroad (1976–1988)   **216**
    Opening the Chapter   217
Section 1 A New Kind of Leader   218
    Building Your Skills: Taking a Test   219
Section 2 Turning Toward Conservatism   220
Section 3 Acting in a Changing World   221
    Closing the Chapter   221
    Assessing the Chapter   222

Chapter 31: Progress and Problems
(1988-2000)   **223**
    Opening the Chapter   224
Section 1 Politics and Presidents   225
Section 2 A New Role in the World   226
Section 3 New Rights and Opportunities   227
    Voices From the Past: Maya Angelou   228
    Closing the Chapter   228
    Assessing the Chapter   229

Chapter 32: A New Century (1990–the future)   **230**
    Opening the Chapter   231
Section 1 Challenges for a New President   232
Section 2 Challenges for All Americans   233
    Closing the Chapter   234
    Assessing the Chapter   235

Bibliography   **236**

Activity Index   **241**

About Pacemaker®

Globe Fearon's Pacemaker® Curriculum has consistently supplied students and educators with materials and techniques that are accessible, predictable, and age-appropriate. Now, in the fourth edition of *United States History*, a wide array of components provide a solid, well-balanced approach to teaching history.

The Pacemaker® Components

The **Student Edition** presents content in manageable sections. All learning is reinforced through consistent review and application. The **Audio CD Program** offers the complete unabridged content of the Student Edition in audio format. Point-of-use strategies and answers are found in the **Teacher's Answer Edition**. Additional review and enrichment are provided in the **Workbook** and **Classroom Resource Binder**. The **Interactive Classroom Resources**, presented in CD-ROM format, is a valuable resource for teachers and students that allows for easy printing, customization, and review. Support for diverse classroom settings is available in the **Teacher's Planning Guide**. Content instruction is enhanced for your Spanish-speaking English-language learners with the **Spanish Supplement**. The **ESL/ELL Teacher's Guide** assists in the customization of lesson plans to support English-language learners. Answers to the Student Edition, Workbook, and Classroom Resource Binder are found in the separate **Answer Key**. Together, these components form a complete U.S. history program.

About This Guide

Benefits of the Planning Guide

Globe Fearon market research shows that using this *Teacher's Planning Guide* can be an important component for every social studies professional. The *Teacher's Planning Guide* is an innovative, comprehensive resource that brings together a wealth of ideas that allows you to plan and customize each lesson to meet your classroom needs.

This guide will help you tailor the teaching of history in a number of ways. You can:

✓ measure concept mastery.

✓ reteach and reinforce concepts.

✓ encourage cooperative learning.

✓ extend and enrich.

✓ assess in multiple formats.

Planning a chapter is made easy with convenient tools, such as Chapter at a Glance, Learning Objectives and Skills, Words to Know, and a Resource Planner.

Addressing the **mixed abilities** of a diverse classroom is possible with a variety of activities for cooperative groups, reteaching, reinforcement, and enrichment.

Meeting the **individual needs** of your students is accomplished through customizing strategies for ESL/LEP, visual, tactile, and auditory learners.

Assessing the diverse classroom can be accomplished using multiple methods, such as standard assessment tools, as well as alternative assessment ideas for lessons, chapters, and units.

Organization of the Planning Guide

This book is presented in a predictable and easy-to-use format. It is specifically organized to correlate to the units and chapters found in the *Pacemaker® United States History* curriculum. The outline below shows the main sections of this guide. A detailed discussion of each section follows.

Unit Overview
- Special Features
- Related Materials

Planning the Chapter
- Chapter at a Glance
- Learning Objectives and Skills
- Words to Know
- Resource Planner

Customizing the Chapter
- Opening the Chapter
- Supporting the Lessons
- Supporting the Features
- Closing the Chapter

Assessing the Chapter
- Traditional Assessment
- Alternative Assessment

Unit Assessment
- Review
- Standardized Test Preparation

Unit Overview

Special Features

The special features of each chapter in a unit are detailed in a chart on the unit overview page. They include *Building Your Skills, Connecting History and...,* and *Voices From the Past.*

Related Materials

Related Globe Fearon programs for remediation and enrichment are highlighted. This includes programs for enhancing content knowledge, appreciating cultural diversity, building skills, and establishing cross-curricular connections through literature. For more information on Globe Fearon materials and other programs, contact:
1-800-321-3106 or www.pearsonlearning.com

Planning the Chapter

Chapter at a Glance

Chapter at a Glance provides a quick preview of the sections and features in each chapter. It also provides page references to the *Pacemaker® United States History* Student Edition.

Learning Objectives and Skills

A list of learning objectives identifies the key concepts for students to demonstrate after completing the chapter. The list at the beginning of each chapter is identical. However, the starred section objectives are new. In each section, a starred (*) objective is further explored as a cooperative activity.

Social Studies Skills, Writing Skills, and Map and Chart Skills are included. These specific skills are addressed in various sections and features of the chapter.

Resource Planner

This chart lists resources from the components of *Pacemaker® United States History,* which include *Workbook Exercises, Teacher's Planning Guide,* and *Classroom Resource Binder.* These resources are referenced to each section being taught. Icons indicate materials appropriate for ⌂ reteaching, ⌇ reinforcement, and ⌂ enrichment. While planning the chapter, use this chart to give students the additional resources they need.

Customizing the Chapter

Opening the Chapter

This section provides activities, vocabulary preview, and chapter objectives information to help motivate students and to prepare them for the content ahead. All of these activities complement the material in the *Pacemaker® United States History* Student Edition. To make history relevant, students can complete the Photo Activity or Portfolio Project. To prepare them for the chapter, students can study the timeline, review Words to Know, and set goals using the Learning Objectives.

Supporting the Lessons

Selections from the *Pacemaker® United States History* Student Edition are supported with:

- Section Objectives
- Words to Know
- Cooperative Group Activities (see p. *ix*)
- Customizing for Individual Needs:
    ESL and Learning Styles (see p. *ix*)
- Mixed Abilities: Reteaching, Reinforcement, or Enrichment Activities (see p. *x*)
- Alternative Assessment (see p. *xi*)

    For more information about this topic, see the pages indicated.

Supporting the Features

Building Your Skills, Connecting History and..., and *Voices From the Past* are features in the *Pacemaker® United States History* Student Edition. They are supported by a variety of materials, including:

- Objectives
- Hands-on Activities
- Role-playing Activities
- Writing Activities

Closing the Chapter

This section provides ideas for summarizing and closing the chapter, including a vocabulary review and checking to ensure that goals were met. Ideas for using Test Tips are also provided. A final group activity provides for a cooperative application of the chapter content. All activities complement the material in the *Pacemaker® United States History* Student Edition.

Assessing the Chapter

Traditional Assessment
A variety of assessment tools are provided in the form of quizzes and tests in the Student Edition and in the *Classroom Resource Binder*.

Alternative Assessment
Many ideas are provided in the *Teacher's Planning Guide* for various modes of assessment. Teachers can interview students, have students apply the social studies concept to an oral or written task, or ask students to make real-life connections.
(See page xi for more on assessment.)

Unit Assessment

Each unit review in *Pacemaker® United States History* provides opportunities for cumulative assessment and standardized test practice. Resources for reviewing a unit are provided in the Student Edition and in the *Classroom Resource Binder*. Unit reviews in these components are in short-answer format. An additional Critical Thinking section provides open-ended and written-response questions.

More About Cooperative Group Activities

Using Materials
Reference materials are powerful learning tools in social studies. They can include anything from an encyclopedia to Internet sites. A suggested list of reference materials is provided in the Bibliography on pages 236–240.

Managing Successful Groups
Students learn best when called upon to collaborate with others in small groups. They learn to make decisions, work cooperatively, negotiate conflicts, and take risks. The teacher's role as facilitator is to create a supportive, effective learning environment.

Teacher Tips:
- Arrange groups so that all students are visible to you.
- Read aloud or post the *Student Rules* shown in next column for group work.
- Explain the task to be accomplished.

- Set a time limit for task completion.
- Avoid interrupting a group that is working well.
- Accept a higher noise level in the classroom.

Student Rules:
1. You are responsible for your own behavior.
2. You are expected to participate.
3. All ideas count.
4. You must help anyone in the group who asks for assistance.
5. Only ask for teacher help if all students in the group need help.

The cooperative group works best when each student participates in the activity. You may wish to assign the following roles to individual students in the group:
- Secretary/Recorder
- Coordinator/Manager
- Encourager

More About Customizing for Individual Needs

Each section is supported with ideas for customizing the cooperative group activity to meet the individual needs of your students. Activities can be completed during any phase of the sections.

ESL Notes
The ESL/LEP population includes not only students for whom English is a second language, but also native English speakers with limited proficiency. ESL notes provide specific activities that will help you address the needs of ESL and LEP (Limited English Proficient) students. Suggestions include hands-on activities, highlighting key words, encouraging peer tutoring and role-playing, labeling visuals, building on prior knowledge, and relating to everyday life. These strategies are designed to address the challenges facing LEP students in social studies where many of the key terms and concepts are not concrete. An early introduction to basic social studies terms such as *map, chart, graph, timeline,* and *cause-and-effect,* is useful to LEP students. Teachers can support students' learning by doing the following:
- Simplify language by using short sentences, pausing frequently, and choosing familiar terms to explain new concepts.
- Avoid slang and culturally coded words.

- Preteach essential vocabulary words for each lesson and limit the number of terms.
- Provide any background knowledge that will enable students to proceed.
- Draw on students' prior knowledge and build their self-esteem by encouraging them to share their information. Encourage students to draw on knowledge of their native country.

Teaching in a language-diverse classroom may seem overwhelming at first. However, there are strategies that work well with students with special needs. Effective strategies that include working in pairs, working with English proficient speakers, or using prior knowledge are included in this guide.

Learning Styles

Learning Styles address the needs of visual, tactile, and auditory learners. Note the following icons:

 Visual Learner: Activities that help a student to see the section concept.

 Tactile Learner: Activities that enable a student to perform hands-on tasks and manipulate objects to absorb the section concept.

 Auditory Learner: Activities that enable a student to hear and verbalize information about the section concept.

Challenged Writing Abilities

Throughout this guide, various alternatives are used to facilitate students with challenged writing abilities. Some of these alternatives include oral presentations, working in pairs, or assigning one group member to make an oral or written report during a group project. These options can be used to customize other activities in this guide in order to better meet the individual needs of each student.

Assessing Students' Writing

One way to assess students' writing is through a process called focused holistic scoring. This process uses specific criteria to score the writing sample as a whole. A score of 1 to 4 is given, with 4 being the highest score. Various writing opportunities are provided throughout the *Pacemaker® United States History* program. The writing prompts can be categorized according to the following modes: descriptive, expository, classificatory, and persuasive. A **descriptive** paragraph involves describing a real or imagined person, place, thing, event, or idea.

An **expository** paragraph involves giving step-by-step instructions explaining how to do something. A **classificatory** paragraph involves comparing and contrasting two ideas or listing the pros and cons of an idea. A **persuasive** paragraph involves choosing one side of an issue and supporting that side in a convincing way. The following general criteria can be used to score the writing activities.

Score of 4 The paragraph has a topic sentence, supporting details, and a concluding sentence. Specific details are given for all aspects of the topic. Ideas are well organized and flow smoothly. Sentence structure is varied. Spelling and mechanical errors are few.

Score of 3 The paragraph addresses the topic and remains focused. Many details are given but are unevenly elaborated. Organization is logical, but a few inconsistencies may exist. Sentence structure and word choice are effective. Spelling and mechanical errors exist but do not interfere with understanding the paragraph.

Score of 2 The paragraph minimally describes the topic. Little or no elaboration is provided for details. Some irrelevant details may be given. Sentence structure and word choice are poor or repetitive. Spelling and mechanical errors impede comprehension.

Score of 1 The paragraph addresses the topic but provides little information or becomes unfocused. Ideas are unorganized and confusing. Sentences are incomplete. Word choice is poor and not descriptive. Spelling and mechanical errors impede comprehension.

More About Mixed Abilities

Reteaching Activities
These activities present another way to teach the section concept by having students use different strategies or models to analyze the information and draw conclusions.

Reinforcement Activities
Students engage in activities that provide additional opportunities to increase comprehension of a section concept.

Enrichment Activities
Enrichment activities encourage the application of newly acquired knowledge to critical thinking tasks.

More About Assessment

Using Alternative Assessment

The *Teacher's Planning Guide* includes an Alternative Assessment for each lesson in the Student Edition. The Alternative Assessment can be used in addition to the traditional paper and pencil assessment to provide a complete picture of student achievement. It provides a different way to check students' mastery of a concept. Alternative Assessment activities are provided in the *Teacher's Planning Guide* for assessing each chapter's objectives.

Making Portfolios

A student's portfolio is a collection of his or her work over a school year. The portfolio provides a long-term record of the student's best efforts, progress, and achievement. Some suggested items to be included in a portfolio are:

1. Book cover with design
2. Table of contents
3. Letter explaining the contents to the viewer
4. Autobiography
5. Paper and pencil tests with student correction of errors
6. Performance assessments
7. Homework samples
8. Journals and writing samples
9. Project results
10. Teacher and student observations

The portfolio of work should be a quality presentation. The following scoring sheet should be provided for student self-assessment:

	POINTS
• Cover design with name, class, title	10
• Table of contents	10
• Cover letter	10
• Autobiography	10
• Includes all required sections	10
• Organized/neat/easy to read	20
• Quality presentation/demonstration of effort	20
• Above and beyond minimum	10

The following is a suggested breakdown of grades for the year that incorporates both traditional and alternative assessment:

• Exams, including the final	30%
• Corrections of exams	5%
• Writing assignments	20%
• Class projects	20%
• Group work, class participation	10%
• Portfolio	5%
• Homework	10%

Using Individual and Group Activity Rubrics

The Individual Activity Rubric and the Group Activity Rubric on pages xii and xiii can be used to score the Portfolio Project and group activities from the Student Edition. They can also be used to assess the individual and cooperative group activities provided in this guide.

The first eight criteria on each rubric are generic. The last two criteria are left blank so that the rubric can be customized for a specific activity or task. This guide gives two suggested criteria for every Portfolio Project and every Group Activity from the *Pacemaker® United States History* Student Edition.

To use either of the rubrics, photocopy the blank master once. Write the two specific criteria in the last boxes. Copy this customized version, making one for each student or group of students. When students complete an activity, evaluate how well each criterion was met. Add the points, and convert to the preferred grading system.

Another way to use the rubric is to have students grade themselves. They can exchange papers with a teammate or grade their own activity. Peer- and self-assessment are valuable learning experiences for students.

Individual Activity Rubric

Name _____ Date _____

Chapter Number _____ Activity _____

Directions
Check ✓ one box in a column to finish each sentence.
Give each check ✓ the assigned number of points.
Add the points in each column. Write the sum. Then add across to find the total score.

POINTS	10	9	8	7	6
For this activity, **Student's** **name** _____	all of the time	most of the time	half of the time	less than half of the time	none of the time
followed directions					
asked questions when help was needed					
worked independently when required					
used appropriate resources and materials					
completed assigned tasks					
showed an understanding of the content					
presented materials without errors					
explained thinking with support					
_____					
_____					
POINTS	+	+	+	+	+ =

TOTAL SCORE

Group Activity Rubric

Name _____ Date _____

Chapter Number _____ Activity _____

Directions

Check ✓ one box in a column to finish each sentence.

Give each check ✓ the assigned number of points.

Add the points in each column. Write the sum. Then add across to find the total score.

POINTS	10	9	8	7	6
For this activity, **Student's** **name** _____	all of the time	most of the time	half of the time	less than half of the time	none of the time
followed directions					
participated in group discussions					
listened carefully to others					
used appropriate resources and materials					
completed assigned tasks					
showed an understanding of the content					
presented materials without errors					
explained thinking with support					
_____					
_____					
POINTS	+	+	+	+	+ =

TOTAL SCORE

Unit Settling the Americas

CHAPTER 1	PORTFOLIO PROJECT	BUILDING YOUR SKILLS	GROUP ACTIVITY	TIMELINE
Early America Prehistory–1492	Series of Letters	Reading a Timeline	Performance of a Scene	Early America

CHAPTER 2	PORTFOLIO PROJECT	CONNECTING HISTORY AND...	GROUP ACTIVITY	TIMELINE
Colonies Are Settled 1519–1733	Travel Journal	Science: Colonial Medicine	Writing a Compact	Settlement of the Americas

CHAPTER 3	PORTFOLIO PROJECT	VOICES FROM THE PAST	GROUP ACTIVITY	TIMELINE
Growth of Colonial Society 1630–1760	Diary Entry	Anna Green Winslow	Performance of a Skit	The Colonies Grow and Change

CHAPTER 4	PORTFOLIO PROJECT	VOICES FROM THE PAST	GROUP ACTIVITY	TIMELINE
The Struggle for Freedom 1754–1783	News Articles	Thomas Jefferson	Role-playing	The Road to Freedom

RELATED MATERIALS

These are some of the Globe Fearon books that can be used to enrich and extend the material in this unit.

Content ▶

Globe Mosaic of American History: Hispanic America to 1776 Focus on exploration in the Americas with Chapter 2.

Literature ▶

Pacemaker® Adapted Classics: The Scarlet Letter Written by Nathaniel Hawthorne. Provides a literary perspective on colonial life.

Skills ▶

Unlocking the Constitution and Declaration of Independence Both documents are presented in their original format and in a simplified narrative to help student understanding.

Chapter 1 • **Early America** Prehistory–1492

Chapter at a Glance

SE page

2		*Opening the Chapter and Portfolio Project*
4	SECTION 1	**The First Americans**
10		*Building Your Skills: Reading a Timeline*
11	SECTION 2	**Europeans Explore New Routes**
14	SECTION 3	**Europeans Search for Wealth**
18		*Chapter Review and Group Activity*

Learning Objectives

- Explain how the first people may have reached the Americas.
- Discuss how the first people may have lived in the Americas.
- Identify the different types of Native American civilizations.
- Describe the reasons Europeans came to the Americas.

Social Studies Skills

- Read a timeline.
- Use a timeline to identify A.D. and B.C. entries.
- Create a timeline of the months of the school year, including important events.
- Act out a scene in which Columbus and his crew ask for money for their voyages.

Writing Skills

- Write a series of letters describing a voyage to an unknown land.
- Write a paragraph about a day in the life of a Mayan worker.
- Write a journal entry from the perspective of a Viking navigator.
- Write a journal entry from the perspective of a sailor on one of Columbus's ships.

Map and Chart Skills

- Use a map to name the present-day continents that the land bridge connected.
- Use a map to locate the Maya, Inca, and Aztec civilizations.
- Use a map to locate the West African kingdoms of Ghana, Mali, and Songhai.
- Use a chart to identify information about explorers and their journeys.

Resource Planner

Chapter 1 Early America	Use the Program Resources below for reteaching, reinforcement, and enrichment. Additional activities for customizing the lessons can be found in this guide. Key Reteaching = ⤺ Reinforcement = ⬇ Enrichment = ⤴

Sections	Program Resources		
	Workbook Exercises	Teacher's Planning Guide	Classroom Resource Binder
The First Americans	1, 2	⤺ p. 3	⤴ Outline Map 5, 6 *North America* *South America*
Building Your Skills: **Reading a Timeline**		⤺ p. 4	Feature Practice 3, 4 ⬇ *Reading a Timeline* ⬇ Graphic Organizer 8 *Timeline*
Europeans Explore New Routes	3	⤺ p. 4	⤺ Outline Map 5, 8 *North America* *Asia*
Europeans Search for Wealth	4	⤴ p. 5	⤴ Outline Map 5, 7 *North America* *Africa*
Chapter 1 Review		p. 6	⬇ Transparency 1 *Voyages of Discovery* ⤺ Concept Builder 1 *Early America* ⬇ Words to Know 1 ⤺ Challenge 5 ⬇ Chapter Tests A & B, 6, 7

Customizing the Chapter

Opening the Chapter
Student Edition, pages 2–3

Photo Activity

Have students look at the photos of the Anasazi pottery and the Anasazi village in present-day Arizona. Ask students what type of climate and weather conditions they think the Anasazi people experienced. Help students conclude that the climate was arid and hot. Explain that the Anasazi were master builders, creating multistoried villages out of mud and rock. The cliff dwellings protected the people from the weather.

Words to Know

Review the Words to Know on page 3 of the Student Edition. To help students remember the words, invite pairs to write down what they think each word means. Then have the pairs look up each word in the Glossary in the Student Edition to verify the accuracy of their definitions. Have each student keep a log of new vocabulary terms for each chapter.

The following words and definitions are covered in this chapter:

nomad a person who travels all the time in search of food

glacier a huge sheet of moving ice

civilization the way of life of a people in one place and time

empire the territories and people under the control of one ruler

colony a settlement ruled by people from another land

navigator a person who plans the direction of a ship

compass an instrument that shows direction

geography the study of climates and land forms

astronomy the study of stars and planets

Portfolio Project

Summary: Students write a series of letters from the perspective of an explorer of an unknown land.

Procedure: Ask students to research an explorer. Students can then assume the role of the explorer by writing a series of letters to family members describing expectations before the voyage, problems during the voyage itself, and what was discovered.

Assessment: Use the Individual Activity Rubric on page *xii* of this guide. Fill in the rubric with the additional information below. For this project, students should have

- written at least three letters.
- written journal entries from the perspective of an explorer.

Learning Objectives

Review the Learning Objectives on page 3 of the Student Edition before starting this chapter. Students can use the list as a learning guide. Suggest they write the objectives in a journal or use the Chapter Goals and Self-Check worksheet found on page PA 6 of the Classroom Resource Binder.

After reading each section of the chapter, have students write an example of what they learned under the appropriate objective. Suggest that students use these worksheets as a practice guide to help them study for the chapter test.

Timeline

Use the timeline to discuss the sequence of events in this chapter. Point out the timeline's title, its time span, and the intervals. After students have read the chapter, have them review the timeline and suggest additional entries.

SECTION 1: The First Americans
Student Edition, pages 4–9

Section Objectives

- Discuss how the first people may have reached the Americas.
- Describe how the lives of Native Americans changed after the Ice Age.
- Identify Native American civilizations in Mexico and in Central and South America.
- * Explain why Native American groups in North America lived in different ways.

Words to Know

nomad, glacier, civilization, empire

Cooperative Group Activity

Haiku Poems About Time Past

Material: Who, What, Where, When, Why, How chart (Classroom Resource Binder, page GO 7)

Procedure: Explain that a haiku poem is an unrhymed verse of Japanese origin that follows this pattern: First line: 5 syllables; second line: 7 syllables; third line: 5 syllables. Divide the class into four groups, and assign each group one of the following ancient civilizations: Olmec, Maya, Inca, and Aztec.

- Groups read about their assigned Native American civilization and create a chart by filling in the following: Who were they? What did they build? Where did they live? When did they live? How did they survive?
- Groups use the information to write a haiku poem about their Native American civilization.
- Students choose two speakers from their group to share the chart and poem with the rest of the class.

Example: The Maya
They built stone temples. (5 syllables)
They carved twenty-ton statues. (7 syllables)
Their home? Mexico. (5 syllables)

Customizing the Activity for Individual Needs

ESL To help students write a haiku, review the definition of a syllable—a part of a word that has one vowel sound. Then have students work in pairs to write their haikus. Remind partners to make sure that their poems follow the haiku syllable pattern.

Learning Styles Students can:

 determine if they have the correct number of syllables by underlining each syllable.

 determine if they have the correct number of syllables by clapping out the syllables in their haiku.

 use a tape recorder to record an oral presentation of their haiku and review the number of syllables in their presentation.

Enrichment Activity

Remind students that the Olmecs developed a writing system that incorporated both symbols and images to represent ideas. Invite volunteers to come to the chalkboard and create symbols and images that could visually represent the ancient civilizations, such as a temple or calendar. Divide the class into four groups and have each group write an interesting fact about their Native American civilization. Students in those groups draw symbols and images to show what their fact was about. Have other groups try to interpret the message.

Alternative Assessment

Students can choose one of the Native American civilizations and write a short paragraph from the perspective of a worker in that society, describing a typical day.

BUILDING YOUR SKILLS: Reading a Timeline
Student Edition, page 10

Objectives

- Social Studies Skill: Use a timeline to organize important events that happened in one day, one week, and one year.
- Social Studies Skill: Compare and contrast materials presented in timelines.

Activities

Hour by Hour
Materials: chart paper; markers

Procedure: Have students choose one day during the school week and create a timeline of six or more events from 7:00 A.M. to 7:00 P.M. Students can share their timelines with the class, comparing and contrasting their day with their classmates'.

Week at a Glance
Materials: chart paper; markers

Procedure: Invite students to create a timeline of their week by choosing the most important event that occurred each day of the seven-day period.

My Life So Far
Materials: chart paper; markers

Procedure: Have students document their own personal history by creating a timeline from birth. Encourage them to think about an event that occurred each year in their lives, such as learning to walk or starting school.

Practice

Have students complete Building Your Skills: Reading a Timeline on page 3 of the Classroom Resource Binder.

SECTION 2: Europeans Explore New Routes
Student Edition, pages 11–13

Section Objectives

- Discuss the reasons why the Vikings explored North America.
- Explain why the colony of Vinland did not succeed.
- Describe what Leif Ericson and Marco Polo learned through their explorations.

Words to Know

colony, navigator

Cooperative Group Activity

Look to the East . . . Look to the West

Materials: reference materials (Unit 1 Bibliography and Internet sites, pages 236–240); Description Web (Classroom Resource Binder, page GO 3); butcher paper; markers

Procedure: Remind students that as Native American empires were growing, Europeans began to explore the world. Students will research the explorations of Leif Ericson, who traveled west, and Marco Polo, who traveled east. Divide the class into two groups.

- Groups use books and Internet sites to research their explorers.
- Groups complete their own Description Web by writing down important facts about the explorer.
- Students use butcher paper to write facts on their description web and name them "Look to the East" or "Look to the West," depending on their group's explorer.
- Student groups present their information to the rest of the class. Encourage students to take notes as they listen to each presentation.

Customizing the Activity for Individual Needs

ESL To help students understand the concept of exploration, have them complete a Description Web about the exploration of their native country. Then have students share their Description Webs with the class. Lead a class discussion on the similarities and differences between the exploration of the Americas and the exploration of the ESL students' countries.

Learning Styles Students can:

 find a map in a reference book that shows the route of their group's explorer. Encourage students to add facts about the explorer to their group's Description Web based on what they learned from the map.

 draw a picture that illustrates Leif Ericson or Marco Polo exploring new lands. The illustration can be used in the Description Web their group is creating.

 work with their group to develop an oral tale about the exploration their group is researching.

Enrichment Activity

Have individual students assume the role of Marco Polo returning from a trip to Asia. Polo explains that he needs to find people to help him return to Asia and bring back treasures. As Polo, each student makes a persuasive speech that will entice people to join him.

Alternative Assessment

Students can demonstrate their knowledge of European exploration by writing two journal entries, one for Leif Ericson and one for Marco Polo. Have them describe where each explorer went and what each explorer discovered on his journey.

SECTION 3: Europeans Search for Wealth
Student Edition, pages 14–17

Section Objectives

- Discuss the reasons why the Portuguese explored Africa.
- Explain what happened when Columbus landed in North America.
- Explain how Columbus financed his exploration.

Words to Know

compass, geography, astronomy

Cooperative Group Activity

Pen a Letter

Materials: tea-stained paper; ribbon

Procedure: Review with students Columbus's struggle to find rulers to finance his voyage across the Atlantic. Then divide the class into pairs and have each pair write a letter from the point of view of Columbus trying to convince King Ferdinand and Queen Isabella of Spain to sponsor a trip across the Atlantic.

- Partners create a list of what to include in their letter, such as the purpose of the trip, what they hope to find, and what they will need for the voyage, such as ships, supplies, and crew members.
- Partners draft letters and hand write them on tea-stained paper. The paper is then rolled up and tied with ribbon.

- One partner assumes the role of Columbus by reading the letter to the rest of the class. Students then decide whether to finance the trip.

Customizing the Activity for Individual Needs

ESL To help students learn new vocabulary words, have them write unfamiliar words on index cards. They should choose words such as *geography* and *compass* from their group's letter. Then pair English-proficient students with ESL students to write definitions for the unfamiliar words on the other side of the index cards. ESL students should use the index cards like flash cards to study the words and their definitions.

Learning Styles Students can:

 fill out a Description Web (Classroom Resource Binder, page GO 3) with the items they will need for their voyage.

 work in pairs to cut out pictures from magazines of items to include on the journey and paste them to index cards. They can then write the name of each item on the back of the card and quiz one another.

 write and tape record a 30-second news flash that begins with "...This just in...." Suggest that the news flash occur when the King and Queen of Spain have just agreed to sponsor Columbus's voyage.

Reteaching Activity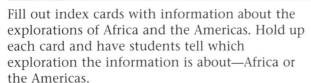

Fill out index cards with information about the explorations of Africa and the Americas. Hold up each card and have students tell which exploration the information is about—Africa or the Americas.

Alternative Assessment

Students can write ten true/false questions about Europeans' search for wealth. Have students exchange papers with a partner. Students then answer the questions and work with partners to verify answers.

Example: Columbus found a shorter route to Asia.
Answer: false

Chapter Vocabulary

Review with students the Words to Know on page 3 of the Student Edition. Then have students quiz each other in pairs.

Have students complete the Vocabulary Review on page 18 of the Student Edition by completing each sentence with a term from the list.

For more vocabulary practice, have them complete the vocabulary exercise on page 1 of the Classroom Resource Binder.

Test Tip

As students study for the Chapter Quiz, have them use a dictionary to look up words they do not understand.

Learning Objectives

Have students review their Chapter Goals and Self-Check worksheet found on page PA 6 of the Classroom Resource Binder. They can check off the goal they have reached. Note that each section of the quiz corresponds to a Learning Objective.

Group Activity

Summary: Students act out scenes in which Columbus asks the rulers of England, Portugal, and Spain to finance his trip.

Procedure: Have student groups write out their scene in play format. Explain to the groups that the dialogue should be written in the first person.

Assessment: Use the Group Activity Rubric on page *xiii* of this guide. You may wish to share this rubric with students at the beginning of the activity. Fill in the rubric with the additional information below. For this project, students should have

- performed cohesive scenes between Columbus and the three rulers.
- included Columbus and his crew in their scene.

RELATED MATERIALS See the Unit Overview page for related Globe Fearon books that can be used to enrich and extend the materials in the chapter.

Traditional Assessment

Chapter Quiz

The Chapter Quiz on page 19 of the Student Edition can be used as an open-book test, a closed-book test, or a homework assignment. Use the quiz to identify concepts in the chapter that students need to review. Chapter Tests can be found in the Classroom Resource Binder on pages 6–7. Workbook pages 1–5 can be used for additional practice.

Chapter Tests

Use Chapter Tests A and B on pages 6–7 in the Classroom Resource Binder to further assess mastery of chapter concepts.

Additional Resources

Use the Resource Planner on page 2 of this guide to assign additional exercises from the Classroom Resource Binder and Workbook.

Alternative Assessment

Student Interview

Write the names of five explorers on the chalkboard. Ask:

• For which country did this person explore?
• What areas were explored?
• What was the outcome of this exploration?
• What difficulties did this explorer experience?

Presentation

Have students explain the concept of exploration to the class. Ask students to illustrate the concept and give two examples. Remind students that they can use maps and pictures in their presentation.

Chapter 2 · **Colonies Are Settled** 1519–1733

Chapter at a Glance

SE page

20 *Opening the Chapter and Portfolio Project*

22 SECTION 1 Spain and France Begin Colonies

26 SECTION 2 The First English Colonies

31 *Connecting History and Science: Colonial Medicine*

32 SECTION 3 The Growth of the Thirteen Colonies

38 *Chapter Review and Group Activity*

Learning Objectives

- Explain the defeat of the Aztec Empire by Spanish conquerors.
- Identify reasons for Spanish and French settlements in the Americas.
- Describe the English colonies at Jamestown, Plymouth, and Massachusetts Bay.
- Identify the colonies in the New England, Middle, and Southern regions.

Social Studies Skills

- Compare and contrast medical practices in colonial times with present technology.
- Read a timeline that illustrates the settling of the Americas between 1519 and 1750.
- Describe the people, economy, and geography of the New England, Middle, and Southern colonies.

Writing Skills

- Write a list of reasons for going to the Americas.
- Write a class compact and explain how these rules will benefit each class member.
- Write a pamphlet describing what life would be like living in one of the thirteen colonies.

Map and Chart Skills

- Use a map to locate the New England, Middle, and Southern colonies.
- Locate and name a geographical feature west of the colonies.
- Use a chart to list the Spanish explorers who conquered land in the Americas.

Resource Planner

Chapter 2 Colonies Are Settled	Use the Program Resources below for reteaching, reinforcement, and enrichment. Additional activities for customizing the lessons can be found in this guide.

Key
Reteaching = ⌒   Reinforcement = ⇩   Enrichment = ⌒

Sections	Program Resources		
	Workbook Exercises	Teacher's Planning Guide	Classroom Resource Binder
Spain and France Begin Colonies	6	⌒ p. 10	⌒ Outline Map 5 North America
The First English Colonies	7	⌒ p. 11	⌒ Transparency 13 U.S. Political Outline
Connecting History and Science: Colonial Medicine		⌒ p. 12	⌒ Feature Practice 10 Connecting History and Science: Making Soap
The Growth of the Thirteen Colonies	8, 9	⇩ p. 12	⇩ Transparency 2 The Thirteen Colonies, 1750
Chapter 2 Review		p. 13	⇩ Words to Know 8 ⌒ Challenge 11 ⇩ Chapter Tests A & B, 12, 13

Customizing the Chapter

Opening the Chapter
Student Edition, pages 20–21

Photo Activity

Invite students to guess why a cradle was selected to accompany a painting of Pilgrims from the *Mayflower*. Explain that the cradle was supposedly brought on the *Mayflower* by Susanna and William White who were anticipating the birth of their child. Mention that their son was born on the *Mayflower* in 1620 after the ship landed in Provincetown Harbor. Because of this momentous journey, the White's named their son Peregrine, which means "traveler" or "pilgrim." Because space and weight were concerns, the Pilgrims could bring very few prized possessions. Ask students what they would have brought with them if they had been traveling on the *Mayflower*. Make a class list of all the possessions, ranking the items according to the ones students think are most important. Then have students categorize the items according to their purpose.

Words to Know

Review the Words to Know on page 21 of the Student Edition. To help students remember the words, invite pairs to find the words in the Glossary on page 660. Have them take turns giving clues that tell about a vocabulary term, without using any part of the term itself. Ask each pair of students to keep track of the number of clues it takes to guess each key term.

The following words and definitions are covered in this chapter:

conquer to take over and control

mission a settlement, built by a church, from which people teach their religion to others

convert to change from one religion or belief to another

joint-stock company a company in which people give money to share costs

charter a written agreement giving certain rights

cash crop crop grown for sale rather than for use by a farmer

indentured servant a person who signs a contract to work for others

treaty a written agreement between two or more nations

debtor a person who owes money to others

Portfolio Project

Summary: Through journal entries, students describe the people, economy, and geography found in the New England, Middle, and Southern colonies.

Materials: reference materials (Unit 1 Bibliography and Internet sites, pages 236–240)

Procedure: Take a class trip to the library or gather reference materials about each of the three regions. Divide the class into three groups representing each of the three colonial regions. Rotate the reference materials so students can take notes on their region. Have students assume the role of a merchant looking for new goods in each region. Students then use their notes to write a journal entry. Students share their entries with the class.

Assessment: Use the Individual Activity Rubric on page *xii* of this guide. Fill in the rubric with the additional information below. For this project, students should have

• used a variety of sources.
• made appropriate and accurate notes.
• presented the material in a clear and concise manner.

Learning Objectives

Review the Learning Objectives on page 21 of the Student Edition before starting this chapter. Students can use the objectives as a learning guide. Suggest that they write the objectives in a journal

or use the Chapter Goals Worksheet found on page PA 6 in the Classroom Resource Binder. After reading each section of the chapter, have students write an example of what they learned about under the appropriate objective. Suggest that students use these worksheets as a practice guide to help them study for the chapter test.

SECTION 1: Spain and France Begin Colonies
Student Edition, pages 22–25

Section Objectives
• Explain the growth of Spain's power in the Americas.
• Describe French exploration in North America.
∗ Compare and contrast how the Spanish and French explorers treated the Native Americans.

Words to Know
conquer, mission, convert

Cooperative Group Activity

Getting Along
Materials: reference materials (Unit 2 Bibliography and Internet sites, pages 236–240); poster paper; markers

Procedure: Explain that both Spanish and French explorers formed different kinds of relationships with the Native Americans. Have students do additional research on Spanish and French exploration in the Americas. Divide students into small groups.

• Each group discusses the ways that the Spanish and French treated the Native Americans.
• Group members assume the role of an explorer in a new land who is meeting the inhabitants for the first time. They then discuss potential problems and explain how to resolve them.
• Groups choose a spokesperson to share with the rest of the class how the group will resolve the problems.

Customizing the Activity for Individual Needs
ESL ESL students can create a list of problems they or their relatives faced as newcomers to a country. Then pair ESL students with English-proficient students to work on solutions to the problems they have listed.

Learning Styles Students can:

 use a Venn diagram to compare and contrast the French and Spanish treatment of Native Americans.

 sort index cards that list problems faced by the Spanish and Native Americans and the solutions. Working in pairs, students try to match each problem with its solution.

 work in pairs to take the role of either a Spanish explorer or a Native American and brainstorm a set of rules that will help them to live and work together.

Enrichment Activity

Explain that one of the ways French explorers worked cooperatively with the Native Americans was to set up trading posts in North America to obtain furs. These furs were sold for a huge profit in Europe and were used for clothing. In turn, the French bartered beads, tools, firearms, brass, and iron kettles with the Native Americans in exchange for the furs. Ask students to set up a trading post by bringing in small items to exchange, such as baseball cards and key chains. Students then explain how the customer and owner need to work cooperatively. Have students list the advantages and disadvantages that trading has over purchasing an item with money.

Alternative Assessment

Students can assume the role of Native Americans to write a short paragraph about their first encounter with explorers.

SECTION 2: The First English Colonies
Student Edition, pages 26–30

Section Objectives

* Describe life in the English colonies at Jamestown, Plymouth, and Massachusetts Bay.
* Explain how the tobacco crop helped Jamestown survive and grow as a colony.
* Explain how Native Americans helped the Pilgrims.
* Describe how the Puritans treated others who lived in their colony.

Words to Know

joint-stock company, charter, cash crop, indentured servant

Cooperative Group Activity

Read All About It!

Materials: reference materials (Unit 1 Bibliography and Internet sites, pages 236–240); computer

Procedure: Tell students they are reporters based in the colonies of Jamestown, Plymouth, and Massachusetts Bay. Explain that they are responsible for writing newspaper articles to inform the people in England about the colonies. Review the questions a news article answers: *who, what, where, when, how,* and *why.* Divide the class into three groups and assign each a news headline such as: *Native Americans Save Pilgrims; Settlers Stay at Massachusetts Bay Colony; Work at Jamestown.* Students may use the Student Edition or additional research to help them write their group's article.

* Groups decide what information will be in the article.
* Groups research their headline topic.
* Groups write an article on their topic.
* One group member keys the article into a computer file.
* Each group hands out and presents its article to the class.

Customizing the Activity for Individual Needs
ESL To help ESL students understand the concept of colonial settlement, have pairs of students draw an illustration that depicts the main point in one of the newspaper articles. Have ESL students write a caption for their illustration.

Learning Styles Students can:

 look at a piece of artwork depicting the Puritans. Students can write a news story based on the picture.

 think of difficulties the colonists experienced, such as planting crops. Students then work in pairs to play a charades guessing game.

 work in pairs and assume the roles of settlers in Jamestown. One student wants to stay in the colony while the other wants to sail back to England. Each student prepares a persuasive speech to convince the colonists why they should or should not give up the effort to settle in Jamestown.

Reteaching Activity

Have students list the colonies that were settled by the English. Next to each colony ask students to list the problems that the colonists faced and tell how these problems were solved.

Alternative Assessment

Students write journal entries from the perspective of settlers in one of the colonies. They discuss what an average day is like, the kind of work that is done, the hardships faced, family life, and favorite activities.

CONNECTING HISTORY AND SCIENCE: Colonial Medicine
Student Edition, page 31

Objectives
- Social Studies Skill: Outline health conditions aboard a ship in colonial times by writing a report.
- Social Studies Skill: Depict colonial and contemporary medical practices by drawing two scenes.
- Social Studies Skill: Compare and contrast medical practices in colonial times with present-day technology and practices.

Activities

Then and Now
Materials: reference materials (Internet sites, pages 236–240)

Procedure: Have students work in pairs to do research about colonial medicine. Each pair lists medical practices in colonial and contemporary times. Students in each pair then assume the role of either a colonial or contemporary doctor and role-play with their partner, discussing the differences in medical practices—then and now.

Is There a Doctor in the House?
Procedure: Invite students to think of a medical condition, such as a sore throat, and how it might be treated in both colonial and contemporary times. Have them draw two scenes, depicting how a doctor would treat a patient—then and now. Ask students to label each scene with the treatment.

Let's Inspect It
Procedure: Ask students to assume the role of a colonial health inspector assigned to passenger ships traveling from Europe to the colonies.

Students can write a brief report that includes their observations aboard ship, an evaluation of conditions on the ship and of the passengers, and recommendations for improvements.

Practice
Have students complete Connecting History and Science from page 10 of the Classroom Resource Binder.

SECTION 3: The Growth of the Thirteen Colonies
Student Edition, pages 32–37

Section Objectives
- Identify the 13 colonies of the New England, Middle, and Southern regions.
- Explain why people left Massachusetts to establish other New England colonies.
- Identify reasons why the Middle colonies were settled.
- Explain how farming differed in the three colonial regions.
- Describe the people, economy, and geography of the New England, Middle, and Southern colonies.

Words to Know
treaty, debtors

Cooperative Group Activity

Who's Who
Materials: reference materials (Unit 1 Bibliography, Internet sites, pages 236–240)

Procedure: Explain to the class that *Who's Who* is a listing of important people. Divide the class into three groups and assign each group a region: New England, Middle or Southern colonies.

- Groups assume the role of editors at *Who's Who*. They need to decide which people from their region should be listed in *Who's Who*.
- Students research their choices and write short, two-paragraph biographies on five people.
- One student from the group presents the *Who's Who* list for its region to the class.

Customizing the Activity for Individual Needs
ESL To help ESL students learn about the *Who's Who* choices, have them write the names of their

groups' *Who's Who* choices on index cards. Then, have ESL students summarize their groups' biographies on the other side of the index cards.

Learning Styles   Students can:

 look at pictures from reference sources of their *Who's Who* choices. What can they tell about each person by their picture?

 design a memorial for one of the *Who's Who* choices. The memorial should incorporate the reason the person made the *Who's Who* list.

 role-play the *Who's Who* choices for one region. Each group member role-plays one *Who's Who* choice. Then the group member tells the rest of the group who the person is and why the person made the *Who's Who* list.

Reinforcement Activity

Divide students into three groups. Have each group think of *Who Am I?* quiz questions about colonists in each of the colonies found in their region. Have them write questions about life in the colonies on one side of an index card and the answers on the back. Then have each group take turns playing a quiz game with the other two groups, awarding points for every correct answer.

Example: We are a group of people in Pennsylvania who are against slavery. Who are we?

Answer: the Quakers

Alternative Assessment

Students can state the names of the 13 American colonies and tell one fact about each colony.

Example: Virginia

Answer: The first colony settled by the English

Closing the Chapter
Student Edition, pages 38–39

Chapter Vocabulary

Review with students the Words to Know on page 21 of the Student Edition. Then have students quiz each other in pairs.

Have students complete the Vocabulary Review questions on page 38 of the Student Edition by completing each sentence with a term from the list.

For more vocabulary practice, have them complete the vocabulary exercise on page 8 in the Classroom Resource Binder.

Test Tip

In pairs, have students practice the test tip when completing the Chapter Quiz. Tell students they have 30 minutes to complete the Chapter Quiz. Have students approximate how much time they can spend on each question.

Learning Objectives

Have the students review their Chapter Goals Worksheet found on page PA 6 in the Classroom Resource Binder. They can check off the goal they have reached. Note that each section of the quiz corresponds to a Learning Objective.

Group Activity

Summary: Students create a new colony, name it, and decide how it will be governed by creating a compact describing its laws.

Materials: Butcher paper; markers

Procedure: Divide the class into four groups. Ask them to brainstorm a name for a new colony and decide how it will be governed. On butcher paper students write a list of the most important laws they think are needed to govern the colony. Students then write their colony's compact on the butcher paper. Each member signs and dates the document. Students choose one group member to read the compact to the rest of the class.

Assessment: Use the Group Activity Rubric found on page *xiii* of this guide. Fill in the rubric with the following additional information. For this activity, students should have

- divided the writing tasks so that each student wrote and contributed information about the new colony.
- worked together to combine the information into a coherent compact, listing laws of the newly formed colony.

RELATED MATERIALS   See the Unit Overview page for related Globe Fearon books that can be used to enrich and extend the materials in the chapter.

Traditional Assessment

Chapter Quiz

The Chapter Quiz on page 39 of the Student Edition can be used as an open-book test, a closed-book test, or a homework assignment. Use the quiz to identify concepts in the chapter that students need to review. Chapter Tests can be found in the Classroom Resource Binder on pages 12–13. Workbook pages 6–9 can be used for additional practice.

Chapter Tests

Use Chapter Tests A and B on pages 12–13 in the Classroom Resource Binder to further assess mastery of chapter concepts.

Additional Resources

Use the Resource Planner on page 9 in this guide to assign additional exercises from the Classroom Resource Binder and Workbook.

Alternative Assessment

Student Interview

Give each student a slip of paper on which the name of one of the 13 colonies is written. Ask:

• When was this colony settled?
• Who settled the colony?
• What problems did the colonists face?

Create a Timeline

• Students scan the chapter and list pertinent dates and events that happened between 1519 and 1733.
• Students list reasons why the colonies were established.
• Students draw timelines that outline the people, places, and events that were important in the colonies.

Chapter 3 · Growth of Colonial Society 1630–1760

Chapter at a Glance

SE page

40		Opening the Chapter and Portfolio Project
42	SECTION 1	Economies of the Colonies
48	SECTION 2	The Growth of Towns and Cities
51		Voices From the Past: Anna Green Winslow
52	SECTION 3	New Ideas in the Colonies
56		Chapter Review and Group Activity

Chapter
3

Learning Objectives

- Identify the economy of each colonial region.
- Explain triangular trade.
- Describe a colonial town.
- Describe how cities grew from towns.
- Explain how new ideas about political and economic rights changed the colonists.

Social Studies Skills

- Explore colonial life in Boston.
- Use a timeline to gather information about colonial development.

Writing Skills

- Write a diary entry from the perspective of a colonist.
- Write a paragraph about a settler coming to a Southern colony.
- Write a list of the things a farmer can do in a colonial town.
- Write a letter to King George III describing the Navigation Acts and the colonists' rights to make their own rules about trade.
- Write and perform a skit about a group of colonists discussing political rights.

Map Skill

- Use a map to explain the concept of triangular trade.

Resource Planner

Chapter 3
Growth of Colonial Society

Use the Program Resources below for reteaching, reinforcement, and enrichment. Additional activities for customizing the lessons can be found in this guide.

Key
Reteaching = ⌒ Reinforcement = ⇩ Enrichment = ⌒

Sections	Program Resources		
	⇩ Workbook Exercises	Teacher's Planning Guide	Classroom Resource Binder
Economies of the Colonies	10, 11	⌒ p. 17	⌒ Concept Builder 3 *Growth of Colonial Society* ⇩ Writing and Test-Taking Tips 5 *Organizing Information by Cause and Effect* ⇩ Outline Map 2 *United States: Physical* ⇩ Graphic Organizer 2 *Cause and Effect* ⌒ Transparency 14, 15 *United States: Physical World: Political*
The Growth of Towns and Cities	12	⇩ p. 18	⌒ Concept Builder 3 *Growth of Colonial Society* ⌒ Graphic Organizer 2 *Cause and Effect* ⇩ Outline Map 2 *United States: Physical* ⇩ Transparency 12 *United States: Political*
Voices From the Past: Anna Green Winslow		⌒ p. 19	⌒ Feature Practice 16 *Voices From the Past: Sarah Kemble Knight*
New Ideas in the Colonies	13	⇩ p. 19	⌒ Concept Builder 3 *Growth of Colonial Society*
Chapter 3 Review		p. 20	⇩ Words to Know 14 ⌒ Challenge 17 ⇩ Chapter Tests A & B, 18, 19

Opening the Chapter
Student Edition, pages 40–41

Photo Activity

Have students study the painting of colonial Philadelphia and the photograph of the silver bowl while a volunteer reads the caption. Then make a class list of how people dressed, how people traveled, and how the city looked. Some items the list might include are long dresses, three-cornered hats, by horseback, by wagon, brick homes, and cobblestone streets.

Words to Know

Review the Words to Know on page 41 of the Student Edition. Organize the students into pairs. Ask one student from each pair to look up a word from the list and read the definition to the other student who should guess the term. Have the students take turns giving clues until all of the words have been identified. Invite pairs to find the words in the Glossary in the Student Edition.

The following words and definitions are covered in this chapter:

economy the way goods, wealth, and services are created and used

export to send goods to another region or country

frontier a newly settled or lightly settled area just outside an area of older settlements

barter to trade a product or service for another product or service

import an item brought into a country or region from another country or region

common an open area shared by all the villagers

political rights rights given to people by the government

jury a group of people who decide whether a person on trial is guilty or innocent

mercantilism the idea that a nation becomes stronger by building up its gold supply and increasing its trade

regulate to control

tax money that must be paid to a government

Portfolio Project

Summary: Students write a diary entry from the point of view of a colonist describing one way the colonies have changed over time.

Material: journal

Procedure: As students read the chapter, have them list some of the ways the colonies changed over time, such as how towns grew into cities. Have students choose one way in which the colonies have changed. Then ask them to write a diary entry from the perspective of a colonist, describing the change and how it impacts the colonist, his or her family, and the community. Divide the class into pairs. Have partners read their diary entries aloud to one another.

Assessment: Use the Individual Activity Rubric on page *xii* of this guide. Fill in the rubric with the additional information below. For this project students should have

- based their diary entry on accurate information.
- written their diary entries in the first-person narrative.

Learning Objectives

Review the Learning Objectives on page 41 of the Student Edition before starting this chapter. Students can use the objectives as a learning guide. Suggest they write the objectives in a journal or use the Chapter Goals and Self-Check worksheet on page PA 6 of the Classroom Resource Binder.

After reading each section of the chapter, have students write an example of what they learned under the appropriate objective. Suggest that students use these worksheets as a practice guide to help them study for the chapter test.

Timeline

Use the timeline to discuss the sequence of events in this chapter. Point out the timeline's title, its time span, and the intervals. After students have read the chapter, have them review the timeline and suggest additional entries.

SECTION 1: Economies of the Colonies
Student Edition, pages 42–47

Section Objectives

- Explain the concept of triangular trade.
- Explain how women contributed to the economy of the colonies.
- Describe the economies of the New England, Middle, and Southern colonies.

Chapter 3

Words to Know

economy, export, frontier

Cooperative Group Activity

Economically Speaking...

Materials: reference materials (Unit 1 Internet sites, pages 236–240); chart paper; markers

Procedure: Divide the class into three groups and assign each group the New England, Middle, or Southern colonies. You may wish to have students do additional research on each region.

- Groups read and take notes about their region, focusing on its economy.
- Groups list kinds of farms, reasons why they were established, crops that were grown, other industries that developed, and whether hired workers or enslaved people were employed to help.
- Each group writes a pamphlet about its region's economy, including illustrations and maps to support the facts.
- Students choose a speaker from their group to share the group's pamphlet with the class.

Customizing the Activity for Individual Needs

ESL To help students understand the concept of colonial regions and their different economies, have ESL students and English-proficient speakers discuss with one another the map of the 13 colonies on page 35 of the Student Edition. Pairs should find and practice the names of the regions and colonies.

Learning Styles Students can:

 fill out a Description Web (Classroom Resource Binder, page GO 3). Students can choose one of the regions and name facts about that region and its economy to include on the Description Web.

 sort index cards labeled with facts about different colonial regions under the headings: *New England Colonies, Middle Colonies, Southern Colonies.*

 work in groups of three to tell each other facts about the economy of one of the three colonial regions.

Enrichment Activity 🎧

Provide students with the following scenario: You are a farmer in one of the colonial regions. A farmer from another region comes to visit your region in order to learn about the economy. Write a paragraph explaining what you and your family do, and what your daily life is like.

Alternative Assessment

Students can present a short oral report about one colonial region. Encourage them to choose the region that most interested them.

SECTION 2: The Growth of Towns and Cities
Student Edition, pages 48–50

Section Objectives

- Name goods and services that were bartered in colonial towns.
- Describe how New England colonists used the town common.
- Identify the locations where colonial cities grew.
- * Explain the concept of bartering goods and services.

Words to Know

barter, import, common

Cooperative Group Activity

I Made It—I Trade It!

Materials: classroom items such as erasers; pencils

Procedure: Review the terms *goods* and *services* with students. Have volunteers discuss the concept of bartering goods and services in colonial times. Divide the class into two groups. Have students in one group think of classroom goods, such as pencils or erasers that they can use to barter. Have the other group members think of services that they can provide, such as helping with homework, babysitting, or giving a guitar lesson. Have students write the services they can provide on index cards.

- Groups choose a day that they will barter their goods and services.
- Groups set up tables around the classroom and display their goods and services.

- Some group members tend their group table while others barter their goods and services. Students within a group switch roles several times.

Customizing the Activity for Individual Needs

ESL To help students understand the concept of bartering goods and services, have each student think of something they can barter. Give examples, such as a bracelet, a soccer ball, or walking a dog. Have students tell whether each one is a good or a service.

Learning Styles Students can:

 look at pictures from magazines that represent the goods and services discussed. Students then barter with each other the goods and services they found in the magazines.

 draw posters advertising their goods or services.

 take turns discussing the goods and services they bartered.

Reinforcement Activity ⇓

Distribute the Description Web on page GO 3 in the Classroom Resource Binder. Write *goods* in the center of the Description Web and have students brainstorm and write a list of goods that they would like to have. Write *services* in the center of another Description Web, then brainstorm and write a list of valuable services. Talk about the value of goods and services, both in colonial times and today.

Alternative Assessment

Students can write about the importance of bartering goods and services in colonial times and explain why bartering was important to colonial economies.

VOICES FROM THE PAST:
Anna Green Winslow
Student Edition, page 51

Objectives
- Social Studies Skill: Describe what colonial life was like by writing diary entries and letters.
- Social Studies Skill: Compare colonial and contemporary ways of life by making a chart.

Activities
More From Anna
Material: journal

Procedure: Based upon what students know about colonial life, have them write a diary entry in the voice of Anna Green Winslow, dated March 3, 1772.

Life in 1772
Procedure: Have students assume the role of a colonial teenager. Students can write a letter to a friend describing life in their family and community.

Anna Then . . . Me Now!
Material: chart paper

Procedure: Ask students to describe activities in their lives and compare them with the activities of Anna Green Winslow. Have students make a chart that lists this information. Afterward, ask students to circle the activities they have in common with Anna.

Practice

Have students complete Voices From the Past: Sarah Kemble Knight on page 16 of the Classroom Resource Binder.

SECTION 3: New Ideas in the Colonies
Student Edition, pages 52–55

Section Objectives
- Explain the concept of the Great Awakening.
- Describe how political rights differed for colonial men and women.
- Explain the economic reasons why England established colonies in North America.
- ＊ Describe how the Navigation Acts controlled trade in the colonies.

Words to Know
political rights, jury, mercantilism, regulate, tax

Cooperative Group Activity

From Cabinet Meeting to Town Meeting
Materials: reference materials (Unit 1 Internet sites, pages 236–240)

Procedure: Have students review the concept of mercantilism, the idea that a nation becomes stronger by building up its gold supply and enlarging its trade. For example, England could increase its wealth by regulating trade and imposing taxes on the colonies. Divide the class into two groups.

- Students in one group assume the roles of King George III and his staff. They conduct a meeting to discuss how the colonies can be used to increase England's wealth.
- Group members discuss the Navigation Acts, why they will benefit England, and how these acts will be enforced.
- Students then write a document to the colonies outlining the Navigation Acts.
- Students in the other group assume the role of colonists who are upset over the new taxes and trade regulations of the Navigation Acts. They discuss the effect of the Navigation Acts on the colonies.
- These group members then write a letter to King George III and his cabinet, outlining the reasons why the colonists oppose the Navigation Acts.
- Each group chooses a speaker to read its letter aloud to the other group.

Customizing the Activity for Individual Needs

ESL To help students reinforce their understanding of colonial rule, encourage students to share what they know about political and economic rights in their native country. Ask them to compare these rights to those of the colonists.

Learning Styles Students can:

 complete a Cause and Effect chart (Classroom Resource Binder, page GO 2) by writing the term *mercantilism* as the "cause." Students then brainstorm and write down how mercantilism affected England and the colonies.

 arrange three index cards to define the term *mercantilism*. The term is written on one index card while the parts of its definition are written on each of the other two index cards.

 tape-record one of the letters and use the tape to take notes.

Reinforcement Activity ⬇

Divide the class into groups to discuss the reasons why the colonists felt that the Navigation Acts were unjust. Have student recorders in each group take notes. Then have group members write an editorial for the newspaper, *The Colonial Times*,

expressing their concern that England will try to take away more of the colonists' freedoms. Student groups choose speakers to share their editorials.

Alternative Assessment

Students can role-play a scene between a spy from England sent to the colonies to attend a town meeting and King George III. In this scene the spy is reporting the colonists' reactions to the Navigation Acts to King George III.

Example: Colonists are beginning to talk about governing themselves.

Closing the Chapter
Student Edition, pages 56–57

Chapter Vocabulary

Review with students the Words to Know on page 41 of the Student Edition. Then have them complete the Vocabulary Review on page 56 of the Student Edition by answering each question as *true* or *false*. Have students rewrite false statements to make them true.

For more vocabulary practice, have students complete the vocabulary exercise on page 14 of the Classroom Resource Binder.

Test Tip

Working in pairs, have students turn to the section titles in Chapter 3 into questions. Then have student pairs review the sections to find the answers.

Learning Objectives

Have students review their Chapter Goals and Self-Check worksheet found on page PA 6 of the Classroom Resource Binder. They can check off the goal they have reached. Note that each section of the quiz corresponds to a Learning Objective.

Group Activity

Summary: Students role-play colonists who meet in a general store. They hold a conversation about political rights in the colonies.

Procedure: Organize students into three groups to write and perform a skit. In their skits students are colonists discussing political rights in the colonies. Students decide how many people meet and talk. A group recorder writes down what each person says. Student groups practice their skits aloud, then perform them for the rest of the class.

Assessment: Use the Group Activity Rubric found on page *xiii* of this guide. Fill in the rubric with the following additional information. For this activity, students should have

- participated in writing the dialogue lines for each member of the skit.

- participated in presenting the skit to the class.

RELATED MATERIALS See the Unit Overview page for related Globe Fearon books that can be used to enrich and extend the materials in the chapter.

Assessing the Chapter

Traditional Assessment

Chapter Quiz
The Chapter Quiz on page 57 of the Student Edition can be used as an open-book test, a closed-book test, or a homework assignment. Use the quiz to identify concepts in the chapter that students need to review. Chapter Tests can be found in the Classroom Resource Binder on pages 18–19. Workbook pages 10–13 can be used for additional practice.

Chapter Tests
Use Chapter Tests A and B on pages 18–19 in the Classroom Resource Binder to further assess mastery of chapter concepts.

Additional Resources
Use the Resource Planner on page 16 of this guide to assign additional exercises from the Classroom Resource Binder and Workbook.

Alternative Assessment

Student Interview
Give each student the role of a New England colonist. Ask:

- What is the main economy of this region?
- How is the economy of the New England region similar to the economies in the Middle and Southern regions?
- How does climate affect the region's economy?

Presentation
- Students scan the chapter to list the political rights of colonial men versus those of colonial women.
- Students write a paragraph using the information from their lists to describe how political rights differed between colonial men and women.

Chapter
3

Chapter 4 · **The Struggle for Freedom** 1754–1783

Chapter at a Glance

SE page

58   *Opening the Chapter and Portfolio Project*

60   SECTION 1   The French and Indian War

63   SECTION 2   The Colonists Unite

67   SECTION 3   The War for Independence

77   *Voices From the Past: Thomas Jefferson*

78   *Chapter Review and Group Activity*

Learning Objectives

- Identify the causes of the French and Indian War.
- Explain how Great Britain gained control of most French lands in North America.
- Identify British laws that angered the colonists.
- Identify the events leading to the War for Independence.

Social Studies Skills

- Explore how Thomas Jefferson wrote the Declaration of Independence.
- Discuss the Declaration of Independence from the perspective of a member of the Second Continental Congress.
- Read a timeline that explains the events that took place during the struggle for freedom.

Writing Skills

- Write a news article describing an event during this time period.
- List what the Native Americans, French, British, and colonists expected to gain from the French and Indian War.
- Write a speech to get members of the Continental Congress to support the cause of independence.
- Compare and contrast the Loyalists, Patriots, and those who remained neutral during the War for Independence.

Map and Chart Skills

- Use a chart to understand the British acts against the colonies.
- Use a map to locate the places where major battles took place during the Revolutionary War.

Resource Planner

Chapter 4 The Struggle for Freedom	Use the Program Resources below for reteaching, reinforcement, and enrichment. Additional activities for customizing the lessons can be found in this guide.

Key
Reteaching = ↶   Reinforcement = ⬇   Enrichment = ↷

Sections	Program Resources		
	⬇ Workbook Exercises	Teacher's Planning Guide	Classroom Resource Binder
The French and Indian War	14	↶ p. 24	↷ Concept Builder 4 *War for Independence* ⬇ Writing and Test-Taking Tips 9 *Writing an Effective Paragraph* ⬇ Graphic Organizer 7 *Who, What, Where, When, Why, How Chart* ↷ Outline Map 2 *United States: Physical* ⬇ Transparency 14 *United States: Physical*
The Colonists Unite	15, 16	↶ p. 25	⬇ Graphic Organizer 7 *Who, What, Where, When, Why, How Chart*
The War for Independence	17	↶ p. 26	↶ Document-Based Questions 1, 2 *The Declaration of Independence* ↶ Graphics Organizer 1 *Sequence of Events Chain* ↶ Transparency 3 *Major Battles for the War for Independence, 1775-1781*
Voices From the Past: Thomas Jefferson		↶ p. 27	↶ Feature Practice 22 *Voices From the Past: Revolutionary Tea*
Chapter 4 Review		p. 27	⬇ Words to Know 20 ↶ Challenge 23 ⬇ Chapter Tests A & B, 24, 25 ⬇ Unit Tests Parts I & II, 26, 27

Chapter
4

Opening the Chapter
Student Edition, pages 58–59

Photo Activity

Have students discuss the painting of the Boston Tea Party. Ask why the words "No Stamp Act" are written on the teapot. Point out that the men on the ship throwing tea into the harbor are colonists dressed as Native Americans. Have students guess why the colonists are disguised and whether they agree with the plan.

Words to Know

Review the Words to Know on page 59 of the Student Edition. To help students remember the words, have volunteers write sentences on the chalkboard, leaving a blank for each term. The class should then try to identify the missing terms. Remind students that they can use the Glossary to help them fill in the missing terms.

The following words and definitions are covered in this chapter:

ally a nation that joins with other nations for the same cause

cede to surrender something

proclamation an official government announcement

representative a person selected to act for others

repeal to end

declaration a public statement

revolution a sudden, complete change of government

militia an army of citizens used in emergencies

blockade an action to keep supplies from getting into or out of an area

Loyalist a colonist who remained loyal to Great Britain

Patriot a colonist who wanted independence from Great Britain

neutral not favoring either side in a quarrel or war

Portfolio Project

Summary: Students write a news article describing the *who, what, when, why, where,* and *how* of an event that took place during the War for Independence.

Materials: reference materials (Unit 1 Bibliography and Internet sites, pages 236–240); *Who, What, Where, When, Why, How* chart (Classroom Resource Binder, page GO 7)

Procedure: Have students choose an event in the chapter to write about. Students may review the timeline on pages 58–59 of the Student Edition for ideas. When students have chosen the event, ask them to write a news article about it, describing what they see and hear. Students should write the questions *who, what, when, why, where,* and *how* in the chart to organize information. After writing the article and giving it a title, have students input the article on a computer. Combine the articles into a class newspaper.

Assessment: Use the Individual Activity Rubric on page *xii* of this guide. Fill in the rubric with the additional information below. For this project students should have:

- answered the questions *who, what, where, when, why,* and *how.*
- written an exciting headline.

Learning Objectives

Review the Learning Objectives on page 59 of the Student Edition before starting this chapter. Students can use the list as a learning guide. Suggest they write the objectives in a journal or use the Chapter Goals and Self-Check worksheet found on page PA 6 of the Classroom Resource Binder.

After students read each section of the chapter, have them write an example of what they learned under the appropriate objective. Suggest that students use these worksheets as a practice guide to help them study for the chapter test.

Timeline

Use the timeline to discuss the sequence of events in this chapter. Point out the timeline's title, its time span, and the intervals. After students have read the chapter, have them review the timeline and suggest additional entries.

SECTION 1: The French and Indian War
Student Edition, pages 60–62

Section Objectives

- Explain why French rulers wanted to control the Ohio River valley.
- Identify the causes of the French and Indian War.
- Explain how Great Britain gained control of most French lands in North America.
- ★ Explain the different ways each side fought in battle.

Words to Know

ally, cede

Cooperative Group Activity

Time for Strategies

Materials: reference materials (Unit 1 Internet sites, pages 236–240)

Procedure: Organize the class into two groups. The first group consists of the French and Native Americans. The second group consists of the British. Tell students that the year is 1754 and that they are soldiers attending a strategy session to make preparations for battle.

- Each group makes a chart that outlines its strategies for winning the war.
- Students should include information such as *who* they will enlist, *why* people will support them, *how* they will defend their land or gain control of the land, *what* battle strategies and fighting techniques they can use, *where* battles will be fought, *when* the most effective time to strike would be, and *why*.
- Groups present their charts to the class. Students then make predictions about who will win the war and why they believe this will be the outcome.

Customizing the Activity for Individual Needs

ESL   To help students understand what happened during the French and Indian War, pair ESL students with English-proficient students. Have student pairs create a Comparison-Contrast chart (Classroom Resource Binder, page GO 4) about the French and British styles of fighting.

Learning Styles   Students can:

 look at a painting from a reference source that depicts a battle scene from the French and Indian War. Have students write down what they learn from the painting.

 establish nonverbal ways to communicate during battles. Mention to students that the French and Native Americans needed to overcome language barriers in order to communicate with each other. Have students take turns using hand signals such as: *stay low* or *move forward*.

 assume the role of army officers presenting a speech to their troops as they move forth in battle. The officers explain how they expect to win and what their strategies are.

Enrichment Activity

Ask students to negotiate a peace treaty for the French and Indian War. Students should consider issues to present, such as dividing the land, establishing borders, or having trade rules. Students list their ideas to present at a treaty meeting. Then they sign and date the document.

Alternative Assessment

Students can write two journal entries—one from the perspective of a French soldier and the other from the perspective of a British soldier. Students describe their first day of battle in terms of what each soldier saw, heard, and felt.

SECTION 2: The Colonists Unite
Student Edition, pages 63–66

Section Objectives

- Describe the Proclamation of 1763.
- Explain why the colonists protested the British acts.
- Describe the events that occurred during the Boston Massacre.
- Explain how the colonists united and reacted to the British tea laws.
- Define the purpose of the First Continental Congress.

Words to Know

proclamation, representative, repeal, declaration, revolution

Cooperative Group Activity

Let's Convene Congress

Materials: reference materials (Unit 1 Bibliography and Internet sites, pages 236–240); chart paper; markers

Procedure: Explain to students that they will be holding the first Continental Congress of 1774. Divide the class into three groups and have each review material on the first Continental Congress.

- On chart paper, students list issues that they think are unfair and write suggestions to rectify the situation.

- Student groups share their charts with the class and organize the issues according to importance.
- Groups then write a *Declaration of American Rights*, or statement, to send to Great Britain.

Customizing the Activity for Individual Needs

ESL To help students make accurate predictions, have them discuss and then make predictions about the British reaction to the *Declaration of American Rights*.

Learning Styles Students can:

 look at a painting from a reference source of the Boston Tea Party and write two paragraphs describing what they see in the painting.

 create bumper sticker slogans or banners that support the colonists' struggle against British control, such as "No taxation without representation."

 assume the role of Patrick Henry giving a speech at the First Continental Congress.

Reteaching Activity

Have students list the major issues presented at the first Continental Congress and organize this information in chart form.

Alternative Assessment

Students can think about some of the issues that were discussed at the Continental Congress and write the minutes for part of that meeting. Students should include names of members and what each said.

SECTION 3: The War for Independence
Student Edition, pages 67–76

Section Objectives

- Explain the events that occurred at Lexington and Concord.
- Describe the issues raised at the Second Continental Congress.
- Identify key points of the Declaration of Independence.
- Describe the differences between Patriots and Loyalists.
- Identify the significance of the Treaty of Paris.
- ★ Report on and track the battles of the Revolution.

Words to Know

militia, blockade, Loyalist, Patriot, neutral

Cooperative Group Activity

The War Room

Materials: reference materials (Unit 1 Bibliography and Internet sites, pages 236–240); map of the 13 colonies

Procedure: Have students track and report on battles of the Revolution. Divide the class into eight groups: George Washington and his advisers and seven groups of armies. Each group assumes the roles of the soldiers.

- Students in the seven armies research or reread information on seven different battles. On slips of paper, students write information that they think is important to report to General Washington and his staff about their group's battle. Groups may include maps and drawings.
- Student groups then choose a messenger to take the information to the General.
- As messengers from each army arrive with updates on the battles, George Washington and his advisers conduct a strategy meeting and take turns writing down suggestions for the messenger to take back to the front line.
- Students report on all seven battles and announce the Treaty of Paris.

Customizing the Activity for Individual Needs

ESL To help students remember important battles fought in the war, have them work in groups using a Description Web (Classroom Resource Binder, page GO 3) to describe each battle that occurred during the Revolutionary War.

Learning Styles Students can:

 find the location of each of the seven battles on a map.

 make and play a board game that consists of a map that traces the battles fought in the Revolutionary War.

 work with a partner to announce "news flashes" about the war.

Reteaching Activity

Have students review the differences between Patriots and Loyalists. Students list the strengths and weaknesses of each position in a chart.

Alternative Assessment

Students can write a brief journal entry from the perspective of George Washington, that describes his thoughts and feelings about at least two battles that occurred during the War for Independence.

VOICES FROM THE PAST:
Thomas Jefferson
Student Edition, page 77

Objectives
• Social Studies Skill: Analyze what Jefferson wrote in the Declaration of Independence.
• Social Studies Skill: Analyze the phrase ". . . all men are created equal . . ."
• Social Studies Skill: Describe freedoms we have in the United States today and write a Declaration of Rights.

Activities

Conduct an Interview
Procedure: Have pairs of students conduct an interview. One student plays the role of Thomas Jefferson. The other student plays the role of a reporter. The reporter should ask Jefferson about his thoughts regarding what he wrote in the Declaration of Independence.

...All Men Are Created Equal...
Procedure: Working in pairs, have students analyze the phrase Thomas Jefferson wrote in the Declaration of Independence that states, ". . . all men are created equal . . ." Ask them to review what it probably meant to the colonists in 1776. Have each pair amend and rewrite that portion of the document to include groups of people such as women, African Americans, and Native Americans, who were also living in the colonies.

A Declaration of Rights
Procedure: Divide the class into small groups to brainstorm a list of rights and freedoms that we have in the United States today, including the freedoms of religion and speech. Ask groups to draft a Declaration of Rights, outlining rights we enjoy in school, in the community, and in our nation.

Practice

Have students complete Voices From the Past: Revolutionary Tea on page 22 of the Classroom Resource Binder.

Closing the Chapter
Student Edition, pages 78–79

Chapter Vocabulary

Review with students the Words to Know on page 59 of the Student Edition.

Have students complete the Vocabulary Review on page 78 of the Student Edition, by writing *true* or *false* after each statement. If the statement is false, have students change the underlined term to make it true.

For more vocabulary practice, have them complete the vocabulary exercise on page 20 of the Classroom Resource Binder.

Test Tip

Working in pairs, have students complete the Chapter Quiz. If they are unsure of an answer, encourage them to find the section in Chapter 4 and take turns rereading and discussing it.

Learning Objectives

Have the students review their Chapter Goals and Self-Check worksheet found on page PA 6 of the Classroom Resource Binder. They can check off the goal they have reached. Note that each section of the quiz corresponds to a Learning Objective.

Group Activity

Summary: Students assume the role of members of the Second Continental Congress. They read part of the Declaration of Independence and discuss it as a group.

Materials: the Declaration of Independence (pages 618–623 of the Student Edition); chart paper

Procedure: Divide the class into small groups. Students choose a portion of the Declaration of Independence and take turns reading the section aloud. Group members discuss the section and list important points on chart paper. Have a speaker from each group share its findings with the class.

Assessment: Use the Group Activity Rubric found on page *xiii* of this guide. Fill in the rubric with the following additional information. For this activity, students should have

• participated in reading aloud and discussing a portion of the Declaration of Independence.
• listed important points on chart paper.

RELATED MATERIALS See the Unit Overview page for related Globe Fearon books that can be used to enrich and extend the materials in the chapter.

Traditional Assessment

Chapter Quiz

The Chapter Quiz on page 79 of the Student Edition can be used as an open-book test, a closed-book test, or a homework assignment. Use the quiz to identify concepts in the chapter that students need to review. Chapter Tests can be found in the Classroom Resource Binder on pages 24–25. Workbook pages 14–17 can be used for additional practice.

Chapter Tests

Use Chapter Tests A and B on pages 24–25 in the Classroom Resource Binder to further assess mastery of chapter concepts. Use Chapter 4 Tests A and B in the Classroom Resource Binder to further assess mastery of chapter concepts.

Additional Resources

Use the Resource Planner on page 23 in this guide to assign additional exercises from the Classroom Resource Binder and Workbook.

Alternative Assessment

Performance

Have students assume the role of Thomas Jefferson and discuss the following:

• the colony he represents
• his role during the Second Continental Congress
• why the Declaration of Independence is an important document

Open-Ended

• Students scan Sections 2 and 3 of the chapter and write down at least five important dates and important events that took place during those years. These dates and events should be different from those shown in the chapter timeline.
• Students use the information to create a timeline.

Unit Assessment

This is the last chapter in Unit 1: Settling the Americas. To assess cumulative knowledge and provide standardized-test practice, have students complete the Unit Review Test on page 80 of the Student Edition, and the Unit 1 Cumulative Test on pages 26–27 of the Classroom Resource Binder.

Unit 2 Growth of a New Nation

CHAPTER 5 Building a New Government 1780–1800	PORTFOLIO PROJECT Journal Entry	BUILDING YOUR SKILLS Reading a Chart	GROUP ACTIVITY Conduct a Meeting	TIMELINE Forming a Government
CHAPTER 6 Economy and Expansion 1800–1830	PORTFOLIO PROJECT Diary Entry	CONNECTING HISTORY AND... Economics: The Cotton Gin	GROUP ACTIVITY Make a Chart	TIMELINE A New Nation Grows
CHAPTER 7 The Changing United States 1820–1850	PORTFOLIO PROJECT Song or Poem	VOICES FROM THE PAST George M. Harkins	GROUP ACTIVITY Present Travel Plans	TIMELINE The United States Expands Westward
CHAPTER 8 Newcomers and New Ideas 1820–1860	PORTFOLIO PROJECT Time Capsule List	VOICES FROM THE PAST Elizabeth Cady Stanton	GROUP ACTIVITY Create Story Boards	TIMELINE Improving American Society

Chapter
5

RELATED MATERIALS

These are some of the Globe Fearon books that can be used to enrich and extend the material in this unit.

Cultural Diversity

Globe Mosaic of American History: Native Americans; The Struggle for the Plains Describes how the arrival of white settlers changed Native Americans' lives

Literature

Pacemaker® Classics: Narrative of the Life of Frederick Douglass Extends content on the conditions of slavery.

Skills

Reading Comprehension Workshop: Perspectives Reinforces the skill of distinguishing fact from opinion within Unit 4, Lesson 7.

Chapter 5 · **Building a New Government** 1780–1800

Chapter at a Glance

SE page

82	*Opening the Chapter and Portfolio Project*
84	SECTION 1 The Articles of Confederation
87	*Building Your Skills: Reading a Chart*
88	SECTION 2 The Constitution and the Bill of Rights
93	SECTION 3 The New Government Begins
98	*Chapter Review and Group Activity*

Learning Objectives

- Discuss the purpose of the Articles of Confederation.
- Analyze the weaknesses of the Articles of Confederation.
- Explain how the Constitution was created.
- Discuss the Bill of Rights.
- Identify the problems facing the first leaders of the nation.

Social Studies Skills

- Read a Main Idea and Details chart.
- Use a timeline to describe how the U.S. government was formed.
- Conduct a meeting from the perspective of a state representative at the Constitutional Convention.

Writing Skills

- Write a journal entry describing how the Articles of Confederation, the U.S. Constitution, and the Bill of Rights made the U.S. government strong.
- Write a paragraph explaining whether Daniel Shays was right or wrong to break the law.
- Write a letter to the newspaper describing either Federalist or Anti-Federalist views about the ratification of the Constitution.
- Write a news article about the Alien and Sedition Acts during John Adams' presidency.

Chart Skill

- Use a chart to explain what each branch of the government does.

Chapter 5 Building a New Government	Use the Program Resources below for reteaching, reinforcement, and enrichment. Additional activities for customizing the lessons can be found in this guide.

Key
Reteaching = ⌒ Reinforcement = ⇓ Enrichment = ⌒

Sections	Program Resources		
	⇓ Workbook Exercises	Teacher's Planning Guide	Classroom Resource Binder
The Articles of Confederation	18	⌒ p. 32	⌒ Outline Map 2 *United States: Physical* ⌒ Transparency 14 *United States: Physical*
Building Your Skills: Reading a Chart		⇓ p. 33	⇓ Feature Practice 30, 31 *Reading a Chart*
The Constitution and the Bill of Rights	19, 20	⇓ p. 33	⌒ Document-Based Questions 3, 4 *The Constitution of the United States*
The New Government Begins	21	⇓ p. 34	
Chapter 5 Review		p. 35	⌒ Concept Builder 5 *Building a New Government* ⇓ Words to Know 28 ⌒ Challenge 32 ⇓ Chapter Tests A & B, 33, 34

Chapter **5**

Customizing the Chapter

Opening the Chapter
Student Edition, pages 82–83

Photo Activity
Explain to students that the painting depicts the signing of the Declaration of Independence in 1776. Point out that quill pens and inkstands like the ones shown were used to sign the document. Ask students to identify the man standing on the podium. Mention that in this chapter they will learn about how Americans built a new government by establishing rules and laws of their own. Using chart paper, have students brainstorm a list of laws and rights they feel the colonists might recommend as they form a new government. After students complete the chapter, have them compare and contrast their list with laws and rights that were established in the actual documents.

Words to Know
Review the Words to Know on page 83 of the Student Edition. To help students remember the words, have them write each term and what they believe the correct definition would be.

Have students refer to the Glossary in the Student Edition to check the accuracy of their definitions. Students can use the following model: *I think that _____ means _____. The Glossary definition is _____.*

The following words and definitions are covered in this chapter:

constitution the laws and plan of a nation's government

territory land that belongs to a national government but is not a state

convention a large gathering of people for a particular reason

compromise a settling of differences where both sides give up something

legislative branch the part of government that makes laws

executive branch the part of government that carries out laws

judicial branch the part of government that settles differences about the meanings of laws

ratify to approve

amendment a change or addition to a document

Cabinet a group of people chosen by the President to give advice

alliance a partnership

Portfolio Project

Summary: Through journal entries, students describe how the Articles of Confederation, the Constitution, and the Bill of Rights helped form a strong nation.

Material: student journals

Procedure: Explain to students that when the American colonists declared independence in 1776, they had to plan a new government. In 1777, leaders wrote the Articles of Confederation. In 1787, the Constitutional Convention was held to develop a better plan of government. By 1790, all the states had ratified the new Constitution. A year later, the Bill of Rights was added to the Constitution. Have students write three journal entries that tell how each document made the U.S. government strong.

Assessment: Use the Individual Activity Rubric on page *xii* of this guide. Fill in the rubric with the additional information below. For this project, students should have

• written three journal entries.

• described how each document provided a framework for our nation's government.

Learning Objectives

Review the Learning Objectives on page 83 of the Student Edition before starting the chapter. Students can use the list as a learning guide. Suggest they write the objectives in a journal or use the Chapter Goals and Self-Check worksheet found on page PA 6 of the Classroom Resource Binder.

After reading each section of the chapter, have students write an example of what they learned under the appropriate objective. Suggest that students use these worksheets as a practice guide to help them study for the chapter test.

Timeline

Use the timeline to discuss the sequence of events in this chapter. Point out the timeline's title, its time span, and the intervals. After students have read the chapter, have them review the timeline and suggest additional entries.

SECTION 1: The Articles of Confederation
Student Edition, pages 84–86

Section Objectives
• Discuss why Daniel Shays led a rebellion.
• Describe the purpose of the Northwest Ordinance.
* Describe the weaknesses of the Articles of Confederation.

Words to Know
constitution, territory

Cooperative Group Activity

Starting From Scratch
Materials: reference materials (Unit 2 Bibliography and Internet sites, pages 236–240); chart paper; markers

Procedure: Explain to students that when the Revolutionary War ended, the colonies had to form a new government. The Articles of Confederation was the first constitution, or plan of government of the new nation. This first plan was weak, however. Leaders needed to develop a stronger national government to help solve postwar problems.

Divide the class into small groups. You may want to have them do additional research on the Articles of Confederation.

- Groups list at least two weaknesses of the Articles of Confederation and brainstorm possible solutions.
- Groups create a class chart that represents the problems and possible solutions that were brainstormed by each group.
- Using the class chart, students write a plan to strengthen the national government.

Customizing the Activity for Individual Needs

ESL To help students understand the word *constitution,* have pairs of students discuss the laws and plans of national governments in countries other than the United States.

Learning Styles Students can:

 underline key concepts in the class chart.

 work in pairs to take turns matching index cards listing problems of the nation's first constitution with cards listing possible solutions.

 describe what a constitution is and why it is important to our nation.

Enrichment Activity

Tell students that they will form a new club, just as the colonists formed a new government. Divide the class into small groups and have each group decide what type of club to form. Groups list how the club will be organized, who will make the decisions, and who will determine the club's rules. Then have each group write a short constitution for their club. Each group presents their club's organization to the class. As a class, discuss the similarities and differences among the clubs.

Alternative Assessment

Students can identify the first constitution of the United States, what it provided for the new country, and who controlled it.

BUILDING YOUR SKILLS: Reading a Chart
Student Edition, page 87

Objectives
- Social Studies Skill: Make a chart to describe how the Articles of Confederation left the national government weak.

- Social Studies Skill: Make a chart to describe the problems that the United States faced after the War for Independence ended.
- Social Studies Skill: Make a chart to describe the reasons why Daniel Shays led a revolt against the government.

Activities

The Government Is Weak
Material: Main Idea and Supporting Details chart (Classroom Resource Binder, page GO 5)

Procedure: Ask students to create a Main Idea and Supporting Details chart that provides supporting details for the following main idea: *The Articles of Confederation made the national government weak.*

The United States Faces Problems
Material: Main Idea and Supporting Details chart (Classroom Resource Binder, page GO 5)

Procedure: Have students work in pairs to fill out a Main Idea and Supporting Details chart for the following main idea: *The United States faced problems after the War for Independence ended.*

Let's Revolt
Material: Main Idea and Supporting Details chart (Classroom Resource Binder, page GO 5)

Procedure: Ask students to complete a Main Idea and Supporting Details chart for the following concept: *Daniel Shays led a revolt against the government in Massachusetts.*

Practice

Have students complete Building Your Skills: Reading a Chart from the Classroom Resource Binder.

SECTION 2: The Constitution and the Bill of Rights
Student Edition, pages 88–92

Section Objectives
- Describe the two ideas agreed upon during the first day of the Constitutional Convention.
- Describe the Great Compromise.
- Explain the Three-fifths Compromise.
- Describe the purpose of the system of checks and balances.
- Compare Federalists and Anti-Federalists.

Words to Know

convention, compromise, legislative branch, executive branch, judicial branch, ratify, amendment

Cooperative Group Activity

Federalists vs. Anti-Federalists

Materials: reference materials (Unit 2 Bibliography and Internet sites, pages 236–240); Description Web (Classroom Resource Binder, page GO3)

Procedure: Divide the class into two groups: Federalists and Anti-Federalists. Student groups debate why each group is for or against the ratification of the Constitution.

- Student groups research the Constitution, Federalists, and Anti-Federalists.
- Student groups complete a Description Web with information about either Federalist or Anti-Federalist beliefs.
- Students organize the information to debate their ideas with the other group.
- Groups choose a delegate to debate the issues. Students switch roles frequently.

Customizing the Activity for Individual Needs

ESL To help students understand the differences between Federalists and Anti-Federalists, write the two headings on the board. Then circle *Anti* and point out that it means "against." Therefore, Anti-Federalists are those against a strong national government.

Learning Styles Students can:

 create a two-column chart that lists the differences between Federalists and Anti-Federalists.

 create cue cards, to be used in the debate, listing the Federalists' ideas or the Anti-Federalists' ideas about the government.

 work in small groups to prepare and present speeches, either supporting Federalists or Anti-Federalists.

Reinforcement Activity

From the perspective of Federalists in favor of a strong national government, students can work in pairs to write letters to a newspaper supporting the Constitution.

Alternative Assessment

Students can cast a vote for or against the ratification of the Constitution on slips of paper. On the back of each slip, have students write the most important factor that helped them make their decision.

SECTION 3: The New Government Begins *Student Edition, pages 93–97*

Section Objectives

- Describe the problems that George Washington faced as President.
- Describe the roles each Cabinet member had in the new government.
- Explain the reason why the Jay Treaty was established.
- Name the states that gave land to build the nation's capital.
- Describe the Alien and Sedition Acts.
- * Explain the differences between the Federalists and the Democratic-Republicans.

Words to Know

Cabinet, alliance

Cooperative Group Activity

The Campaign Trail

Materials: reference materials (Unit 2 Internet sites, pages 236–240)

Procedure: Divide the class in half and have one group support the views of the Federalists, while the other group supports the views of the Democratic-Republican party.

- Students conduct research to learn more about the two-party system in the late 1700s.
- Groups discuss and chart their views about how the nation should be governed, from either the Federalist or Democratic-Republican point of view.
- Each group chooses a member to represent their candidate for President: John Adams (Federalist) or Thomas Jefferson (Democratic-Republican).
- Each group writes campaign speeches for its candidate, which the candidates then present to the class.
- Hold a class election so students can cast their vote for President.

Customizing the Activity for Individual Needs

ESL To help students understand the concept of a two-party political system, pair ESL students with English-proficient students. Have ESL students discuss the political system in their native land.

Learning Styles Students can:

 use Description Webs (Classroom Resource Binder, page GO 3) to take notes on each of the candidates.

 create ballots for the class election. Ballots should list the candidates and their positions.

 work in pairs to express the point of view of either the Federalists or Democratic-Republicans.

Enrichment Activity

Hold a class election. Have two groups of students create their own political parties and define their parties' beliefs. Each group then chooses candidates to run for the office of President and Vice President, and writes a campaign speech for their candidate to present to the class. Students may create political posters to hang up around the room. After candidates present their speeches, conduct a class election.

Alternative Assessment

Students can write a journal entry that explains this quote by Thomas Jefferson: "The government that governs best governs least."

Closing the Chapter
Student Edition, pages 98–99

Chapter Vocabulary

Review with students the Words to Know on page 83 of the Student Edition. Then have them complete the Vocabulary Review on page 98 of the Student Edition, by completing each sentence with a word from the list.

For more vocabulary practice, have them complete the vocabulary exercise on page 28 of the Classroom Resource Binder.

Test Tip

Have students create a timeline for the events covered in this chapter. After students have created their timelines, have them compare their timelines with the chapter timeline on pages 82–83.

Learning Objectives

Have students review their Chapter Goals and Self-Check worksheet found on page PA 6 of the Classroom Resource Binder. They can check off the goal they have reached. Note that each section of the quiz corresponds to a Learning Objective.

Group Activity

Summary: Students assume the role of state delegates sent to the Constitutional Convention in Philadelphia in 1787 to argue for their state's interests.

Materials: chart paper; markers

Procedure: Divide the class into five groups. Each group will represent one state. Have each group make a list of what their state hopes to gain at the Convention. Conduct a mock Constitutional Convention together as a class. A spokesperson from each group presents their ideas and argues for their state's interest at the convention.

Assessment: Use the Group Activity Rubric on page *xiii* of this guide. Fill in the rubric with the following additional information. For this activity, students should have

- worked collaboratively to prepare a list of relevant issues to present at a mock Constitutional Convention.

- presented a cohesive argument for their states' interests.

RELATED MATERIALS See the Unit Overview page for related Globe Fearon books that can be used to enrich and extend the materials in the chapter.

Traditional Assessment

Chapter Quiz
The Chapter Quiz on page 99 of the Student Edition can be used as an open-book test, a closed-book test, or a homework assignment. Use the quiz to identify concepts in the chapter that students need to review. Chapter Tests can be found in the Classroom Resource Binder on pages 33–34. Workbook pages 18–21 can be used for additional practice.

Chapter Tests
Use Chapter Tests A and B on pages 33–34 in the Classroom Resource Binder to further assess mastery of chapter concepts.

Additional Resources
Use the Resource Planner on page 31 in this guide to assign additional exercises from the Classroom Resource Binder and Workbook.

Alternative Assessment

Student Interview
Write *Articles of Confederation, Bill of Rights,* and the *Constitution* on the chalkboard. Ask:
- What was the purpose of each of these documents?
- How are these documents similar? How are they different?
- How are these documents used today?

Presentation
Have students write and present their own version of George Washington's farewell speech, given at the end of his presidency. Have them include information such as
- problems that President Washington and his country faced after the War for Independence ended.
- Washington's accomplishments while in office.
- future issues that Washington felt still needed to be addressed after he left office.

Chapter 6 · **Economy and Expansion** 1800–1830

Chapter at a Glance

SE page

100   *Opening the Chapter and Portfolio Project*

102   SECTION 1   Growth and Conflict

109   SECTION 2   Northern Manufacturing

112   SECTION 3   Southern Agriculture

115   *Connecting History and Economics: The Cotton Gin*

116   *Chapter Review and Group Activity*

Learning Objectives

- Explain how the United States grew in the early nineteenth century.
- Describe the events that led to the War of 1812.
- Discuss how the Industrial Revolution affected the economies in the North and South.

Social Studies Skills

- Explore how the cotton gin changed the economy of the South.
- Use a timeline to describe how the nation grew in the early nineteenth century.

Writing Skills

- Write a diary entry describing important events that occurred in the early 1800s.
- Write a paragraph explaining the importance of the Monroe Doctrine.
- Write two paragraphs comparing and contrasting life on a farm and life in a factory during the early 1800s.
- Write an ad describing the benefits of the cotton gin.

Map and Chart Skills

- Use a map to trace the route of Lewis and Clark's expedition.
- Use a map to locate the area and natural boundaries of the Louisiana Purchase.
- Use a chart to describe the problems that the Americans and the British faced during the War of 1812.

Chapter
6

Chapter 6 Economy and Expansion	Use the Program Resources below for reteaching, reinforcement, and enrichment. Additional activities for customizing the lessons can be found in this guide.

Key
Reteaching = ↰   Reinforcement = ⇩   Enrichment = ↰

Sections	Program Resources		
	⇩ Workbook Exercises	Teacher's Planning Guide	Classroom Resource Binder
Growth and Conflict	22, 23	↰ p. 39	↰ Concept Builder 6 *Economy and Expansion* ↰ Outline Map 1 *United States: Political* ↰ Transparency 4, 12 *United States: Political The War of 1812*
Northern Manufacturing	24	⇩ p. 40	↰ Concept Builder 6 *Economy and Expansion*
Southern Agriculture	25	↰ p.41	↰ Concept Builder 6 *Economy and Expansion* Document-Based Question 6 *Darling Nellie Gray*
Connecting History and Economics: The Cotton Gin		↰ p. 42	↰ Feature Practice 37 *Connecting History and Economics: City Populations Grow*
Chapter 6 Review		↰ p. 43	⇩ Words to Know 35 ↰ Challenge 38 ⇩ Chapter Tests A & B, 39, 40

Customizing the Chapter

Opening the Chapter
Student Edition, pages 100–101

Photo Activity
Ask students to study the painting and the photo. Explain that during the early 1800s, the United States began to expand its economy. Mention that new growing industries, such as the cotton industry, needed factory workers to spin cotton. Ask students how they think this factory compares with modern factories today. What are some differences? On chart paper, have students list products made today. Next to each item, have them write whether they think the product is made by a factory worker, a machine, or both.

Words to Know

Review the Words to Know on page 101 of the Student Edition. To help students remember the words, have pairs of students write the words and their definitions on separate index cards. Have them take turns matching a word with the correct definition. Students can use the Glossary in the Student Edition to look up each vocabulary term to check for accuracy. Then have them write the words and definitions in their journals.

The following words and definitions are covered in this chapter:

elector a person selected to vote for the President and Vice President

impressment the act of forcing a person into public service, especially into a navy

embargo a government order that stops trade with other countries

nationalism pride in one's country

doctrine a set of beliefs

industry the making or producing of goods by businesses and factories

textile woven cloth

interchangeable part a part that can be used in place of another part in manufactured products

mass production a method of making large numbers of goods quickly and cheaply

cotton gin a machine that separates cotton from its seeds

overseer a person who watches over and directs the work of others

Portfolio Project

Summary: Students choose two of the following topics and write diary entries from the perspective of a person living in the United States in the early 1800s: *the Louisiana Purchase, the Lewis and Clark expedition, the War of 1812,* or *mass production of goods.*

Materials: student journals; reference materials (Unit 2 Bibliography and Internet sites, pages 236–240)

Procedure: Have students choose two topics and take notes on these topics as they reread the chapter. Students may conduct further research on their topics. Ask students to write a diary entry about each topic from the perspective of someone living in the United States in the early 1800s.

Assessment: Use the Individual Activity Rubric on page *xii* of this guide. Fill in the rubric with the additional information below. For this project, students should have

- written a diary entry from the perspective of someone living in the 1800s.
- described feelings about major events of the time.

Learning Objectives

Review the Learning Objectives on page 101 of the Student Edition before starting the chapter. Students can use the list as a learning guide. Suggest they write the objectives in a journal or use the Chapter Goals and Self-Check worksheet found on page PA 6 in the Classroom Resource Binder.

After reading each section of the chapter, have students write an example of what they learned under the appropriate objective. Suggest that students use these worksheets as a practice guide to help them study for the chapter test.

Timeline

Use the timeline to discuss the sequence of events in this chapter. Point out the timeline's title, its time span, and the intervals. After students have read the chapter, have them review the timeline and suggest additional entries.

SECTION 1: Growth and Conflict
Student Edition, pages 102–108

Section Objectives

* Explain the importance of the Louisiana Purchase.
* Describe the Lewis and Clark expedition.
* Describe the relationship between Great Britain and the United States in the 1800s.
* Describe the War of 1812.
* Explain the main purpose of the Monroe Doctrine.

Words to Know

elector, impressment, embargo, nationalism, doctrine

Cooperative Group Activity

Power to the Country

Materials: reference materials (Unit 2 Bibliography and Internet sites, pages 236–240); KWL chart (Classroom Resource Binder, page GO 6); poster paper; markers

Procedure: Divide the class into three groups and assign each group one of the following topics: *the Louisiana Purchase and the Lewis and Clark Expedition, the War of 1812,* or *the Monroe Doctrine.* Distribute a KWL chart to each group. Explain to students that a KWL chart helps you organize what you <u>k</u>now, what you <u>w</u>ant to know, and what you <u>l</u>earned.

- Student groups work together to complete the first and second sections of the KWL chart on their topics.
- Groups conduct additional research on their topics.
- Groups complete the final sections of their KWL charts, listing as many supporting details as possible.
- Groups develop their presentations. They recreate their KWL charts on poster paper to use during their presentations.
- Each group presents its project to the class, using its KWL poster.
- Encourage students to take notes during presentations.

Customizing the Activity for Individual Needs

ESL   To help ESL students understand the major events in U.S. history during the 1800s, write each of the three events on the chalkboard and ask them to summarize the events in their own words.

Learning Styles   Students can:

 look at a map of the United States that shows its expansion in the 1800s. Then point to the places where the major events took place.

 sort index cards with items from each section of the KWL chart.

 work with partners to discuss the importance of the three events.

Enrichment Activity

Point out that Francis Scott Key wrote the poem "The Star Spangled Banner," as he watched the Americans defend themselves against a British attack on Fort McHenry during the War of 1812. Give students copies of the poem; have them read each line of the poem; and then write about what Francis Scott Key might have been thinking, feeling, and seeing on the night he wrote the poem.

Alternative Assessment

Students can assume the role of a U.S. soldier fighting in the War of 1812 to write a short paragraph about the reasons for fighting.

SECTION 2: Northern Manufacturing
Student Edition, pages 109–111

Section Objectives
- Describe the Industrial Revolution.
- Identify the events that helped factories grow in the North.
- Explain the concept of mass production.

Words to Know
industry, textile, interchangeable part, mass production

Cooperative Group Activity

Mention Your Invention
Materials: Who, What, Where, When, Why, How chart (Classroom Resource Binder, page GO 7); chart paper; markers

Procedure: Organize the class into small groups to brainstorm a list of inventions that can be mass-produced.

- Groups then vote on the invention they think would be most valuable and popular.
- Groups use the *Who, What, Where, When, Why, How* chart to describe their inventions.
- Group members name their invention and work together to write a detailed description about the invention using their completed chart.
- Groups choose a spokesperson to read their descriptions to the class.

Customizing the Activity for Individual Needs

ESL   To help students understand the concept of mass production, have partners choose one of the inventions and discuss how it could be built. Partners discuss the steps needed to mass-produce the invention.

Learning Styles   Students can:

 look up pictures of the inventions in an encyclopedia.

 draw pictures of what the inventions might look like.

work in pairs to discuss why this invention/product is useful and should be purchased.

Reinforcement

Ask students to write on separate index cards eight key words or phrases that pertain to the Industrial Revolution. Students may scan the Student Edition for key words or phrases, such as: *textile mill, Eli Whitney, interchangeable parts, mass production, steam engine, textile, Lowell,* and *factory.* Students place the cards face down and then take turns turning the cards over and explaining how the words or phrases relate to the Industrial Revolution.

Alternative Assessment

Students can explain two economic benefits of the Industrial Revolution.

Sample Answers: The Industrial Revolution provided Americans with many more jobs. More products could be produced in less time.

SECTION 3: Southern Agriculture
Student Edition, pages 112–114

Section Objectives
- Explain how the cotton gin changed the economy.
* Describe some conditions of slavery in the South.
* Identify people who led protests against slavery.

Words to Know
cotton gin, overseer

Cooperative Group Activity

Documentary Filmmakers
Materials: reference materials (Unit 2 Internet sites, page 236–240); oak tag

Procedure: Organize students into groups of five or six. Have them prepare an outline and a script for a documentary film about the life and times of enslaved African Americans working on plantations in the South during the early 1800s. Students may conduct additional research for this project.

- Groups brainstorm a list of topics for their films. Their list should include conditions of slavery in the 1800s and important people to highlight,

such as Nat Turner, who led one of the largest slave revolts in U.S. history.
- Some group members then write a script for their documentary and give it a title.
- Other group members can draw illustrations and maps to visually describe their film.
- One group member presents the concept for their documentary to the rest of the class.

Customizing the Activity for Individual Needs

ESL To help students understand what a documentary is, explain that it is a kind of film that is based on facts rather than a story. It is nonfiction presented in dramatic form. Then brainstorm phrases that describe a documentary— *tells facts, true story, fact film.*

Learning Styles Students can:

 fill in a KWL chart to organize information for the topic of their group's documentary.

 choose a scene from their documentary and draw what that scene might look like.

 choose music to accompany their documentary, such as spirituals, or songs that enslaved African Americans passed on by word of mouth.

Enrichment Activity

Explain to students that music and singing played important roles in the lives of enslaved African Americans. Provide music or have students take a trip to the library to listen to African American songs on recordings and to conduct research on African American music. Have students make a presentation to the class about their findings.

Alternative Assessment

Students can explain why enslaved African Americans were necessary to the southern economy.

Sample Answer: Enslaved people did most of the work on southern plantations, such as farming, cooking, and making tools. These goods were then sold for profit.

CONNECTING HISTORY AND ECONOMICS: The Cotton Gin
Student Edition, page 115

Objectives
- Social Studies Skill: Create a flow chart to describe the process of growing and selling cotton.
- Social Studies Skill: Write a journal entry describing life in the cotton fields.
- Social Studies Skill: Design a newspaper advertisement that explains the benefits of the cotton gin.

Activities

From Field to Store
Material: chart paper

Procedure: As a class, discuss the steps involved in growing cotton in the 1800s, and later manufacturing it into clothing. List responses on the chalkboard such as *cotton was grown in fields in the South and tended by enslaved Africans; Cotton was cleaned using the cotton gin; cotton fiber was then woven into cloth in factories; cloth was sent to clothing manufacturers in the North to be made into dresses, shirts, and suits; clothing was shipped around the world and sold in stores.*

Invite students to create a flow chart to describe each step.

Life in the Cotton Field
Material: journal

Procedure: Have students write a journal entry that describes a typical day for an enslaved person working in the cotton fields of a Southern plantation in the 1800s. Students may wish to illustrate their entry.

Coming Soon!
Materials: markers; poster paper

Procedure: Invite students to design a 1794 newspaper advertisement that promotes the cotton gin. Have students include reasons why plantation owners would want this invention. Working in groups, have students write a persuasive ad and draw an illustration to include in the advertisement.

Practice
Have students complete Connecting History and Economics: City Populations Grow on page 37 of the Classroom Resource Binder.

Closing the Chapter
Student Edition, pages 116–117

Chapter Vocabulary
Review with students the Words to Know on page 101 of the Student Edition.

Have students complete the Vocabulary Review on page 116, by completing each sentence with a term from the list.

For more vocabulary practice, have them complete the vocabulary exercise on page 35 of the Classroom Resource Binder.

Test Tip
Have students practice the test tip in the Chapter Quiz. Have students write the questions on a separate sheet of paper and underline or circle the important words.

Learning Objectives
Have the students review their Chapter Goals Worksheet found on page PA 6 in the Classroom Resource Binder. They can check off the goal they have reached. Note that each section of the quiz corresponds to a Learning Objective.

Group Activity
Summary: Students create a two-column chart. One column shows improvements that resulted from America's growth during the 1800s. The other column shows problems that were caused by each new change.

Procedure: Divide students into two groups. Each group makes a two-column chart that shows the improvements and problems resulting from the growth of the United States during the early 1800s.

The two groups then quiz each other about problems and improvements that are included on their lists.

Assessment: Use the Group Activity Rubric found on page *xiii* of this guide. Fill in the rubric with the following additional information. For this activity, students should have

- participated in creating two lists outlining improvements and problems.
- asked questions and volunteered answers in a group setting.

RELATED MATERIALS   See the Unit 2 Overview page for related Globe Fearon books that can be used to enrich and extend the materials in the chapter.

Traditional Assessment

Chapter Quiz
The Chapter Quiz on page 117 of the Student Edition can be used as an open-book test, a closed-book test, or a homework assignment. Use the quiz to identify concepts in the chapter that students need to review. Chapter Tests can be found in the Classroom Resource Binder on pages 39–40. Workbook pages 22–25 can be used for additional practice.

Chapter Tests
Use Chapter Tests A and B on pages 39–40 in the Classroom Resource Binder to further assess mastery of chapter concepts.

Additional Resources
Use the Resource Planner on page 38 in this guide to assign additional exercises from the Classroom Resource Binder and Workbook.

Alternative Assessment

Student Interview
List these events on the chalkboard: *War of 1812; Louisiana Purchase;* and *Industrial Revolution.* Ask:
• What led to each event?
• What is the importance of each event?
• How did each event help the nation grow?

Performance
Have students perform a scene set in the early 1800s. They assume the roles of the characters needed to perform the scene. For example, students may wish to act out a scene involving Lewis, Clark, and Sacajawea during their expedition.

Chapter
6

Chapter 7 · **The Changing United States** 1820–1850

Chapter at a Glance

SE page

118   *Opening the Chapter and Portfolio Project*

120   SECTION 1   The Policies of Adams and Jackson

124   *Voices From the Past: George M. Harkins*

125   SECTION 2   Moving West

131   SECTION 3   Gold and California

134   *Chapter Review and Group Activity*

Learning Objectives

- Explain how Andrew Jackson was different from previous Presidents.
- Identify ways people traveled west.
- Explain why people moved west.
- Discuss the reasons for and the results of the war with Mexico.
- Discuss how the discovery of gold led to California becoming a state.

Social Studies Skills

- Explore the point of view of a Choctaw district chief.
- Use a timeline to describe events that occurred during the westward expansion of the United States.
- Create a travel plan from the perspective of a settler heading west.

Writing Skills

- Write a song or poem describing how Native Americans or settlers may have felt about their land in the 1800s.
- Write a persuasive paragraph explaining why Andrew Jackson would be a good president, from the perspective of a Jackson supporter.
- Write a descriptive paragraph about an 1850s journey between the Mississippi River and the Pacific coast.
- Write a letter describing the California gold rush from the perspective of someone finding gold for the first time.

Map Skill

- Use a map to identify territories that were gained during the westward expansion of the United States.

Resource Planner

Chapter 7
The Changing United States

Use the Program Resources below for reteaching, reinforcement, and enrichment. Additional activities for customizing the lessons can be found in this guide.

Key
Reteaching = ↶   Reinforcement = ↓   Enrichment = ↷

Sections	Program Resources		
	↓ Workbook Exercises	Teacher's Planning Guide	Classroom Resource Binder
The Policies of Adams and Jackson	26	↓ p. 46	
Voices From the Past: George M. Harkins		↶ p. 47	↶ Feature Practice 43 *Voices From the Past: Washington Irving*
Moving West	27, 28	↶ p. 47	↷ Document-Based Question 5 *The American Frugal Housewife* ↓ Outline Map 2 *United States: Physical* ↓ Transparency 13 *United States: Political*
Gold and California	29	↓ p. 48	↶ Geography and Economics 2 *Trails West*
Chapter 7 Review		p. 49	↓ Concept Builder 6 *Economy and Expansion* ↓ Words to Know 41 ↶ Challenge 44 ↓ Chapter Tests A & B, 45, 46

Chapter
7

Customizing the Chapter

Opening the Chapter
Student Edition, pages 118–119

Photo Activity

Ask students to study the painting and think about where the people are going, the difficulty of the trip, and why they are traveling in covered wagons.

Explain that as the United States grew in the early 1800s, people began traveling west. Point out the photo of the lantern. Mention that the only sources of light that travelers had were the sun, the moon and stars, their campfires, and the lanterns they could light in the evening. Discuss why people traveled westward. Encourage students to think about the travelers' hopes, dreams, and what they might be searching for.

Words to Know

Review the Words to Know on page 119 of the Student Edition. To help students remember the words, invite pairs of students to locate the words in the Glossary in the Student Edition. Have students take turns giving clues that tell about a vocabulary word, without using any part of the word itself. Ask each pair of students to keep track of the number of clues it takes to guess each key word.

The following words and definitions are covered in this chapter.

tariff a tax on goods brought into a country

spoils system the system of giving government jobs to people who had helped to get the winner elected

canal a human-made waterway

mountain man a fur trapper and trader who lived in the mountains and knew the wilderness

forty-niner a person who went to California in 1849 to find gold

ranch a large farm with grazing land for raising horses, cattle, or sheep

Portfolio Project

Summary: Students write a poem or song reflecting how the Native Americans might have felt when settlers came to their land in the 1800s.

Materials: journals

Procedure: Have students consider how Native Americans felt when settlers moved onto their lands. Have students write their thoughts in their journals, then use this information to write a poem or song expressing their feelings. Help students select simple melodies for their songs. Encourage students to recite their songs or poems for the rest of the class.

Assessment: Use the Individual Activity Rubric on page *xii* of this guide. Fill in the rubric with the additional information below. For this project, students should have

- written a poem or song about the Native Americans' or settlers' feelings about the land.
- used information from the chapter to create their poems or songs.

Learning Objectives

Review the Learning Objectives on page 119 of the Student Edition before starting the chapter. Students can use the list as a learning guide. Suggest that they write the objectives in a journal or use the Chapter Goals and Self-Check worksheet found on page PA 6 of the Classroom Resource Binder.

After reading each section of the chapter, have students write an example of what they learned under the appropriate objective. Suggest that students use these worksheets as a practice guide to help them study for the chapter test.

Timeline

Use the timeline to discuss the sequence of events in this chapter. Point out the timeline's title, its time span, and the intervals. After students have read the chapter, have them review the timeline and suggest additional entries.

SECTION 1: The Policies of Adams and Jackson
Student Edition, pages 120–123

Section Objectives

* Describe how John Quincy Adams won the election of 1824.
* Explain why the Tariff of 1828 was unpopular.
* Identify ways in which Andrew Jackson was different from the Presidents before him.
* Describe the spoils system.
* Describe the Indian Removal Act.

Words to Know

tariff, spoils system

Cooperative Group Activity

In the News

Materials: Who, What, Where, When, Why, How chart (Classroom Resource Binder, page GO 7); reference materials (Unit 2 Bibliography and Internet sites, pages 236–240)

Procedure: Have students write newspaper articles for a class newspaper, focusing on events that occurred during the Adams and Jackson administrations. Divide the class into five groups and assign each group one of the following topics: *the election of 1824; the election of 1828; the Tariff of 1828; the spoils system;* or *the Indian Removal Act.*

- Groups research their topics and use the *who, what, where, when, why, how* chart to help them list relevant facts.
- Groups brainstorm different ways that they can write about their topics in a newspaper.
- Some group members write newspaper articles. Others write headlines and draw cartoons for the articles.

- If possible, one group member inputs the articles on computer and prints out a copy.
- Groups combine their articles for a class newspaper.

Customizing the Activity for Individual Needs

ESL   To help students, turn one group's article into cloze paragraphs, deleting every fifth word. Have ESL students complete the article by filling in the blanks.

Learning Styles   Students can:

 look at political cartoons in current newspapers and then draw a cartoon of their own that focuses on their topic.

 draw a picture to accompany their article and label it.

 work in pairs to tape-record their articles.

Reinforcement Activity

Have students write journal entries from the perspective of a Cherokee living in 1838. Journal entries should tell what happened to Cherokee families when they were forced from their homeland.

Alternative Assessment

Students can write brief statements in response to each of the following three questions:
- Would you have supported the Tariff of 1828? Explain your answer.
- Would you have voted for Andrew Jackson in 1828? Explain your answer.
- How would you have changed policies concerning Native Americans in 1830?

VOICES FROM THE PAST: George M. Harkins
Student Edition, page 124

Objectives
- Social Studies Skill: List reasons why the practice of treating Native Americans differently was unfair.
- Social Studies Skill: Describe how the people of the Choctaw nation might have felt leaving about their homeland.

- Social Studies Skill: Identify reasons why the people of the Choctaw nation wanted to stay in their homeland.

Activities
What If?
Procedure: Explain to students that in the 1800s, Native Americans were treated differently from other Americans. Their land taken was away from them and their families split up. Have students work in small groups to discuss why this practice was unfair. Students can write their responses on index cards. Groups then exchange cards and read and discuss each other's responses.

My People's Sorrow
Procedure: Ask students to write a four-line poem expressing the sadness, frustration, and anger the people of the Choctaw nation must have felt when they were forced to leave their homeland. Students may wish to set their poem to music.

I Believe...
Materials: copy of the Declaration of Independence (pages 618–623 of the Student Edition)

Procedure: Ask students to write a speech to present to government officials from the perspective of George M. Harkins, district chief of the Choctaw nation. Have them provide reasons why the people of the Choctaw nation should be able to stay in their homeland. Suggest that students cite the Declaration of Independence to support their argument.

Practice
Have students complete Voices From the Past: Washington Irving on page 43 of the Classroom Resource Binder.

SECTION 2: Moving West
Student Edition, pages 125–130

Section Objectives
- Describe modes of travel in the 1800s.
- Compare traveling by railroads with other forms of transportation.
- Describe the westward movement.
- Explain Manifest Destiny.
- Describe how Americans settled Texas.

- Identify the reasons that led to the war between the United States and Mexico.
- * Make a map of the United States.

Words to Know

canal, mountain man

Cooperative Group Activity

Mapmaking

Materials: reference materials (historical maps; outline map of United States (Classroom Resource Binder, page T 14); colored pencils

Procedure: Divide the class into three groups and assign each group one of the following years: 1800, 1825, or 1850. Students can use reference materials, such as historical maps, to help them complete the activity.

- Students fill in the outline map of the United States based on their assigned year.
- Students should include: major cities, transportation routes, landforms, bodies of water, boundary lines; territories, state names, important sites, and a map key.
- Student groups share their maps with the class, pointing out the differences between them.

Customizing the Activity for Individual Needs

ESL To help students understand map skills, have them bring in a map of their native countries and compare them with one of the maps drawn in class. Ask what geographical features the two countries have in common.

Learning Styles Students can:

 place the three maps side by side and work in pairs to describe the progress that was made during this fifty-year time frame.

 illustrate one of the transportation modes of the 1800s.

 work in pairs to give each other directions using one of the maps.

Enrichment Activity

Group the students and have them write rap verses that describe how people traveled from the eastern portion of the United States to the West coast. Have each group share their rap with the class. Tape-record each performance.

Example: We're going on a trip across miles of land. We'll travel over mountains. We'll travel through sand. We can't take a car, a bike, or a plane. They haven't been invented, so we'll take a train!

Alternative Assessment

Students can use the three maps to write brief descriptions of the changes that occurred between 1800–1820 and 1820–1850.

SECTION 3: Gold and California
Student Edition, pages 131–133

Section Objectives

- Describe the events that took place at Sutter's Mill.
- * Explain the events that occurred during the gold rush and the significance of the term *forty-niners*.

Words to Know

forty-niner, ranch

Cooperative Group Activity

Spread the News!

Material: Sequence of Events Chain (Classroom Resource Binder, page GO1)

Procedure: Divide the class into small groups. Review the discovery of gold at Sutter's Mill, where two gold nuggets have just been discovered. Distribute the Sequence of Events Chain to each group.

- Groups brainstorm and list how news of the discovery of gold could spread rapidly throughout the United States and the entire world. Examples include: by a letter to friends; by a newspaper article; by telling another person.
- Group members complete a Sequence of Events Chain with three of their ideas on how the discovery at Sutter's Mill could spread throughout the world.
- Groups share their Sequence of Events Chain with the class.

Customizing the Activity for Individual Needs

ESL To help students understand the term *gold rush,* explain that people *rushed* to California to seek *gold* in 1849. Have students discuss whether they know of family members or friends who have left their homelands in search of a better life elsewhere, and how this compares with immigration during the Gold Rush era.

Learning Styles   Students can:

 find a painting or photo of a forty-niner from a reference source. Write a paragraph describing the forty-niner.

 use a world map to trace routes from New York, Europe, and China to Sutter's Mill in California.

 work in pairs to role-play a scene in which one of Marshall's workers speaks to a local shopkeeper about the discovery of gold.

Reinforcement Activity ⇩

Have students review the term *forty-niner*. Ask them to write a letter, from the perspective of someone who went to California in 1849 to find gold and about their experiences once they arrived in California. Encourage students to include as much description as possible in their letters.

Alternative Assessment

Students can list five ways in which the gold rush affected individuals, the nation, and the world.

Closing the Chapter
Student Edition, pages 134–135

Chapter Vocabulary

Review with students the Words to Know on page 119 of the Student Edition. Then have them complete the Vocabulary Review on page 134 of the Student Edition, by writing *true* or *false* next to each sentence. If the sentence is false, have students change the underlined term to make it true.

For more vocabulary practice, have them complete the vocabulary exercise on page 41 of the Classroom Resource Binder.

Test Tip

Working in pairs, have students answer the Critical Thinking questions in the Chapter Quiz. As they review the section, have students write the main ideas of the paragraphs in order to answer the questions in their own words.

Learning Objectives

Have the students review their Chapter Goals and Self-Check worksheet found on page PA 6 of the Classroom Resource Binder. They can check off the goal they have reached. Note that each section of the quiz corresponds to a Learning Objective.

Group Activity

Summary: Students make travel plans that settlers starting a new life in the West might have made. They present their plans to the class.

Procedure: Divide the class into groups of three or four. Have students brainstorm travel ideas for settlers living on the East coast in the mid-1800s who will be moving to California in two months. Have groups list preparations for their journey, such as determining the route they will take, their mode of transportation, how long the trip will take, and the supplies they will need. Have groups share their travel plans with the class and discuss the similarities and differences of each plan.

Assessment: Use the Group Activity Rubric found on page *xiii* of this guide. Fill in the rubric with the following additional information. For this activity, students should have

• worked cooperatively to prepare a list of travel plans.

• presented their ideas in a clear, cohesive manner.

RELATED MATERIALS   See the Unit Overview page for related Globe Fearon books that can be used to enrich and extend the materials in the chapter.

Traditional Assessment

Chapter Quiz

The Chapter Quiz on page 135 of the Student Edition can be used as an open-book test, a closed-book test, or a homework assignment. Use the quiz to identify concepts in the chapter that students need to review. Chapter Tests can be found in the Classroom Resource Binder on pages 45–46. Workbook pages 26–29 can be used for additional practice.

Chapter Tests

Use Chapter Tests A and B on pages 45–46 in the Classroom Resource Binder to further assess mastery of chapter concepts.

Additional Resources

Use the Resource Planner on page 45 of this guide to assign additional exercises from the Classroom Resource Binder and Workbook.

Alternative Assessment

Student Interview

Give students sheets of paper on which the following events are written: Texas gains independence, gold rush, War with Mexico, Trail of Tears, John Quincy Adams elected President. Ask:

- Which of these events occurred first?
- Which event occurred last?
- Which event is the cause of another event?
- Which event do you think was most important? Why?

Open-Ended

- Students create a timeline of at least five events and their dates as found in the chapter. These should be events other than those found in the chapter timeline.
- Encourage students to scan the map "Expansion of the United States" for possible timeline entries.

Chapter 8 · **Newcomers and New Ideas** 1820–1860

Chapter at a Glance

SE page

136   *Opening the Chapter and Portfolio Project*

138   SECTION 1   New Ways and New People

142   SECTION 2   Women and Political Rights

146   *Voices From the Past: Elizabeth Cady Stanton*

147   SECTION 3   Working for Reform

150   *Chapter Review and Group Activity*

Learning Objectives

- Discuss reasons that cities grew between 1820 and 1860.
- Identify the main immigrant groups who came to the United States in the mid-1800s.
- Describe the struggle of women for equal rights.
- Discuss the movement to reform U.S. society.

Social Studies Skills

- Explore Elizabeth Cady Stanton's view on raising young girls.
- Explain events that occurred in U.S. history between 1820 and 1860 by creating a time capsule for future generations.
- Use a timeline to identify events related to social and political reform.
- Create a storyboard showing reactions to the Seneca Falls Convention.

Writing Skills

- Write a journal entry describing an experience from the perspective of an immigrant from China during the 1840s.
- Create a poster to persuade women to attend the Seneca Falls Convention.
- Write a letter to an editor of a newspaper supporting public education.

Map and Chart Skills

- Use a chart to show the ways in which women worked to gain equal rights for all U.S. citizens.

Chapter
8

Resource Planner

Chapter 8 Newcomers and New Ideas	Use the Program Resources below for reteaching, reinforcement, and enrichment. Additional activities for customizing the lessons can be found in this guide.

Key
Reteaching = ⟲   Reinforcement = ⬇   Enrichment = ⟳

Sections	Program Resources		
	Workbook Exercises	Teacher's Planning Guide	Classroom Resource Binder
New Ways and New People	30	⟳ p. 53	⟳ Concept Builder 8 *Newcomers and New Ideas* ⟲ Outline Maps 3, 8 *Europe, Asia*
Women and Political Rights	31, 32	⬇ p. 54	⟳ Concept Builder 8 *Newcomers and New Ideas*
Voices From the Past: Elizabeth Cady Stanton		⟲ p. 55	⟳ Feature Practice 49 *Voices From the Past: Elizabeth Blackwell*
Working for Reform	33	⟲ p. 55	⟳ Concept Builder 8 *Newcomers and New Ideas*
Chapter 8 Review		p. 56	⬇ Words to Know 47 ⟲ Challenge 50 ⬇ Chapter Tests A & B, 51, 52 ⬇ Unit Tests Parts I & II, 53, 54

Customizing the Chapter

Opening the Chapter
Student Edition, pages 136–137

Photo Activity
Have students look at the painting of immigrants arriving in the Unites States. Then point out the photograph of the soup bowl. Explain to students that in the mid-1800s, groups of immigrants from around the world came to the United States in search of a better life. Ask students how the immigrants traveled to America, what they might have brought with them, and what their expectations might have been. As students read the chapter, have them compare their ideas with the immigrants' actual experiences.

Words to Know

Review the Words to Know on page 137 of the Student Edition. To help students remember the words, ask them to skim the text and find each boldfaced word and its definition. Remind students to use the Glossary in the Student Edition to help them.

The following words and definitions are covered in this chapter:

rural having to do with the country

urban having to do with the city

immigrant a person who comes to a country for the purpose of living there

famine a time when people in a place starve because there is not enough food

equal rights rights that all people in a society should have

suffrage the right to vote

reformer a person who works for a cause that improves the way something is done in a society

temperance a reform movement that is against drinking alcohol

Portfolio Project

Summary: Students create a time capsule to help future generations better understand U.S. history between 1820 and 1860.

Materials: plastic jars and lids

Procedure: Students scan the chapter to list important events. Students construct a time capsule that includes their list of facts and other items, such as objects that represent this time in history, drawings, maps, or news ads. Students present their capsule to the class. Have the class vote on the most imaginative time capsule.

Assessment: Use the Individual Activity Rubric on page *xii* of this guide. Fill in the rubric with the additional information below. For this project, students should have

- collected relevant facts about the time period.
- used a variety of resources to assemble time capsules.

Learning Objectives

Review the Learning Objectives on page 137 of the Student Edition before starting the chapter. Students can use the list as a learning guide. Suggest they write the objectives in a journal or use the Chapter Goals and Self-Check worksheet found on page PA 6 of the Classroom Resource Binder.

After reading each section of the chapter, have students write an example of what they learned under the appropriate objective. Suggest that students use these worksheets as a practice guide to help them study for the chapter test.

Timeline

Use the timeline to discuss the sequence of events in this chapter. Point out the timeline's title, its time span, and the intervals. After students have read the chapter, have them review the timeline and suggest additional entries.

SECTION 1: New Ways and New People
Student Edition, pages 138–141

Section Objectives

- Identify reasons why people moved to cities.
- Explain the reasons why German and Irish immigrants came to the United States between 1830 and 1850.
- Explain the reasons why Chinese men came to California in the mid-1800s.

Words to Know

rural, urban, immigrant, famine

Cooperative Group Activity

"Log Me In" Data Sheets

Materials: reference materials (Unit 2 Internet sites, pages 236–240)

Procedure: Organize students into three groups. Each group represents the following countries: Germany, Ireland, and China. Explain to students that they will make data sheets for immigrants who entered the United States from 1830 to 1860. Students may wish to do additional research for this project.

- Most students in each group assume the roles of immigrants. They create scenarios for themselves based on historical information: a date they might have arrived in the United States, their country of origin, their U.S. destination, their occupation, their reasons for leaving their homeland, their intended length of stay, and their health status.
- One student from each group compiles the information in data sheets after interviewing each immigrant.

- After students have completed their data sheets, have them share their information with the rest of the class.

Customizing the Activity for Individual Needs

ESL To help students understand the concept of immigration, have students share an experience they or someone they know had when they immigrated to this country.

Learning Styles Students can:

 look at a map to locate the countries that immigrants came from in the early 1800s.

 play a trivia game about immigration facts that they have written on index cards.

 make oral presentations about the various reasons that immigrants came to the United States.

Enrichment Activity

Have students create their own family tree. Have students find out who was the first member of their family to come to the United States. Why did that person emigrate? Where was the person from? Students can present their family trees to the class.

Alternative Assessment

Students can write three journal entries, one each from the perspective of a German, Irish, and Asian immigrant. The entries should include the reasons for leaving their homeland as well as their hopes and dreams for a new life in America.

SECTION 2: Women and Political Rights
Student Edition, pages 142–145

Section Objectives
- Identify leaders who fought for equal rights in the early 1800s.
- ∗ Explain reasons why the Seneca Falls Convention took place.

Words to Know
equal rights, suffrage

Cooperative Group Activity

A Fight for Rights! Poster

Materials: reference materials (Unit 2 Bibliography and Internet sites, pages 236–240); poster paper; markers

Procedure: Organize students into five groups and assign each group one of the following rights for which women were fighting at the Seneca Falls Convention of 1848: *voting in elections, earning wages, owning property, having a career, having equal say about children after a divorce.*

- Groups brainstorm a list of strategies for convincing members of the Seneca Falls Convention of 1848 to support the right they have been assigned.
- Group members create posters listing the benefits of supporting this right.
- Groups choose a spokesperson to present their posters to the class. Encourage students to take notes on each presentation.

Customizing the Activity for Individual Needs

ESL To help students understand the concept of *suffrage*, pair ESL students with English-proficient students to role-play a scene between two people: one who supports suffrage and one who does not.

Learning Styles Students can:

 highlight the important words on the posters that describe why women's rights are just.

 use posterboard and safety pins to make buttons supporting the women's movement. Each button should have a slogan.

 prepare and tape-record a speech that outlines the list of demands for women's rights.

Reinforcement Activity

Ask students to make a chart to compare and contrast the ways in which life would be different today if women did not have the right to vote in elections, earn wages, own property, have a career, have equal say about children after a divorce.

Alternative Assessment

Students can write a letter to a newspaper from the perspective of a person living in 1850, stating the reasons why women should have equal rights.

VOICES FROM THE PAST: Elizabeth Cady Stanton
Student Edition, page 146

Objectives
- Social Studies Skill: Compare and contrast ways in which girls should be raised.
- Social Studies Skill: Discuss how girls and boys are raised, and debate the nature versus nurture theory.
- Social Studies Skill: Identify gender issues that are being raised in today's society.

Activities

A New Approach to Raising Girls Interview
Procedure: Have students review the ways in which Stanton believed girls should be raised. Using this information, have students create a series of questions to ask Stanton in a class interview. Select one student to play the role of Stanton.

Nature vs. Nurture
Procedure: Ask students to think about the following questions: Are girls nurtured, cared for, and raised differently from boys? Do girls naturally prefer to play with dolls, while boys prefer trucks? Have students take either a nature or nurture stance and debate the issue.

Gender Roles
Procedure: Have students think about current issues being raised in today's society about the roles of men and women. Have students make a list of issues in the form of questions, such as *Should women be allowed to fight in wars? Should a man be able to take a leave of absence from work when he and his wife have a baby?* Have students present their lists and vote on each issue.

Practice
Have students complete Voices From the Past: Elizabeth Blackwell from the Classroom Resource Binder.

SECTION 3: Working for Reform
Student Edition, pages 147–149

Section Objectives
- Explain why people believed education reform was important.
- Identify why the temperance movement was established.
- Describe mental health conditions that Dorothea Dix helped to reform.
* Describe the changes reformers worked toward in the mid-1800s.

Words to Know
temperance, reformer

Cooperative Group Activity

Petitions for Reform
Materials: reference materials (Unit 2 Bibliography and Internet sites, pages 236–240); chart paper; markers

Procedure: Explain to students that a petition is a written request to the government asking for change. Divide the class into three groups and assign one of the following topics to each group: *education; alcohol abuse;* or *mental health.* You may wish to have students do additional research on their topics.

- Group members use chart paper and markers to write the title of their topic and the following headings: *Present Conditions; Changes That Are Needed; Why Changes Are Needed;* and *Benefits of Changes.*
- Students list relevant information under each category.
- Groups then use their charts to write a petition.
- Groups choose a spokesperson to read their petitions aloud.
- Students vote on whether to support the petition.

Customizing the Activity for Individual Needs
ESL To help students understand the meaning of the word *petition,* point out that it is a formal request, usually accompanied by documents and signatures. Pair students to brainstorm a list of synonyms, such as *request,* or *ask.*

Learning Styles Students can:

 complete a Cause and Effect chart (Classroom Resource Binder, page GO 2) on one of the topics for reform.

 sort index cards that list statements about each reform into categories representing each reform movement.

 role-play a scene between a reporter and a leader in the reform movement.

Chapter **8**

Enrichment Activity

List on the chalkboard the improvements that the United States has made in education, alcohol abuse, and mental health since the 1800s. Have students brainstorm additional changes they think are needed and chart them. Then have students use this information to write a class petition that can be circulated throughout the school and, if appropriate, sent to their local congressperson.

Alternative Assessment

Students can write a journal entry about each reform from the perspective of the following people: Emma Willard (Education); Horace Mann (Education); Dorothea Dix (Mental Health).

Closing the Chapter
Student Edition, pages 150–151

Chapter Vocabulary

Review with students the Words to Know on page 137 of the Student Edition. Then have them complete the Vocabulary Review on page 150 of the Student Edition, by labeling each sentence as *true* or *false*. If the sentence is false, have students change the underlined term to make it true.

For more vocabulary practice, have them complete the vocabulary exercise on page 47 of the Classroom Resource Binder.

Test Tip

Encourage students to look over the test before they begin to answer questions. Tell them to set aside enough time to complete all questions. If, however, they are having difficulty completing one question, they should move to the next one.

Learning Objectives

Have students review their Chapter Goals and Self-Check worksheet found on page PA 6 of the Classroom Resource Binder. They can check off the goal they have reached. Note that each section of the quiz corresponds to a Learning Objective.

Group Activity

Summary: Students create storyboards that illustrate reactions to topics and events of the 1848 Seneca Falls Convention.

Materials: oak tag; markers

Procedure: Divide the class into small groups and have them review details of the 1848 Seneca Falls Convention. Have group members discuss and list the demands that the convention attendees decided upon, and then brainstorm a list of reactions that they think some people might have had when they learned of these demands. Have students use this information to draw a series of four or five frames, or storyboards, that illustrate people's reactions. They should write captions under each visual.

Assessment: Use the Group Activity Rubric found on page *xiii* of this guide. Fill in the rubric with the following additional information. For this activity, students should have

• created at least four frames for the storyboard.

• incorporated ideas about the Seneca Falls Convention in their frames.

RELATED MATERIALS See the Unit Overview page for related Globe Fearon books that can be used to enrich and extend the materials in this chapter.

Traditional Assessment

Chapter Quiz

The Chapter Quiz on page 151 of the Student Edition can be used as an open-book test, a closed-book test, or a homework assignment. Use the quiz to identify concepts in the chapter that students need to review. Chapter Tests can be found in the Classroom Resource Binder on pages 51–52. Workbook pages 30–33 can be used for additional practice.

Chapter Tests

Use Chapter Tests A and B on pages 51–52 in the Classroom Resource Binder to further assess mastery of chapter concepts.

Additional Resources

Use the Resource Planner on page 52 of this guide to assign additional exercises from the Classroom Resource Binder and Workbook.

Alternative Assessment

Performance

Have students explain the role of a reformer to the rest of the class. Then have students assume the roles of different reformers. Students explain:

• what reform movement this person was involved with.
• when this person worked for reforms.
• the outcome of this person's work.
• how this person's work affected other people's lives.

Real-Life Connection

Students explain how the following social reforms of the 1800s affect life today: *Immigration, Equal Rights, Education, Temperance,* and *Mental Health.*

Unit Assessment

This is the last chapter in Unit 2, Growth of a New Nation. To assess cumulative knowledge and to provide standardized-test practice, have students complete the Unit Review Test on page 152 of the Student Edition, and the Unit 2 Cumulative Test on pages 53–54 of the Classroom Resource Binder.

Chapter

8

Unit 3 ▷ A Nation Divided

CHAPTER 9	PORTFOLIO PROJECT	BUILDING YOUR SKILLS	GROUP ACTIVITY	TIMELINE
North and South Disagree 1820–1861	A Dialogue	Reading a Map	Arguing a Case	The North and South Grow Apart

CHAPTER 10	PORTFOLIO PROJECT	CONNECTING HISTORY AND...	GROUP ACTIVITY	TIMELINE
The Civil War 1861–1865	Timeline	Technology: The Technology of War	Debating an Issue	War Divides the Nation

CHAPTER 11	PORTFOLIO PROJECT	VOICES FROM THE PAST	GROUP ACTIVITY	TIMELINE
Rebuilding a Divided Nation 1865–1877	Oral History	Tempie Cummins	Performance of a Skit	Reconstruction

RELATED MATERIALS

These are some of the Globe Fearon books that can be used to enrich and extend the material in this unit.

Literary ▷

Pacemaker® Classics: The Red Badge of Courage Written by Stephen Crane. Explores the life of a soldier during the Civil War.

Cultural Diversity ▷

The African American Experience: A History Offers in-depth coverage of the Underground Railroad, the Dred Scott case, John Brown's raid, and Reconstruction.

Skills ▷

Newspaper Workshop Reinforce the skill of interpreting political cartoons with Unit 5, Lesson 2.

Chapter 9 · North and South Disagree 1820–1861

Chapter at a Glance

SE page

154   *Opening the Chapter and Portfolio Project*

156   SECTION 1   Expansion and Compromise

161   *Building Your Skills: Reading a Map*

162   SECTION 2   Northerners Change Their Thinking

165   SECTION 3   Troubles Build

172   *Chapter Review and Group Activity*

Learning Objectives

- Describe how lawmakers tried to settle slavery issues.
- Identify reasons why slavery divided the country.
- Explain how abolitionists worked to end slavery.
- Discuss how Abraham Lincoln's election in 1860 affected the Union.

Social Studies Skills

- Read a map.
- Use a timeline to identify events that led to the war between the North and South.
- Hold a mock trial to teach a decision in the Dred Scott case.

Writing Skills

- Write a dialogue between a historical figure and an interviewer.
- Make a sign describing a position on being taxed on goods from other countries.
- Write an editorial explaining an abolitionist's point of view.
- Write a journal entry identifying how a Union soldier might have felt on April 12, 1861.

Map and Chart Skills

- Use a map to identify free states and slave states.
- Use a chart to compare and contrast issues on taxes, immigration, and slavery in the North, South, and West.

Chapter
9

Resource Planner

Chapter 9
North and South Disagree

Use the Program Resources below for reteaching, reinforcement and enrichment. Additional activities for customizing the lessons can be found in this guide.

Key
Reteaching = ⌒ Reinforcement = ⇓ Enrichment = ⌒

Sections	Program Resources		
	⇓ Workbook Exercises	Teacher's Planning Guide	Classroom Resource Binder
Expansion and Compromise	34, 35	⌒ p. 61	⌒ Writing and Test-Taking 9 *Writing an Effective Paragraph* ⇓ Graphic Organizer 7 *Who, What, Where, When, Why, How Chart* ⌒ Outline Map 2 *United States: Physical*
Building Your Skills: Reading a Map		⇓ p. 62	⇓ Feature Practice 57, 58 *Reading a Map*
Northerners Change Their Thinking	36	⇓ p. 63	
Troubles Build	37	⇓ p. 63	⌒ Transparency 5 *Slavery and the Civil War, 1861*
Chapter 9 Review		p. 64	⇓ Concept Builder 9 *The North and South Disagree* ⇓ Words to Know 55 ⌒ Challenge 59 ⇓ Chapter Tests A & B 60, 61

Customizing the Chapter

Opening the Chapter
Student Edition, pages 154–155

Photo Activity
Invite students to look at the painting depicting enslaved African Americans escaping from the South. Then direct their attention to the photo of the reward poster. Have students brainstorm reasons why African Americans wanted freedom, and how reward posters might have affected their escape.

Words to Know
Review the Words to Know on page 155 of the Student Edition. To help students remember the words, invite pairs of students to write each word and its possible definition. Then, have them use the Glossary in the Student Edition to find correct definitions.

The following words and definitions are covered in this chapter:

free state a state in which slavery was not allowed

slave state a state in which slavery was allowed

sectionalism loyalty to one region of a country instead of to the whole country

fugitive a person who runs away or escapes

abolitionist a person who wanted to end slavery

Underground Railroad a network of secret escape routes enslaved African Americans followed to reach freedom in the North

popular sovereignty a system that allowed people in a territory to make their own decisions

extremist a person whose opinions are very different from those of most people

secede to break away from, as a state leaving the Union

civil war a war between regions or groups of people in the same country

Portfolio Project

Summary: Students interview an important person in United States history who lived between 1820 and 1861.

Materials: reference materials (Unit 3 Bibliography and Internet sites pages 236–240)

Procedure: Have students make a list of important people as they read the chapter. For this project, students may conduct further research on a historical figure. Students choose an important historical figure who lived between 1820 and 1861, and create a list of questions to ask the historical figure. After each question, students write an answer from the perspective of the historical figure. Based on the questions and answers, students write a dialogue between the news reporter and the historical figure.

Assessment: Use the Individual Activity Rubric on page *xii* of this guide. Fill in the rubric with the additional information below. For this project, students should have

• written appropriate questions and answers.

• written a dialogue based on their questions and answers.

Learning Objectives

Review the Learning Objectives on page 155 of the Student Edition before starting the chapter. Students can use the list as a learning guide. Suggest they write the objectives in a journal or use the Chapter Goals and Self-Check worksheet found on page PA 6 in the Classroom Resource Binder. After reading each section of the chapter, have students write an example of what they learned under the appropriate objective. Suggest that students use these worksheets as a practice guide to help them study for the chapter test.

Timeline

Use the timeline to discuss the sequence of events in this chapter. Point out the timeline's title, its time span, and the intervals. After students have read the chapter, have them review the timeline and suggest additional entries.

SECTION 1: Expansion and Compromise
Student Edition, pages 156–160

Section Objectives

• Describe the main points of the Missouri Compromise.

• Identify the results of the Compromise of 1850.

★ Discuss the issues that were debated among people of the North, South, and West.

Words to Know

free state, slave state, sectionalism, fugitive

Cooperative Group Activity

A Three-Way Discussion

Materials: reference materials (Unit 3 Bibliography and Internet sites, pages 236–240)

Procedure: Have students review the concept of sectionalism. You may wish to have them conduct further research on the topic. Then divide the students into three groups, and assign each group one of the following regions of the United States in the 1840s: *North, South,* or *West.*

• Groups review and research issues important to their region involving these topics: *taxes, immigration,* and *slavery.* Groups then make a chart that lists the reasons why their region has taken a particular stance on each issue.

• Each group chooses representatives to debate the first issue, *taxes,* with other group representatives.

• Representatives decide on a compromise that satisfies all three regions.

Chapter **9**

- Groups choose different representatives to debate each of the other two issues, *immigration* and *slavery*.

Customizing the Activity for Individual Needs

ESL To help ESL students understand the different regions of the United States, have them divide an outline map of the country (Classroom Resource Binder, page OM 1) into the regions— North, South, and West.

Learning Styles Students can:

 highlight states in each of the regions— North, South, and West—on a map. Which states were free states and which states were slave states?

 sort index cards listing state names into three piles, each representing a region of the United States in the 1840s.

 work with a partner to play a game of "20 Questions" about each region of the United States in the 1840s.

Enrichment Activity

Initiate a discussion about issues in the classroom or in the school that need resolution, such as dress codes. Have students list these on the chalkboard. Have students think of possible resolutions to each issue, and write these next to the issue. Then, divide the class into groups and assign each group one of the issues. Group members discuss the issue and decide on a solution, compromising if the group is divided on its solution. Have each group present its issue and its resolution or compromise.

Alternative Assessment

Students can work with partners to take turns quizzing each other with true/false questions pertaining to facts about the three regions.

Example: The West wanted to be allowed to make its own decisions about slavery.

Answer: True

BUILDING YOUR SKILLS:
Reading a Map
Student Edition, page 161

Objectives

- Social Studies Skill: Compare and contrast a map of the Compromise of 1850 with a current U.S. political map.
- Social Studies Skill: Identify boundaries, states, territories and geographical features on a map from 1850.
- Social Studies Skill: Label an outline map of United States.

Activities

Maps Then and Now

Materials: Map of the Compromise of 1850; current U.S. political map; Comparison-Contrast chart (Classroom Resource Binder, page GO 4)

Procedure: Have students compare and contrast a map of the Compromise of 1850 with a current U.S. political map. Distribute copies of the Comparison-Contrast chart and ask students to complete the chart by writing in the similarities and differences between the maps.

Go North, South, or West!

Procedure: Have students brainstorm a series of trivia questions based on the map of the Compromise of 1850, and write these questions on index cards. Have students form small groups to play a game of map trivia.

Be a Cartographer

Materials: colored pens; outline map of the United States (Classroom Resource Binder, page OM 2)

Procedure: Have students label an outline map of the United States based on the map of the Compromise of 1850. Students should include state labels, territories, boundary lines, major landforms, rivers, and other geographical and political features.

Practice

Have students complete Building Your Skills: Reading a Map on page 57 of the Classroom Resource Binder.

SECTION 2: Northerners Change Their Thinking
Student Edition, pages 162–164

Section Objectives
- Describe the Underground Railroad and the people important to its success.
- Identify the writers who influenced Northerners to turn away from slavery.
- * Describe the abolitionists and their accomplishments in the mid-1800s.

Words to Know
abolitionist, Underground Railroad

Cooperative Group Activity

Biography of an Abolitionist
Materials: reference materials (Unit 3 Bibliography and Internet sites, pages 236–240)

Procedure: Divide the students into small groups and have them choose an abolitionist to write about, such as Frederick Douglass, Harriet Tubman, or William Lloyd Garrison. Groups may use library reference materials or information from the Internet to learn more about the abolitionist.

- Groups read and take notes, organizing their material into sections, similar to chapters of a book.
- Students use their research to write biographies of their abolitionists, using the sections of their research as different chapters of their biographies.
- Groups choose a member to input the biography on a computer and print it.
- Groups create a title page and table of contents for their biographies.

Customizing the Activity for Individual Needs
ESL To help students, pair ESL students with English-proficient students to play a game of "Who Am I?" about famous abolitionists.

Learning Styles Students can:

 complete a *Who, What, Where, When, Why, How* chart (Classroom Resource Binder, page GO 7) with information about famous abolitionists.

 create informative pamphlets advertising a meeting of abolitionists to be held in one of the northern states.

 assume the role of a famous abolitionist, such as Frederick Douglass, and give a speech about why slavery is wrong.

Reinforcement Activity

Ask students to assume the roles of northern abolitionists. Have the students work in small groups to hold discussions about participating in the Underground Railroad. Have group members discuss their reasons for participating, the pros and cons of participation, and the value of Harriet Tubman's work with the Railroad. Groups can share their views.

Alternative Assessment

Students can write a letter to a publishing house, asking if there is interest in publishing the biography they have written about an abolitionist. Tell students to write the letter from the perspective of an author living in 1860. Encourage students to provide a brief synopsis of the book, as well as reasons why the book is timely and should be published.

SECTION 3: Troubles Build
Student Edition, pages 165–171

Section Objectives
- Describe the Kansas-Nebraska Act.
- Explain the Dred Scott case and its outcome.
- Contrast the beliefs of Stephen Douglas and Abraham Lincoln.
- * Explain the secession of many southern states in 1860.
- * Describe events that occurred at Fort Sumter.

Words to Know
popular sovereignty, extremist, secede, civil war

Cooperative Group Activity

Abe's Private Journal
Materials: reference materials (Unit 3 Bibliography and Internet sites, pages 236–240)

Procedure: Divide the class into two groups to write journal entries of Abraham Lincoln from December 1860 to April 12, 1861. Students may wish to conduct further research on President Lincoln for this activity.

Chapter 9

- Students use their research to write a series of entries on one of the following topics: Southern States Seceding and Fort Sumter.
- Encourage group members to include facts about the event, Lincoln's feelings about the event, his concerns about the Union, and his hopes for the future.
- Students can include drawings, maps, and newspaper clippings about each event.
- Groups choose a spokesperson to read the journal entries.

Customizing the Activity for Individual Needs

ESL To help students understand how issues can divide a nation, help them compile a list of national issues that have led other countries into civil wars.

Learning Styles Students can:

 describe the attack on Fort Sumter by viewing the visual on page 170 of the Student Edition.

 place index cards listing events between December 1860 and April 12, 1861 in chronological order.

 work with a partner to role-play a debate between northerners and southerners on April 13, 1861.

Reinforcement Activity

Divide the class into groups of three or four students and have them write an acceptance speech for Abraham Lincoln after he won the presidential election of 1860. Encourage students to include Lincoln's hopes and goals for the future as well as his concerns over major issues confronting the nation. Have students share their speeches.

Alternative Assessment

Students can create a timeline of events that led to the Civil War. Have students begin their timeline in 1854 and end it with the events that took place at Fort Sumter in 1861.

Closing the Chapter
Student Edition, pages 172–173

Chapter Vocabulary

Review with students the Words to Know on page 155 of the Student Edition. Then have students complete the Vocabulary Review on page 172 of the Student Edition, by completing each sentence with a word from the list.

For more vocabulary practice, have them complete the vocabulary exercise on page 55 of the Classroom Resource Binder.

Test Tip

Remind students to quickly look over tests before starting them. Tell them it is important to read all direction lines carefully before starting the test. If they do not understand the direction lines, they should ask the teacher for help before taking the test.

Learning Objectives

Have students review their Chapter Goals and Self-Check worksheet found on page PA 6 of the Classroom Resource Binder. They can check off the goal they have reached. Note that each section of the quiz corresponds to a Learning Objective.

Group Activity

Summary: Working in groups, students assume the roles of lawyers and judges who argue and decide the case concerning Dred Scott.

Procedure: Have students review the Dred Scott case. Then divide the class into groups of five students. Have each group choose three students to act as judges and two students to act as lawyers, one lawyer arguing for the freedom of Dred Scott, and the other arguing for the slaveholder. The lawyers present their cases to the judges. The judges then present their individual opinions about the case, and confer about their final decision. A judge from each group shares the judges' decision with the rest of the class.

Assessment: Use the Group Activity Rubric on page *xiii* of this guide. Fill in the rubric with the following additional information. For this activity, students should have

- reviewed information on the Dred Scott case.
- presented information in a clear and concise manner.

RELATED MATERIALS See the Unit Overview page for related Globe Fearon books that can be used to enrich and extend the materials in the chapter.

Traditional Assessment

Chapter Quiz

The Chapter Quiz on page 173 of the Student Edition can be used as an open-book test, a closed-book test, or a homework assignment. Use the quiz to identify concepts in the chapter that students need to review. Chapter Tests can be found in the Classroom Resource Binder on pages 60–61. Workbook pages 34–37 can be used for additional practice.

Chapter Tests

Use Chapter Tests A and B on pages 60–61 in the Classroom Resource Binder to further assess mastery of chapter concepts.

Additional Resources

Use the Resource Planner on page 60 of this guide to assign additional exercises from the Classroom Resource Binder and Workbook.

Alternative Assessment

Student Interview

Have individual students choose one event and one person that they have learned about in this chapter. Ask:

- Why was this event important in U.S. history?
- What was the outcome of the event?
- What contributions did this individual make during the mid-1800s?
- Do you agree or disagree with the actions of this individual? Explain.

Presentations

- Students scan the chapter to review information about the differences that existed between the North and the South.
- Students write a summary that lists the reasons why a compromise between the North and the South could no longer work in 1861 and why a confrontation was inevitable.
- Students who believe that a compromise could have prevented a war between the states can write an argument that supports their beliefs. Students then present their arguments to the class.

Chapter 10 · The Civil War 1861–1865

Chapter at a Glance

SE page

174   *Opening the Chapter and Portfolio Project*

176   SECTION 1   Preparing for War

179   SECTION 2   The Early Years of War

184   SECTION 3   Life at Home

189   *Connecting History and Technology: The Technology of War*

190   SECTION 4   The End of the War

194   *Chapter Review and Group Activity*

Learning Objectives

- Identify the strengths of the North and the South.
- Identify the important battles of the early war years.
- Describe life at home during the war.
- Discuss how the war ended.

Social Studies Skills

- Explore how new technology made the Civil War the first modern war.
- Use a timeline to identify the events that took place during the Civil War.
- Debate the fairness of total war.

Writing Skills

- Describe major events that took place during the Civil War by drawing a timeline.

- Describe how the Anaconda Plan used geography to try to defeat the South.
- Describe a battle by writing a news article from either a northern or southern perspective.
- Identify reasons to encourage men to join the war effort by creating a poster for either the Union or Confederate army.
- List reasons why the government needed to spend money on the Civil War.

Map and Chart Skills

- Use a chart to identify the strengths of the North and the South.
- Use a map to compare how many battles the North and the South won early in the war.
- Use a chart to identify and describe major battles of the Civil War.

Chapter 10 The Civil War	Use the Program Resources below for reteaching, reinforcement, and enrichment. Additional activities for customizing the lessons can be found in this guide.

Key
Reteaching = ⟲   Reinforcement = ⇩   Enrichment = ⟳

Sections	Program Resources		
	Workbook Exercises	Teacher's Planning Guide	Classroom Resource Binder
Preparing for War	38	⟳ p. 68	⟲ Outline Map 1 *United States: Political* ⟲ Transparency 12 *United States: Political*
The Early Years of War	39, 40	⟲ p. 69	⟳ Geography and Economics 3 *The Civil War* ⟳ Transparency 15 *World: Political*
Life at Home	41	⟳ p. 70	
Connecting History and Technology: The Technology of War		⟳ p. 70	⟲ Feature Practice 64 *Connecting History and Technology: The Ironclad Ship*
The End of the War	42	⟳ p. 71	⟳ Transparency 6 *Some Civil War Battles, 1861–1865*
Chapter 10 Review		p. 72	⟳ Concept Builder 10 *Civil War* ⇩ Words to Know 62 ⟲ Challenge 65 ⇩ Chapter Tests A & B, 66, 67

Customizing the Chapter

Opening the Chapter
Student Edition, pages 174–175

Photo Activity
Have students view the picture of Union soldiers resting in their camp before going into battle against the Confederate Army. Point out the hats worn by both groups of soldiers. Ask groups of students to write a poem entitled "On the Eve of Battle." Have them include thoughts and feelings the soldiers might have experienced as they entered the battle.

Words to Know
Review the Words to Know on page 175 of the Student Edition. To help students remember the words, have them write the words on index cards.

As students read the words in the section, have them write at least one synonym or similar phrase for each of the words on the back of each index card.

Example: assassinate: murder or destroy

The following words and definitions are covered in this chapter:

border state a slave state between the North and the South that remained in the Union during the Civil War

martial law rule by an army instead of by elected officials

casualty a person killed, injured, or captured in war

civilian a person who is not a soldier

conscription drafting of people for military service

discrimination unjust treatment of a person based on false ideas about a particular group

total war the destruction of food, equipment, and anything else of use to soldiers and civilians

assassinate to murder a political leader like a President

veteran a person who has served in the armed forces

Portfolio Project

Summary: Students supplement the Chapter 10 timeline with five new events.

Procedure: Ask students to look at the timeline on pages 174–175 of their Student Edition, and read each event of the Civil War. As students read each section of the chapter, have them take notes about other important events. After students have completed the chapter, they create their own Civil War timeline, adding five new entries.

Assessment: Use the Individual Activity Rubric on page *xii* of this guide. Fill in the rubric with the additional information below. For this project, students should have

• taken accurate notes on each chapter section.

• used their notes to make a Civil War timeline, adding five major events.

Learning Objectives

Review the Learning Objectives on page 175 of the Student Edition before starting the chapter. Students can use the list as a learning guide. Suggest that they write the objectives in a journal or use the Chapter Goals and Self-Check worksheet found on page PA 6 in the Classroom Resource Binder.

After reading each section of the chapter, have students write an example of what they learned under the appropriate objective. Suggest that students use these worksheets as a practice guide to help them study for the chapter test.

Timeline

Use the timeline to discuss the sequence of events in this chapter. Point out the timeline's title, its time span, and the intervals. After students have read the chapter, have them review the timeline and suggest additional entries.

SECTION 1: Preparing for War
Student Edition, pages 176–178

Section Objectives

• Describe what Union supporters learned from the Battle of Bull Run.

• Explain the Anaconda Plan.

• Identify the ways in which the nation divided further during the first days of the Civil War.

* Compare the strengths of the Northern and Southern governments.

Words to Know

border state, martial law

Cooperative Group Activity

The Army Wants You!

Materials: colored markers; drawing paper

Procedure: Explain to students that men were enthusiastic about joining the war effort because no one believed that war would last more than three months. Divide the class into two groups, one representing the North and one representing the South.

• Group members discuss and list reasons why people should join the army and fight for their side.

• Using their list as a guide, students design flyers and pamphlets encouraging men to enlist. Have students include patriotic messages in their flyers.

• Each group chooses a spokesperson to present its pamphlet or flyer to the class.

Customizing the Activity for Individual Needs

ESL To help students understand the term *patriotism*, share some patriotic slogans from other U.S. wars, such as "Uncle Sam Wants You!"

Learning Styles Students can:

 look at the photo of Union soldiers on page 174 of the Student Edition and tell a story about them based on their photographs.

 sort index cards with facts about the Union and Confederate armies into the appropriate categories.

 work in groups to hold recruitment meetings for each army by giving speeches to convince people to enlist.

Enrichment Activity

Have students review information about the Union and Confederate armies. Divide the class into small groups and have them make a list of each army's strengths and weaknesses. The class then discuss the issues and list the reasons why they think one side will win and the other side will lose. Groups reconvene to discuss their predictions.

Alternative Assessment

Students can write a journal entry from the perspective of either a Union or Confederate soldier that describes the reasons for enlisting in the army and concerns about fighting in the war.

SECTION 2: The Early Years of War
Student Edition, pages 179–183

Section Objectives

- Explain the reasons why General Lee felt the South could win the war.
- Describe the sea battle between the Virginia and the Monitor.
- Explain why the city of New Orleans was important to the South.
- Identify the reasons why the Battle of Gettysburg became the turning point of the war.
- * Identify the important battles of the early war years.

Words to Know

casualty, civilian

Cooperative Group Activity

The General's Report

Materials: reference materials (Unit 3 Bibliography and Internet sites, pages 236–240)

Procedure: Divide the class into five groups and assign each group one of the following Civil War battles: *Seven Days' Battle, Battle of Antietam, Battle between the Virginia and the Monitor, Battle of New Orleans,* or *Battle of Gettysburg.* You may want students to do additional research on their assigned battle.

- Group members list facts about their battle including how the battle was executed, highlights and disappointments of the battle, casualties, and the battle's outcome.
- Groups use the information to write two reports: one from the perspective of a Union general and one from the viewpoint of a Confederate general.
- Groups choose a spokesperson to present the highlights of their reports to the class.

Customizing the Activity for Individual Needs

ESL To help students remember important details about early Civil War battles, pair them with English-proficient students to review each battle and the significance of its outcome.

Learning Styles Students can:

 look at the map on page 180 of the Student Edition to pinpoint the location of each battle.

 make and play a trivia-style board game that has students answer questions about a battle and move markers on the board in order to win.

 have pairs discuss a particular battle. One student will take the perspective of a Union soldier, while the other speaks from the viewpoint of a Confederate soldier.

Reteaching Activity

Have students work in small groups to review each battle and whether it was won by the Union or Confederate army. Students then decide if additional recruitment of soldiers is needed by the North or the South after those battles.

Alternative Assessment

Students can choose one of the battles. From the perspective of a soldier, have students write a letter to their families describing the battle and why they are homesick.

SECTION 3: Life at Home
Student Edition, pages 184–188

Section Objectives

- Describe what was stated in the Emancipation Proclamation.
- Describe women's contributions to the war effort.
- Explain the dangers that African Americans faced as soldiers in the Union army.
- * Explain the reasons why some Northerners opposed the war.

Words to Know

conscription, discrimination

Cooperative Group Activity

Dear Mr. President

Materials: reference materials (Unit 3 Bibliography and Internet sites, pages 236–240)

Procedure: Remind students that the Civil War affected many groups of people in different ways. Divide the class into the following six groups: *Copperheads in the North, women and families who were left at home, women nurses and doctors who helped the armies, women army spies, African American soldiers in the Union Army,* and *men drafted into army service.* Groups may conduct additional research on their topics.

- Group members discuss the effect war has had on them, and chart their responses.
- Students use their charts to decide whether they are "pro" war or in opposition to the Civil War.
- Group members compose a letter to President Lincoln expressing their views about the war and how the war is impacting their group.
- A spokesperson from each group reads the letters aloud.

Customizing the Activity for Individual Needs

ESL To help students understand the term *Copperhead,* explain how a poisonous snake uses venom to attack its enemies. The Copperheads wanted to use any means available to end the war.

Learning Styles Students can:

 create a Description Web (Classroom Resource Binder, page GO 3) to organize information about one of the six groups.

 create postage stamps that depict scenes of outstanding contributions made by courageous people in one of the six groups during the war.

 tell a partner their own views about the Civil War.

Enrichment Activity

Have students review information about African Americans in the Union army. Explain to students that many people were opposed to having African Americans fight for the Union, and that these soldiers were often discriminated against once the war began. Read to students the following quote by Abraham Lincoln: "You say you will not fight to free [African Americans]. Some of them seem willing to fight for you."

Have students tell what they think the quote means, and write a summary explaining their ideas.

Alternative Assessment

Students can choose a person or a group of people they think deserves to have been named the "person or group of the year" in 1864. Have students write a list of five reasons why this person or group of people deserves the award.

CONNECTING HISTORY AND TECHNOLOGY: The Technology of War
Student Edition, page 189

Objectives

- Social Studies Skill: Compare and contrast the technology used in the Civil War and the War for Independence.
- Social Studies Skill: Describe current warfare technologies.
- Social Studies Skill: Identify a strategic plan that combines modern technology and warfare tactics.

Activities

Past Wars, Past Technologies

Materials: Comparison-Contrast chart (Classroom Resource Binder, page GO 4); reference materials (Unit 3 Bibliography and Internet sites, pages 236–240)

Procedure: Have pairs of students complete a Comparison-Contrast chart that compares and contrasts technologies used in the Civil War with technologies used in the War for Independence. Pairs can do additional research.

Technology Today

Materials: newspapers and magazines

Procedure: Invite students to bring in newspaper and magazine articles about current war technology. Divide the class into groups of three or four and have them write a paragraph about the impact that technology has on fighting wars.

A Strategic Plan

Procedure: Have students review information about the minié ball, a bullet that could travel greater distances than bullets of the past. Mention that during Pickett's charge at Gettysburg, the Confederate army relied on a frontal attack, marching across open fields. When the Confederate army came within 200 yards, Union forces opened fire using minié balls, killing or wounding 7,000 Confederate soldiers within 30 minutes. Have students develop a strategic plan for the Confederates that would take into account this new form of technology.

Practice

Have students complete Connecting History and Technology: The Ironclad Ship on page 64 of the Classroom Resource Binder.

SECTION 4: The End of the War
Student Edition, pages 190–193

Section Objectives

- Describe Sherman's march through Georgia and into Atlanta.
- Explain the terms of surrender that ended the war at Appomattox Court House.
- * Explain why General Grant was willing to use total war against General Lee and the Confederacy.

Words to Know

total war, assassinate, veteran

Cooperative Group Activity

A Total War

Materials: reference materials (Unit 3 Bibliography and Internet sites, pages 236–240)

Procedure: Review the concept of "total war." You may wish to have students research facts about the implementation of total war. Divide the class into small groups.

- Groups discuss how General Grant might have felt about implementing total war.
- Students compose a journal entry that expresses General Grant's feelings about implementing total war.
- Group members write their own views about implementing total war.
- A spokesperson from each group reads the journal entries aloud.

Customizing the Activity for Individual Needs

ESL   To help students understand the concept of total war, review with students information about total war, and list facts on the chalkboard. Then, pair ESL students with English-proficient students to complete a Cause and Effect chart (Classroom Resource Binder, page GO 2) with information about the effects that total war had on the southern states.

Learning Styles   Students can:

 read their group's journal and highlight the adjectives used to describe total war.

 draw pictures of cities destroyed by total war.

 debate in small groups the pros and cons of implementing total war in 1864.

Enrichment Activity

Have students research and report on other events in history that employed total war techniques, such as the bombing of Hiroshima during World War II. Divide the class into small groups and have them choose an event in history in which total war was used. Students write facts on chart paper that describe this event. Have each group report on their findings to the class.

Alternative Assessment

Students can recall information about total war tactics by answering questions.

Example: Name one tactic of total war and explain how it helps to defeat the enemy.

Answer: Destroying the food supply of enemy soldiers will weaken their army.

Closing the Chapter
Student Edition, pages 194–195

Chapter Vocabulary

Review with students the Words to Know on page 175 of the Student Edition. Then have students complete the Vocabulary Review on page 194 of the Student Edition, by completing each sentence with a term from the list.

For more vocabulary practice, have them complete the vocabulary exercise on page 62 of the Classroom Resource Binder.

Test Tip

To help prepare students for taking a chapter test, encourage them to turn section titles into questions and write them down. Have students look for the answers as they read. Remind students that this is a good tip to use in other subject areas.

Learning Objectives

Have students review their Chapter Goals and Self-Check worksheet found on page PA 6 of the Classroom Resource Binder. They can check off the goal they have reached. Note that each section of the quiz corresponds to a Learning Objective.

Group Activity

Summary: Students debate the issue of total war and whether it is necessary to use it.

Procedure: Divide the class into groups of six students. Have groups review information about the implementation of total war during the Civil War. In each group, students choose three people to represent the South and three to represent the North. Student representatives then debate whether total war is fair from their point of view. During the debate, have students cite reasons for their points of view.

Assessment: Use the Group Activity Rubric found on page *xiii* of this guide. Fill in the rubric with the following additional information. For this activity, students should have

• participated in a debate.
• given reasons for a particular point of view.

RELATED MATERIALS   See the Unit Overview page for related Globe Fearon books that can be used to enrich and extend the materials in the chapter.

Traditional Assessment

Chapter Quiz

The Chapter Quiz on page 195 of the Student Edition can be used as an open-book test, a closed-book test, or a homework assignment. Use the quiz to identify concepts in the chapter that students need to review. Chapter Tests can be found in the Classroom Resource Binder on pages 66–67. Workbook pages 38–42 can be used for additional practice.

Chapter Tests

Use Chapter Tests A and B on pages 66–67 in the Classroom Resource Binder to further assess mastery of chapter concepts.

Additional Resources

Use the Classroom Resource Planner on page 67 of this guide to assign additional exercises from the Classroom Resource Binder and Workbook.

Alternative Assessment

Student Interview

Write the names of three Civil War battles on the chalkboard. Ask:

- When was the battle fought?
- What are some highlights of this battle?
- Which side won the battle?
- What effect did the outcome of this battle have on the North and on the South?

Presentation

- Students review the chapter and chart the strengths and weaknesses of both the Union and Confederate armies.
- Based on information from the chart, students share reasons why they think the North won the war.

Chapter 11 · Rebuilding a Divided Nation 1865–1877

Chapter at a Glance

SE page

196   Opening the Chapter and Portfolio Project

198   SECTION 1   Reconstruction Begins

202   SECTION 2   Congress Takes Charge

206   SECTION 3   African Americans Work to Build New Lives

211   Voices From the Past: Tempie Cummins

212   Chapter Review and Group Activity

Learning Objectives

- Compare the plans of President Lincoln, President Johnson, and Congress for rebuilding the South.
- Identify the Thirteenth, Fourteenth, and Fifteenth Amendments.
- Discuss the impeachment trial of Andrew Johnson.
- Identify how the lives of African Americans changed after the Civil War.

Social Studies Skills

- Explore the feelings of a freed slave after the Civil War.
- Use a timeline to identify events that occurred during the Reconstruction period.

Writing Skills

- Describe what life was like for an African American family after the Civil War from the perspective of a historian.
- Write a letter to a newspaper explaining conditions in the South under the Johnson plan.
- Identify reasons why most African Americans supported the Republicans during Reconstruction.
- Write a newspaper article about the mission of the Freedmen's Bureau.
- Write a statement supporting the Reconstruction plan of either President Johnson or the Radical Republicans.

Resource Planner

**Chapter 11
Rebuilding a Divided Nation**

Use the Program Resources below for reteaching, reinforcement, and enrichment. Additional activities for customizing the lessons can be found in this guide.

Key
Reteaching = ⌒   Reinforcement = ⇓   Enrichment = ⌒

Sections	Program Resources		
	⇓ Workbook Exercises	Teacher's Planning Guide	Classroom Resource Binder
Reconstruction Begins	43, 44	⇓ p. 76	
Congress Takes Charge	45	⌒ p. 77	
African Americans Work to Build New Lives	46	⌒ p. 78	⌒ Outline Map 1 *United States: Political* ⌒ Transparency 12 *United States: Political*
Voices From the Past: Tempie Cummins		⌒ p. 79	⌒ Feature Practice 70 *Voices From the Past: Harriet Jacobs*
Chapter 11 Review		p. 79	⇓ Concept Builder 11 *Rebuilding a Divided Nation* ⇓ Words to Know 68 ⌒ Challenge 71 ⇓ Chapter Tests A & B, 72, 73 ⇓ Unit Tests Parts I & II, 74, 75

Customizing the Chapter

Opening the Chapter
Student Edition, pages 196–197

Photo Activity
Direct students' attention to the photograph of Richmond, Virginia, and the five-dollar bill that was produced in the South. Use the photo of the five-dollar bill as a springboard to discuss the cost of rebuilding the South after the war. Encourage students to think about the first steps in the reconstruction process: providing food and shelter to thousands of homeless Southerners; rebuilding houses, communities, and entire cities such as Richmond; and offering job opportunities to those in need. As students read the chapter, have them add new issues to their lists.

Words to Know
Review the Words to Know on page 197 of the Student Edition. To help students remember the words, have them look up each word in the Glossary in the Student Edition and write a sentence for each one.

The following words and definitions are covered in this chapter:

Reconstruction the time period after the Civil War when the United States began to rebuild the South

black codes a series of southern laws to limit the freedom of African Americans

civil rights rights belonging to all citizens

impeach to accuse a high public official (like the President of the United States) of a crime

segregation the separation of people by race

carpetbagger a name for a Northerner who went to the South after the Civil War

scalawag a name for a white Southerner who supported the Reconstruction government

freedman a person freed from slavery

sharecropping farming someone else's land and paying a share of the crops raised for rent

poll tax a tax paid before someone can vote

Portfolio Project

Summary: From the perspective of a historian, students write a story about an African American family living in the South after the Civil War.

Materials: reference materials (Unit 3 Bibliography, pages 236–240; Internet sites)

Procedure: For this project, you may want students to do additional research on the following topics: *Freedmen's Bureau, black codes, Civil Right's Act, Thirteenth–Fifteenth Amendments,* and *sharecropping.* Students assume the role of a historian who is interviewing an African American family living in the South in 1866. Students use their interview questions to write and illustrate a story about the African American family.

Assessment: Use the Individual Activity Rubric on page *xii* of this guide. Fill in the rubric with the additional information below. For this project, students should have

- written a story that is based on an interview and has a beginning, middle, and end.
- drawn pictures to accompany their story.

Learning Objectives

Introduce the Learning Objectives on page 197 of the Student Edition before starting the chapter. Students can use the list as a learning guide. Suggest that they write the objectives in a journal or use the Chapter Goals and Self-Check worksheet found on page PA 6 in the Classroom Resource Binder.

After reading each section of the chapter, have students write an example of what they learned under the appropriate objective. Suggest that students use these worksheets as a practice guide to help them study for the chapter test.

Timeline

Use the timeline to discuss the sequence of events in this chapter. Point out the timeline's title, its time span, and the intervals. After students have read the chapter, have them review the timeline and suggest additional entries.

SECTION 1: Reconstruction Begins
Student Edition, pages 198–201

Section Objectives

- Identify issues raised by Radical Republicans concerning Johnson's plan.
- Discuss Lincoln's Reconstruction plan.
- Describe what Johnson's plan required of southern states.
- Explain what happened to African Americans under Johnson's plan to rebuild the South.
- Identify African American rights under the Civil Rights Act.
- Describe the Fourteenth Amendment.

Words to Know

Reconstruction, black codes, civil rights

Cooperative Group Activity

What's the Plan?

Materials: reference materials (Internet sites, pages 236–240)

Procedure: Remind students that Johnson's plan for rebuilding the South met with opposition from a large group of congressmen, the Radical Republicans. Divide the class into two groups and give each group one of the following roles: *Radical Republicans,* or *supporters of President Johnson.*

- Group members write a paragraph expressing their views on one of the postwar issues: *Johnson's plan for Reconstruction, Lincoln's plan for Reconstruction; black codes, violence toward African Americans, the Civil Rights Act,* or *the Fourteenth Amendment.*
- Representatives from each group hold a panel discussion of their differing viewpoints on the issues. Rotate representatives often.

Customizing the Activity for Individual Needs

ESL To help students understand Johnson's plan for rebuilding the South, have them work in pairs with English-proficient students to complete a KWL chart (Classroom Resource Binder, page GO 6) on the topic.

Learning Styles Students can:

 complete a Main Idea and Supporting Details chart (Classroom Resource Binder, page GO 5) to help them organize their paragraphs.

 organize index cards listing facts about each Reconstruction plan into three piles, each representing whose plan it was.

 work in pairs to discuss how President Lincoln might have reacted to President Johnson's plan for rebuilding the South.

Reinforcement Activity

Divide the class into groups and have them create a chart that lists and describes the following information: *Lincoln's reconstruction plan, Johnson's reconstruction plan, black codes, the Civil Rights Act,* and *the Fourteenth Amendment.*

Alternative Assessment

From the perspective of freed African Americans living in 1865, have students present and explain to the class the significance of the Fourteenth Amendment.

SECTION 2: Congress Takes Charge
Student Edition, pages 202–205

Section Objectives
- Describe the Reconstruction Act of 1867.
- Identify the groups who comprised Republican state governments in the South.
- Explain why carpetbaggers and scalawags were often disliked.
- * Explain why Congress voted to impeach President Johnson.

Words to Know
impeach, segregation, carpetbagger, scalawag

Cooperative Group Activity

Mock Impeachment
Materials: reference materials (Internet sites, pages 236–240)

Procedure: Divide the class into three groups to hold a mock impeachment trial. One group will assume the role of the prosecution, another will be President Johnson's defense team, and the third group will act as the Senate. Students may want to do additional research on President Johnson's impeachment.

- Groups meet to write their arguments. Students in the Senate jury meet to choose someone who will act as Chief Justice and preside over the trial.
- The Chief Justice calls the court to order.
- A group assuming the role of the prosecution presents its case to the Senate. When it is done, the defense group presents its defense to the Senate.
- Members of the Senate cast their votes on the President's guilt or innocence. The Chief Justice tallies the votes and announces the verdict.

Customizing the Activity for Individual Needs

ESL To help students understand how impeachment works as a part of this country's system of checks and balances, have them share with the class the system used in their native country to ensure that leaders follow the laws.

Learning Styles Students can:

 tally the votes of guilt or innocence on the chalkboard as the votes come in.

 illustrate a scene from President Johnson's impeachment.

 role-play a discussion between senators discussing the trial.

Enrichment Activity

Have students brainstorm a plan of their own for rebuilding the South. Encourage them to think of ways to eliminate segregation and fight for the civil rights of African Americans, as well as ways to rebuild the economy of the southern states. Students write a summary of their plan and share it with the class.

Alternative Assessment

Students can write a journal entry from the perspective of either an African American, a Radical Republican, or a white Southern Democrat. Explain that the entries should reflect each person's views and feelings regarding one of the following issues:

- President Johnson's plan for Reconstruction
- The Reconstruction Act of 1867
- The impeachment of President Johnson
- The laws passed by new Republican state governments against segregation

SECTION 3: African Americans Work to Build New Lives
Student Edition, pages 206–210

Section Objectives
- Describe the role of the Freedmen's Bureau.
- Describe the Fifteenth Amendment.
- ∗ Explain how sharecropping was similar to slavery.
- ∗ Describe how white southern lawmakers took away the rights of African Americans.

Words to Know
freedman, sharecropping, poll tax

Cooperative Group Activity

Loss of Rights

Materials: reference materials (Unit 3 Internet sites, pages 236–240)

Procedure: Remind students that after the Reconstruction period came to an end, white Democrats seized control of state governments and began to take away the rights of African Americans. Divide the class into four groups and assign one of the following topics to each group: *sharecropping, poll taxes, segregation laws (Jim Crow laws),* and the *Ku Klux Klan.* You may wish to have students do additional research on these topics for this project.

- Group members review and research information about their topic, taking notes that focus on how African Americans were treated and on the violations of their civil rights.
- Students write a diary entry from the perspective of African Americans from the South who are being impacted by this issue. Have students write about their loss of rights and how this makes them feel.

- Group members select a spokesperson to read their journal entry to the class.

Customizing the Activity for Individual Needs
ESL To help students understand the loss of civil rights, have them create a collage combining words and pictures that show what life was like for African Americans after the Reconstruction.

Learning Styles Students can:

 complete a Cause and Effect chart (Classroom Resource Binder, page GO 2) by writing about what occurred when white southern Democrats, mostly Confederate leaders, came into power at the end of Reconstruction.

 organize their notes on index cards and use them to write their diaries.

 assume the role of an African American leader giving a speech that focuses on the loss of rights and how African Americans can bring about change.

Enrichment Activity

Divide the class into groups and have them scan newspapers and magazines for articles focusing on the continuing struggle for Civil Rights and equal opportunity by African Americans and other groups in the United States today. Have students take notes and list the issues that are still a problem in this country. Have students write a possible resolution next to each listed issue.

Alternative Assessment

Students can write a poem focusing on rights that were taken away from African Americans after Reconstruction. Each sentence of the poem should begin with the words *I should have the right to . . .* Encourage students to include lines in their poems that tell why the rights of African Americans should not have been taken away.

VOICES FROM THE PAST:
Tempie Cummins
Student Edition, page 211

Objectives
- Social Studies Skill: Identify one method in which enslaved African Americans used special ways to communicate with one another.
- Social Studies Skill: Describe the services provided by the Freedmen's Bureau by creating a flyer.
- Social Studies Skill: Describe the concept of freedom by creating a symbol, or logo, that represents four million freed African Americans.

Activities
A Song About Freedom
Procedure: Remind students that songs were used among enslaved people for a variety of reasons, including preserving secrecy. For example, African Americans traveling the Underground Railroad often received coded messages in songs about directions for escaping north toward freedom. Have students think of a current tune and create lyrics to send a coded message telling enslaved people that they have been freed.

Spread the Word
Materials: poster paper; colored markers

Procedure: Have students create a flyer that could be distributed to former enslaved African Americans about services of the Freedmen's Bureau, such as food, clothing, medicine, and job searches. Remind them that many African Americans at the time could not read, having had no formal schooling, so they should include illustrations to support their text.

A Symbol of Freedom
Materials: poster paper; colored markers

Procedure: Tell students they have been hired by the Freedmen's Bureau to create a symbol, or logo, of freedom that will represent the four million recently freed African Americans.

Practice
Have students complete Voices From the Past: Harriet Jacobs on page 70 of the Classroom Resource Binder.

Closing the Chapter
Student Edition, pages 212–213

Chapter Vocabulary
Review with students the Words to Know on page 197 of the Student Edition. Then have them complete the Vocabulary Review on page 212 of the Student Edition, by completing each sentence with a term from the list.

For more vocabulary practice, have them complete the vocabulary exercise on page 68 of the Classroom Resource Binder.

Test Tip
Have students scan the chapter and look for names, dates, and facts that will help them prepare for their history test.

Learning Objectives
Have students review their Chapter Goals and Self-Check worksheet found on page PA 6 of the Classroom Resource Binder. They can check off the goal they have reached. Note that each section of the quiz corresponds to a Learning Objective.

Group Activity
Summary: Students assume different roles to write a short statement describing a position on Reconstruction.

Procedure: Divide students into two groups and assign each group one of the following roles: *a supporter of Andrew Johnson* or *a supporter of the Radical Republicans*. Group members review the chapter to take notes about the views of their assigned person. Students use their notes to write a statement describing their position on Reconstruction. They should be prepared to explain why this position is valid. Group members choose a spokesperson to read their statement to the rest of the class and answer questions about their position that are posed by classmates.

Assessment: Use the Group Activity Rubric found on page *xiii* of this guide. Fill in the rubric with the following information. For this activity, students should have

- written their position on Reconstruction in a clear and precise manner.
- shared their position with the class.

RELATED MATERIALS See the Unit Overview page for related Globe Fearon books that can be used to enrich and extend the materials in the chapter.

Traditional Assessment

Chapter Quiz

The Chapter Quiz on page 213 of the Student Edition can be used as an open-book test, a closed-book test, or a homework assignment. Use the quiz to identify concepts in the chapter that students need to review. Chapter Tests can be found in the Classroom Resource Binder on pages 72–73. Workbook pages 43–46 can be used for additional practice.

Chapter Tests

Use Chapter Tests A and B on pages 72–73 in the Classroom Resource Binder to further assess mastery of chapter concepts.

Additional Resources

Use the Resource Planner on page 75 of this guide to assign additional exercises from the Classroom Resource Binder and Workbook.

Alternative Assessment

Student Interview

Give individual students a slip of paper on which is written one of the following topics: *Freedmen's Bureau, sharecropping, Reconstruction, impeachment,* or *carpetbagger*. Ask:
- What is this topic about?
- What is most important about this topic?
- Who are the people involved or affected?

Presentation

- Students scan the chapter to list facts about rights African Americans gained after the Civil War.
- Students scan the chapter to list facts about rights African Americans lost when Reconstruction ended.
- Students create a chart using the information listed and then present their chart to the class.

Unit Assessment

This is the last chapter in Unit 3: A Nation Divided. To review and assess cumulative understanding and provide standardized-test practice, have students complete the Unit Review Test on page 214 of the Student Edition, and the Unit 3 Cumulative Test on pages 74–75 of the Classroom Resource Binder.

Unit 4 ▶ A Growing Nation

CHAPTER 12

Americans Move West
1860–1890

PORTFOLIO PROJECT	BUILDING YOUR SKILLS	GROUP ACTIVITY	TIMELINE
Descriptive Notes	Distinguishing Fact From Opinion	Help-Wanted Ads	Westward Movement

CHAPTER 13

The Growth of Industry
1860–1900

PORTFOLIO PROJECT	VOICES FROM THE PAST	GROUP ACTIVITY	TIMELINE
Notes for a Speech	Andrew Carnegie	Debating an Issue	Inventions and Industries

CHAPTER 14

Cities and Immigration
1880–1920

PORTFOLIO PROJECT	CONNECTING HISTORY AND...	GROUP ACTIVITY	TIMELINE
Journal Entries	Technology: Skyscrapers, Streetcars, and Bridges	Writing Laws	The Age of Immigration

RELATED MATERIALS

These are some of the Globe Fearon books that can be used to enrich and extend the material in this unit.

Cultural Diversity

Content

Skills

Globe Mosaic of American History: Native Americans: The Struggle for the Plains
Enrich understanding of the conflict between Native Americans and settlers.

Globe Mosaic of American History: Women in the U.S. Work Force: 1876–1914
Expand understanding of industrial working conditions in the 1800s.

Unlocking Research and Writing Skills for the Social Studies
Reinforce the skill of identifying primary sources with Chapter 14.

Chapter 12 · **Americans Move West** 1860–1890

Chapter at a Glance

SE page

216   *Opening the Chapter and Portfolio Project*

218   SECTION 1   Joining the Nation Together

221   *Building Your Skills: Distinguishing Fact From Opinion*

222   SECTION 2   Problems on the Great Plains

227   SECTION 3   Life on the Great Plains

232   *Chapter Review and Group Activity*

Learning Objectives

- Discuss reasons for the first transcontinental railroad.
- Describe how railroads affected the West.
- Identify events that forced Native Americans onto reservations.
- Describe what life was like in mining towns.
- Identify the ways that groups of farmers helped one another.

Social Studies Skills

- Distinguish fact from opinion.
- Use a timeline to identify important events that occurred during the westward movement.
- Create a display to show the people, places, and things seen on a train trip between Nebraska and California.

Writing Skills

- Draw a poster showing why farmers should settle on the Great Plains.
- Write a news article describing what happened at the Battle of Little Bighorn.
- Write a letter describing land features, weather conditions, and ways to make a living in Montana.
- Describe the responsibilities of a railroad worker, a soldier, a cowhand, a miner, and a farmer by writing a help-wanted ad for each job.

Map and Chart Skills

- Use a map to identify mining areas and cattle trails in the western region of the United States.
- Use a chart to describe a cowhand's life on a cattle drive.

Resource Planner

Chapter 12 Americans Move West	Use the Program Resources below for reteaching, reinforcement, and enrichment. Additional activities for customizing the lessons can be found in this guide.

Key
Reteaching = ⌒   Reinforcement = ↓   Enrichment = ⌒

Sections	Program Resources		
	↓ Workbook Exercises	Teacher's Planning Guide	Classroom Resource Binder
Joining the Nation Together	47	↓ p. 84	⌒ Geography and Economics 4 *Railroads, Industry, and Mining*
Building Your Skills: Distinguishing Fact From Opinion		↓ p. 85	↓ Feature Practice, 78, 79 *Distinguishing Fact From Opinion*
Problems on the Great Plains	48	⌒ p. 85	
Life on the Great Plains	49, 50	↓ p. 86	
Chapter 12 Review		p. 87	⌒ Concept Builder 12 *Americans Move West* ↓ Words to Know 76 ⌒ *Challenge* 80 ↓ Chapter Tests A & B, 81, 82

Chapter **12**

Customizing the Chapter

Opening the Chapter
Student Edition, pages 216–217

Photo Activity

Explain to students that many Americans relocated to other parts of the country as the United States expanded its territories westward. Have students look at the photo of frontier families as well as the photo of an iron stove that was used in frontier homes across the nation. Then have students create a list of items frontier families planning a trip across the country would need to take on their journey. Encourage students to think of supplies such as food, tools, blankets, clothing, cooking stoves, and medicines that would fit into the wagons used for the journey.

Words to Know

Review the Words to Know on page 217 of the Student Edition. To help students remember the words, invite pairs of students to skim the chapter looking for the words. Have them draw a chart listing each word and its definition.

The following words and definitions are covered in this chapter:

transcontinental across a continent

prairie a large area of level or slightly rolling land

homesteader a person who received land under the Homestead Act of 1862

reservation public land set aside by the government for the use of a particular group of people

tradition the handing down of information, beliefs, and customs from one generation to another

prospector a person who searches for gold, silver, or other valuable minerals

boom town a camp that grows into a town almost overnight

Portfolio Project

Summary: Students create notes for a museum display about a train journey from Nebraska to California in 1870.

Procedure: Have students take descriptive notes about the transcontinental railroad and the western region of the United States as they read the chapter in the Student Edition. Student notes should include information about weather conditions, physical features, Native American reservations, and cities.

Assessment: Use the Individual Activity Rubric on page *xii* of this guide. Fill in the rubric with the additional information below. For this project, students should have

- prepared accurate notes.
- described the sights of their train journey westward.

Learning Objectives

Review the Learning Objectives on page 217 of the Student Edition before starting the chapter. Students can use the list as a learning guide. Suggest that they write the objectives in a journal or use the Chapter Goals and Self-Check worksheet found on page PA 6 of the Classroom Resource Binder.

After reading each section of the chapter, have students write an example of what they learned under the appropriate objective. Suggest that students use these worksheets as a practice guide to help them study for the chapter test.

Timeline

Use the timeline to discuss the sequence of events in this chapter. Point out the timeline's title, its time span, and the intervals. After students have read the chapter, have them review the timeline and suggest additional entries.

SECTION 1: Joining the Nation Together
Student Edition, pages 218–220

Section Objectives

* Describe the transcontinental railroad and identify the people who built it.
* Describe the Homestead Act and the settling of the Great Plains.

Words to Know

transcontinental, prairie, homesteader

Cooperative Group Activity

Great Nation, Great Plains

Materials: reference materials (Unit 4 Bibliography, pages 236–240); U.S. map

Procedure: Divide the class into two groups. Have one group research the construction of the transcontinental railroad, while the other group researches the Homestead Act. Explain to students that they will create a magazine from the year 1862 that documents the time period and features their assigned topic.

- Group members draw a series of pictures, maps, and illustrations about their topic. Underneath each picture and map, they should write a short caption that clearly explains the visual or provides background information.
- Groups should use a variety of sources, such as maps and Internet sites to include as many facts as they can in their picture essay.
- Both groups then combine their work to create the magazine. Students should choose a title for their magazine, such as *Great Plains Life in 1862*.

Customizing the Activity for Individual Needs

ESL To help students understand the Words to Know in this section, have them create picture cards. On one side of an index card, students write the word and its definition. On the other side of the index card, students draw a picture to illustrate the word's meaning.

Learning Styles Students can:

 view the visual showing of the completion of the transcontinental railroad on page 219 of the Student Edition to describe the event.

 design covers for their class magazine.

 discuss in pairs why the Homestead Act was successful in attracting people to settle the Great Plains.

Reinforcement Activity

Have students assume the role of a homesteader who is about to clear newly purchased land in order to build a house and plant crops. Students then write a letter to a relative describing the hardships, frustrations, and possible rewards of homesteading.

Alternative Assessment

Students can design an advertisement encouraging people to either help build the transcontinental railroad or settle the Great Plains.

BUILDING YOUR SKILLS: Distinguishing Fact From Opinion
Student Edition, page 221

Objectives
- Social Studies Skill: Identify facts about building the transcontinental railroad.
- Social Studies Skill: Identify opinions about reactions to the Homestead Act.
- Social Studies Skill: Distinguish between fact and opinion.

Activities

Just the Facts
Procedure: As reporters for the *Railway Times*, have students write a brief newspaper article that describes the building of the transcontinental railroad. Remind them to report just the facts, or information that can be proved.

It's My Opinion
Procedure: Have students assume the role of settlers who are taking advantage of the Homestead Act. Ask them to write letters to family members living in Massachusetts, describing their feelings about the Homestead

Act and explaining why they think it provides a good opportunity. Remind students that an opinion can tell how someone feels about a certain issue.

Fact or Opinion?
Procedure: Using index cards, have students write facts and opinions they have read about the Homestead Act and the transcontinental railroad. *Example*: In 1862, Congress passes the Homestead Act. (fact) On the reverse side of each card, have students write whether each statement is a fact or an opinion. Working in pairs, have students take turns reading cards and asking whether each statement is a fact or an opinion.

Practice
Have students complete Building Your Skills: Distinguishing Fact From Opinion on page 78 of the Classroom Resource Binder.

SECTION 2: Problems on the Great Plains
Student Edition, pages 222–226

Section Objectives
- Describe the victories and defeats experienced by Native Americans.
- Explain why reformers wanted to change the way Native Americans were treated.
- ☆ Identify promises made to Native Americans that were broken in the 1860s.

Words to Know
reservation, tradition

Cooperative Group Activity

Time for Reform
Materials: reference materials (Unit 4 Bibliography and Internet sites, pages 236–240)

Procedure: Organize students into small groups and have each group review information about the treatment of Native Americans in the late 1800s. Students may wish to do additional research for this project.

- Group members list ways in which Native Americans and their ways of life were threatened in the late 1800s.

Chapter **12**

- Students write a letter to a 1865 newspaper editor describing the unfair treatment of Native Americans and how positive changes could be implemented to help correct the situation.
- Groups choose a spokesperson to read their letter aloud.

Customizing the Activity for Individual Needs

ESL To help students understand the problems that Native Americans faced, have them share with the class some customs and traditions from their native land. Ask students how they have continued these customs and traditions in a new country.

Learning Styles Students can:

 use a Description Web (Classroom Resource Binder, page GO 3) to list the problems that Native Americans faced.

 work with partners to play a cause-and-effect matching game that uses index cards listing events, such as *killing buffalo to clear land for railroads* (cause) and *loss of food supply to Native Americans* (effect).

 tell a story from the perspective of a Native American who tried to protect his or her land and traditions.

Enrichment Activity

Have students work in small groups to brainstorm a list of traditions that are important to them. Have students discuss how they would react if the government forced them to alter these traditions or declared them unlawful. Group members then write a poem that expresses their feelings. Have each group share its poem with the class.

Alternative Assessment

Students can work in pairs to write a list of reforms they think are needed to aid Native Americans living in 1870.

SECTION 3: Life on the Great Plains
Student Edition, pages 227–231

Section Objectives
- Explain how mining created boom towns.
- Describe farming techniques on the Great Plains.
- * Describe the life of a cowhand, farmer, and miner.

Words to Know
prospector, boom town

Cooperative Group Activity

Short Stories

Materials: reference materials (Unit 4 Bibliography and Internet sites, pages 236–240)

Procedure: Organize the class into the following three groups: farmers, cowhands, and miners. You may want students to conduct additional research on their topic for this project.

- Group members make a list of important facts about their topic. They use these facts to write a short story for young children.
- Group members draw illustrations that support each page of their text.
- Students then create a title and cover page for their story and bind the pages together to make a book.

Customizing the Activity for Individual Needs

ESL To help them understand the work of farmers, cattle herders, and miners, have students make three index cards describing the types of jobs each group did. Then have one student read from the list of jobs, while another student guesses who did the job.

Learning Styles Students can:

 use the photo of Nat Love on page 228 of the Student Edition to infer what type of work cowhands did.

 play a game of charades in which they take turns miming the actions of the three workers.

 work in pairs to interview each other about the daily life of a Great Plains farmer living in the 1870s.

Reinforcement Activity

Have students create three riddles for each of the jobs they have learned about. Explain that each riddle will consist of four lines, with the second and fourth lines rhyming. Mention that they should write facts about each of the workers in their riddles.

Example: I eat fried bacon, biscuits and <u>beans</u>. I wear a sombrero and a pair of <u>jeans</u>. Who am I?

Answer: a cowhand

Alternative Assessment

Students can choose one of the three jobs: farmer, cowhand, or miner. Students list the duties that this worker performs each day, and in the order the worker would do first, next, and last. Students can then create a timeline of this worker's duties during one 24-hour period.

Closing the Chapter
Student Edition, pages 232–233

Chapter Vocabulary

Review with students the Words to Know on page 217 of the Student Edition. Then have them complete the Vocabulary Review on page 232 of the Student Edition by answering each statement with a *true* or *false* answer. If the answer is false, have students change the underlined term to make the statement true.

For more vocabulary practice, have them complete the vocabulary exercise on page 76 of the Classroom Resource Binder.

Test Tip

Remind students that before beginning a test, they should try to set aside enough time to complete all the questions. Students can practice this skill when they complete the Chapter Quiz.

Learning Objectives

Have students review the Chapter Goals and Self-Check worksheet found on page PA 6 of the Classroom Resource Binder. They can check off the goal they have reached. Note that each section of the quiz corresponds to a Learning Objective.

Group Activity

Summary: Students write help-wanted ads for workers living in the late 1800s.

Procedure: Divide the class into five groups and assign each group one of the following jobs: *railroad worker, soldier, cowhand, miner,* or *farmer.* Have students review information in the Student Edition to make a list of the qualifications required to perform each job. Group members then write a help-wanted ad that would entice prospective employees to apply for the position.

Assessment: Use the Group Activity Rubric found on page *xiii* of this guide. Fill in the rubric with the following additional information. For this activity, students should have

- completed a list of job qualifications.
- assisted in writing a help-wanted ad.

RELATED MATERIALS See the Unit Overview page for related Globe Fearon books that can be used to enrich and extend the materials in the chapter.

Traditional Assessment

Chapter Quiz

The Chapter Quiz on page 233 of the Student Edition can be used as an open-book test, a closed-book test, or a homework assignment. Use the quiz to identify concepts in the chapter that students need to review. Chapter Tests can be found in the Classroom Resource Binder on pages 81–82. Workbook pages 47–51 can be used for additional practice.

Chapter Tests

Use Chapter Tests A and B on pages 81–82 in the Classroom Resource Binder to further assess mastery of chapter concepts.

Additional Resources

Use the Resource Planner on page 83 in this guide to assign additional exercises from the Classroom Resource Binder and Workbook.

Alternative Assessment

Presentation

Write the following on the chalkboard: *Americans Move West*. Then, make two columns under the main heading and write *Pro* at the top of one column and *Con* at the top of the other.

- Students list positive outcomes and benefits that resulted during the westward movement in the *Pro* column.
- Students then list negative outcomes that occurred as a result of westward expansion in the *Con* column.

Open-Ended

- Students list reasons why the Homestead Act succeeded in 1862.
- Students write whether they think a similar act would be popular and successful today, and explain their answer.

Chapter 13 • The Growth of Industry 1860–1900

Chapter at a Glance

SE page

234   Opening the Chapter and Portfolio Project

236   SECTION 1   The Machine Age

240   SECTION 2   The Rise of Big Business

244   Voices From the Past: Andrew Carnegie

245   SECTION 3   The Work Force

250   Chapter Review and Group Activity

Chapter
13

Learning Objectives

- Explain how new inventions changed the lives of Americans.
- Explain how the steel and oil industries became so powerful.
- Identify ways that powerful business leaders controlled the lives of workers.
- Describe how the rise of industries affected workers.

Social Studies Skills

- Explore the ideas of Andrew Carnegie.
- Use a timeline to identify new inventions and industries from 1869 through 1893.

Writing Skills

- Write notes for a speech comparing and contrasting the views of a wealthy business owner and a factory worker living in the 1880s.

- Write a newspaper editorial describing the work conditions in a steel plant from the perspective of a factory worker.
- Write a speech that a farmer might give to lawmakers describing monopolies.
- Explain the effects of violence and riots on strikes.
- Describe the different points of view between union workers and management.

Map and Chart Skills

- Use a chart to identify inventions and inventors from the late 1800s.

Resource Planner

Chapter 13 The Growth of Industry	Use the Program Resources below for reteaching, reinforcement, and enrichment. Additional activities for customizing the lessons can be found in this guide.

Key
Reteaching = ⌒   Reinforcement = ⬇   Enrichment = ⌒

Sections	Program Resources		
	Workbook Exercises	Teacher's Planning Guide	Classroom Resource Binder
The Machine Age	52, 53	⌒ p. 91	⌒ Concept Builder 13 *The Growth of Industry*
The Rise of Big Business	54	⬇ p. 92	⌒ Concept Builder 13 *The Growth of Industry*
Voices From the Past: Andrew Carnegie		⌒ p. 93	⌒ Feature Practice 85 *Voices From the Past: Child Labor*
The Work Force	55	⌒ p. 93	⌒ Concept Builder 13 *The Growth of Industry*
Chapter 13 Review		p. 94	⬇ Words to Know 83 ⌒ Challenge 86 ⬇ Chapter Tests A & B, 87, 88

Customizing the Chapter

Opening the Chapter
Student Edition, pages 234–235

Photo Activity

Explain to students that the workers in the painting are turning iron into steel, which is a strong alloy or metal. Mention that steel is primarily made up of iron, carbon, and other metals. Point out that the object below the painting is a gear made from steel. Discuss why steel is often the most useful building material and what it is used for today.

Words to Know

Review the Words to Know on page 235 of the Student Edition. To help students remember the words, invite pairs of students to write each word and its possible definition. Ask them to use the Glossary in the Student Edition to verify their definition. Have students use the following model: *I think _____ means _____ . The definition of _____ is _____ .*

The following words and definitions are covered in this chapter:

patent a government grant that allows only the inventor to make, use, and sell an invention for a certain time

pollution damage to land, air, and water from harmful materials

corporation a large company formed by a group of investors

monopoly the complete control of an industry by one company or person

company town a community set up and run by a company for its workers

labor union a group of workers that tries to help its members

strike to refuse to work until certain demands, such as higher wages or better working conditions, are met

Portfolio Project

Summary: Students write speeches about social conditions in the 1880s from the perspective of a wealthy business owner or a factory worker.

Procedure: Students assume the role of a wealthy business owner or a factory worker. As students read the chapter, they take notes to write a speech about social conditions in the 1880s. Students in the role of the factory worker write a speech that includes the working conditions they encounter, their pay, their schedule, and their employer. Students in the role of the wealthy business owner write a speech about the social conditions of the times, good and bad. Students present their speeches to the class.

Assessment: Use the Individual Activity Rubric on page *xii* of this guide. Fill in the rubric with the additional information below. For this project, students should have

- written notes to make an informative and persuasive speech.
- presented their speech to the class.

Learning Objectives

Review the Learning Objectives on page 235 of the Student Edition before starting the chapter. Students can use the list as a learning guide. Suggest they write the objectives in a journal or use the Chapter Goals and Self-Check worksheet found on page PA 6 of the Classroom Resource Binder.

After reading each section of the chapter, have students write an example of what they learned under the appropriate objective. Suggest that students use these worksheets as a practice guide to help them study for the chapter test.

Timeline

Use the timeline to discuss the sequence of events in this chapter. Point out the timeline's title, its time span, and the intervals. After students have read the chapter, have them review the timeline and suggest additional entries.

SECTION 1: The Machine Age
Student Edition, pages 236–239

Section Objectives

- Identify inventions that were created and how an inventor's work became protected.
- Describe the oil industry and identify two early uses of oil.
- Describe the steel industry and the Bessemer process.
- Explain the changes and problems that workers in the oil and steel industries faced.
- ★ Describe how inventions changed lives between 1860 and 1900.

Words to Know

patent, pollution

Cooperative Group Activity

The Invention Factory

Materials: reference materials (Unit 4 Bibliography and Internet sites, pages 236–240)

Procedure: Discuss with students the ways that inventions and industry changed how people in the United States lived, worked, and traveled. You may want students to do additional research on inventions and inventors between 1860 and 1900. Divide the class into small groups and have them assume the role of inventors from the late 1800s.

- Students list inventions of the period and how each impacted people's lives.
- Students conduct additional research on inventions in order to brainstorm an invention of their own.
- Group members write a proposal for their invention that includes the following information: *how the invention will change the lives of Americans; what the invention will allow people to do; why the invention is necessary; where it will be sold;* and *how much the new invention will cost.*

Customizing the Activity for Individual Needs

ESL To help ESL students, pair them with an English-proficient student to play a game of 20 Questions about the inventions of the 1800s.

Learning Styles Students can:

 look at pictures in reference materials of some inventions of the 1800s, such as the railroad sleeping car, the cash register, and the telephone. Then have students look at modern-day versions of these inventions and describe the differences.

 build a model of their group's invention.

 tape-record a discussion between a group of students about the phonograph. Then compare and contrast it with the listening and recording devices of today.

Reteaching Activity

Have students review the list of inventions of the 1800s and determine which inventions they still use today. Students can then create a two-column chart. One column lists inventions; the other column lists the ways each invention has made their lives easier or better.

Alternative Assessment

Students can write a paragraph about the oil and steel industries. Remind students to include both good and bad points about these industries.

SECTION 2: The Rise of Big Business
Student Edition, pages 240–243

Section Objectives
- Explain how businesses changed in the late 1800s.
- Identify the leaders in big business and describe the industries they controlled.
- Explain the concept of monopolies and how lawmakers proposed to control them.

Words to Know
corporation, monopoly

Cooperative Group Activity

To Control or Not to Control

Materials: reference materials (Unit 4 Bibliography and Internet sites, pages 236–240)

Procedure: Remind students that during the late 1800s, many people were concerned about the growth of some businesses. As a result, lawmakers took steps to control big business. You may want to have students do additional research about this issue. Organize the class into three groups and assign each group one of the following positions: *Big Business, Small Business,* or *Government Official.*

- Students who are assigned the position of *Big Business* write a letter to government officials to convince them not to enact laws that will control and limit the power of large businesses.
- Students who are assigned the position of *Small Business* write a letter to government officials to convince them to establish laws that will put limits on big businesses.
- Students who are assigned the position of *Government Official* review the letters received by both big business and small business owners. Group members then discuss their position and make a list of laws that they think are necessary to implement.

Customizing the Activity for Individual Needs
ESL To help students understand the concept of big business, have them play a true/false game with an English-proficient partner using index cards with statements about big business.

Example: Andrew Carnegie controlled almost the entire oil industry in the United States. (false)

Learning Styles Students can:

 complete a Cause and Effect chart (Classroom Resource Binder, page GO 2). Students list big businesses and describe the impact each had on society during the late 1800s.

 create posters with slogans and pictures that describe their position on big business from the perspective of a small business owner.

 work in pairs to prepare arguments for or against controls or limits on big business.

Reinforcement Activity

Divide the class into small groups and ask them to make a list of small businesses in their city or community. Have students prepare a list of questions they would like to ask these small business owners, such as: *How are you able to compete with larger stores? Are there laws that protect your rights?* Invite one or two owners of these small businesses into the class and conduct a class interview.

Alternative Assessment

Students, working with partners, can list the benefits of big business under the heading *Pros*, and then list the problems that occurred as a result of the growth of big business under *Cons*.

VOICES FROM THE PAST:
Andrew Carnegie
Student Edition, page 244

Objectives
- Social Studies Skill: Describe the life of Andrew Carnegie.
- Social Studies Skill: Explain working conditions in a steel mill, from the perspective of a worker.
- Social Studies Skill: Analyze quotes by Andrew Carnegie that describe his views on big business and wealth.

Activities

Biography of Andrew Carnegie
Procedure: Have students write a biographical sketch of big business owner, Andrew Carnegie. Ask students to draw illustrations that support the biography and include quotes made by Carnegie.

A Cotton Worker's Perspective
Procedure: Have students assume the role of a "bobbin-boy" who worked with young Andrew Carnegie in a cotton factory. Have them write a letter to a family member describing what life is like working at the cotton factory.

You Can Quote Me
Procedure: Divide the class into three groups and have each group read and analyze a quote from Andrew Carnegie on page 244 of the Student Edition. Students should analyze each quote by deciding what Carnegie is trying to say. Students can then rewrite the quote in their own words.

Practice
Have students complete Voices From the Past: Child Labor on page 85 of the Classroom Resource Binder.

SECTION 3: The Work Force
Student Edition, pages 245–249

Section Objectives
- Describe working conditions in factories.
- Describe the reasons why company towns were created.
- Explain why workers joined labor unions.
- * Explain why strikes occurred and how they affected company owners.

Words to Know
company town, labor union, strike

Cooperative Group Activity

Investigative Reporters
Materials: reference materials (Unit 4 Bibliography and Internet sites, pages 236–240)

Procedure: Organize the class into three groups and assign each group one of the following: *Haymarket Square Riot, Homestead Strike,* or *Pullman Strike.* Have groups do additional research on their topic.

- Group members assume the roles of newspaper reporters, members of the union, and big business owners.
- Newspaper reporters prepare questions to ask union members and big business owners. Union members and big business owners research their side's position.
- Each group holds a round table discussion on their strike for the class.

Customizing the Activity for Individual Needs
ESL To help students understand the concept of strikes, discuss the effects of a strike on unions and on business owners.

Learning Styles Students can:

 look at the photo of the Haymarket Square Riot on page 248 of the Student Edition and write a paragraph describing it.

 create a storyboard of events that led to one of the strikes.

 tape-record the roundtable discussions and take notes from their tapes.

Reteaching Activity

Have students list ways in which employers mistreated employees in the late 1800s. Next to each mistreatment, have students write a possible solution to the problem. Using their list as a guide, students write a plan of action that explains how big businesses can improve working conditions.

Alternative Assessment

Students can propose five important laws they think should be implemented to improve working conditions for men, women, and children in the nineteenth century.

Closing the Chapter
Student Edition, pages 250–251

Chapter Vocabulary

Review with students the Words to Know on page 235 of the Student Edition. Then have them complete the Vocabulary Review on page 250 of the Student Edition, by matching each definition with a term from the list.

For more vocabulary practice, have them complete the vocabulary exercise on page 83 of the Classroom Resource Binder.

Test Tip

Ask students to make an outline as they review the chapter. Students can scan each section of the chapter to write titles and subtitles found in boldface print. They can then list brief facts under each of these titles. Encourage students to use their outline to help them study for the chapter test.

Learning Objectives

Have students review their Chapter Goals and Self-Check worksheet found on page PA 6 of the Classroom Resource Binder. They can check off the goal they have reached. Note that each section of the quiz corresponds to a Learning Objective.

Group Activity

Summary: Students assume the role of union workers and managers at a steel mill and debate the mill's decision to lower workers' wages.

Procedure: Organize students into two groups. Assign one group the role of union workers at a steel mill. Have students in the second group assume the role of managers at the steel mill. Set the stage by explaining to students that union workers have asked to meet with managers at the steel mill to discuss the lowering of their wages. Students in both groups make a list of issues to raise and debate. Groups conduct a debate, using their lists of issues, between union workers and management. Students in both groups vote to lower wages (pro management) or to keep wages stable (pro worker).

Assessment: Use the Group Activity Rubric found on page *xiii* of this guide. Fill in the rubric with the following additional information. For this activity, students should have

* prepared a list of issues to use in a debate.
* participated in the debate.

RELATED MATERIALS See the Unit Overview page for related Globe Fearon books that can be used to enrich and extend the materials in the chapter.

Traditional Assessment

Chapter Quiz

The Chapter Quiz on page 251 of the Student Edition can be used as an open-book test, a closed-book test, or a homework assignment. Use the quiz to identify concepts in the chapter that students need to review. Chapter Tests can be found in the Classroom Resource Binder on pages 87–88. Workbook pages 52–55 can be used for additional practice.

Chapter Tests

Use Chapter Tests A and B on pages 87–88 in the Classroom Resource Binder to further assess mastery of chapter concepts.

Additional Resources

Use the Resource Planner on page 90 of this guide to assign additional exercises from the Classroom Resource Binder and Workbook.

Alternative Assessment

Student Interview

Have students think about what their lives would be like if they were living in the United States during the late 1800s. Ask:

- Which inventions of this time would affect your daily life? How?
- If you were a child worker in a coal mine, what would your life be like?
- Why did many Americans of the time look up to Andrew Carnegie?

Presentation

- Students scan the chapter to list inventions of the 1800s and how each affected business in the United States.
- Student volunteers share their lists with the class.

Chapter
13

Chapter 14 · Cities and Immigration 1880–1920

Chapter at a Glance

SE page

252		*Opening the Chapter and Portfolio Project*
254	SECTION 1	Immigrants From Southern and Eastern Europe
260		*Connecting History and Technology: Skyscrapers, Streetcars, and Bridges*
261	SECTION 2	Immigrants From Asia and Latin America
265	SECTION 3	African Americans Move North
268		*Chapter Review and Group Activity*

Learning Objectives

- Explain reasons for immigration to the United States in the late 1800s.
- Identify problems and advantages of city life.
- Explain reasons for Asian and Latin American immigration.
- Describe why some native-born Americans disliked the new immigrants.
- Discuss why many African Americans moved to the North.

Social Studies Skills

- Explore ways that technology changed U.S. cities.
- Use a timeline to identify events associated with the Age of Immigration.

Writing Skills

- Describe experiences from the perspective of an immigrant arriving in the United States during the late 1880s by writing a journal entry.

- Write a news article describing the Triangle Shirtwaist Company fire.
- Describe what life is like from the perspective of a Mexican immigrant by writing a letter to family members.
- Explain the importance of the NAACP by writing an editorial that might have appeared in a northern newspaper.
- Write five laws to protect the health and safety of people living in cities.

Map and Chart Skills

- Use a chart to trace the shift in European immigration.
- Use a map to locate the states where African Americans settled between 1910 and 1920.

Resource Planner

Chapter 14 Cities and Immigration	Use the Program Resources below for reteaching, reinforcement, and enrichment. Additional activities for customizing the lessons can be found in this guide.

Key
Reteaching = ↶   Reinforcement = ⇩   Enrichment = ↷

Sections	Program Resources		
	⇩ Workbook Exercises	Teacher's Planning Guide	Classroom Resource Binder
Immigrants From Southern and Eastern Europe	56	⇩ p. 98	↷ Outline Map 3 *Europe*
Connecting History and Technology: Skyscrapers, Streetcars, and Bridges		↶ p. 99	↶ Feature Practice 91 *Connecting History and Technology: The Dumbbell Tenement*
Immigrants From Asia and Latin America	57	↶ p. 99	↶ Outline Map 8 *Asia*
African Americans Move North	58, 59	⇩ p. 100	
Chapter 14 Review		p. 101	⇩ Words to Know 89 ↶ Challenge 92 ⇩ Chapter Tests A & B, 93, 94 ⇩ Unit Tests Parts I & II, 95, 96

Chapter
14

Customizing the Chapter

Opening the Chapter
Student Edition pages, 252–253

Photo Activity

Have students examine the image of immigrants viewing the Statue of Liberty as they sailed into New York Harbor. Explain to students that like the Pilgrims, who came to America in 1620, some immigrants of the late 1800s and early 1900s were searching for freedom they did not have in their native homeland. Direct students' attention to the trunk in the lower right corner. Explain that many immigrants came to the United States with only a suitcase or trunk of personal possessions and the clothing on their backs. Ask students to make a list of items they would pack if they were leaving their homeland. Then, have students rank the items, listing the most important one at the top of the list.

Words to Know

Review the Words to Know on page 253 of the Student Edition. To help students remember the words, invite pairs of students to scan the chapter to find the words and their definitions. Ask them to draw a chart listing each word and its definition.

The following words and definitions are covered in this chapter:

ghetto a neighborhood where people of the same race, religion, or country live

tenement an apartment house with poor safety, sanitation, and comfort conditions

skyscraper a very tall building with many floors, elevators, and a steel frame

nativism a feeling of citizens who are against immigrants

exclusion keeping a person or a group from coming in

migration a movement of people within a country or area

racism feelings against people because of their skin color

Portfolio Project

Summary: From the perspective of immigrants arriving in the United States during the late 1880s, students write a journal entry that describes the sights and experiences that have made an impact on them.

Procedure: Have students write five journal entries about their initial experiences and impressions of the United States from the perspective of an immigrant. Students should include details about their first viewing of the Statue of Liberty, what the first day was like in a new land, and some of the sights that were different from those in their homeland.

Assessment: Use the Individual Activity Rubric on page *xii* of this guide. Fill in the rubric with the additional information below. For this project, students should have

- written journal entries about immigrant experiences.
- composed five journal entries that show an understanding of the chapter.

Learning Objectives

Review the Learning Objectives on page 253 of the Student Edition before starting the chapter. Students can use the list as a learning guide. Suggest they write the objectives in a journal or use the Chapter Goals and Self-Check worksheet found on page PA 6 of the Classroom Resource Binder.

After students read each section of the chapter, have them write an example of what they learned under the appropriate objective. Suggest that students use these worksheets as a practice guide to help them study for the chapter test.

Timeline

Use the timeline to discuss the sequence of events in this chapter. Point out the timeline's title, its time span, and the intervals. After students have read the chapter, have them review the timeline and suggest additional entries.

SECTION 1: Immigrants From Southern and Eastern Europe
Student Edition, pages 254–259

Section Objectives

- Explain why the journey to America was difficult for immigrants.
- Explain how cities changed as a result of ghettos formed by groups of immigrants.
- Describe the Triangle Shirtwaist Company fire.
- * Describe the similarities among new immigrants arriving in the United States.

Words to Know

ghetto, tenement, skyscraper

Cooperative Group Activity

Profile of an Immigrant

Materials: reference materials (Unit 4 Bibliography and Internet sites, pages 236–240)

Procedure: Remind students that the "new" immigrants, who began arriving from southern and eastern Europe in the late 1870s, were similar in many ways. You may want students to do additional research on immigration during this time. Divide the class into groups and have each group read and take notes about immigration from the late 1800s to the early 1900s.

- Group members write detailed profiles of two "new" immigrants that include information about the immigrants' country of origin, religion, age, health, work skills, reasons for immigrating, experiences with city living.

- Group members choose a spokesperson to read their profiles to the class and relate similarities among new immigrants. Groups then discuss the similarities and differences among all the immigrant profiles.

Customizing the Activity for Individual Needs

ESL To help students understand the experiences immigrants had in the late 1800s, have them compare these experiences to the ones they or members of their family had when they came to the United States.

Learning Styles Students can:

 complete a *Who, What, Where, When, How, Why* chart (Classroom Resource Binder, page GO 7) about the two new immigrants.

 write the similarities between the new immigrants on index cards. Have students use the index cards to study.

 tell a story to a partner about a new immigrant's journey to America in 1880.

Reinforcement Activity

Remind students that new immigrants faced many challenges after arriving in the United States. Have students work in pairs to scan the first section of the chapter to create an outline of immigrant experiences. Students should title their outlines *New Immigrants: 1880–1920*. Remind students to use the boldfaced section titles in the Student Edition as headings for their outlines and to list pertinent facts under these headings.

Alternative Assessment

Students can write a magazine article from the perspective of a new immigrant. Articles should include *reasons for immigrating, a description of new experiences in the United States, feelings about city life and work environments,* and *thoughts about future hopes and dreams.* Encourage students to write a final statement explaining why they feel that coming to the United States was or was not the right choice.

CONNECTING HISTORY AND TECHNOLOGY: Skyscrapers, Streetcars, and Bridges
Student Edition, page 260

Objectives
- Social Studies Skill: Describe the space that is for rent in a recently built skyscraper by writing a newspaper ad.
- Social Studies Skill: Describe city life by drawing a map that includes city streets, bridges, waterways, streetcars, and skyscrapers.
- Social Studies Skill: Describe city life in the 1880s by writing a poem.

Activities
Space for Rent
Procedure: Have students write a newspaper ad that will attract people living in 1900 to rent space in a newly built skyscraper. Students should include information about the size of the space for rent, its location, safety advantages, and appeal.

Map it
Materials: 11 x 14 sheets of paper; colored markers

Procedure: Have students design a map of a growing city in the late 1880s. They should include city streets, waterways, bridges, streetcars, parks, homes, and skyscrapers in their maps. Remind students to include a map key.

City Life
Materials: poster paper; colored markers

Procedure: Students work in groups of three or four to create poems that describe city life in the 1880s. Encourage students to include descriptions of the sights and sounds of city life, such as the noise of streetcars, the bustle of people moving from place to place, the cries of street vendors, and the sounds of skyscrapers or bridges being built. Have students illustrate their poems.

Practice

Have students complete Connecting History and Technology: The Dumbbell Tenement on page 91 of the Classroom Resource Binder.

SECTION 2: Immigrants From Asia and Latin America
Student Edition, pages 261–264

Section Objectives
- Explain the negative feelings some Americans had toward immigrants.
- Describe the Exclusion Act and how it affected Asian immigrants.
- Describe the Treaty of Guadalupe Hidalgo and the boundary it settled.
- Describe how Chinese, Japanese, and Filipino immigrants were treated.

Words to Know
nativism, exclusion

Cooperative Group Activity

A Historian's Perspective

Materials: reference materials (Unit 4 Bibliography and Internet sites, pages 236–240)

Procedure: Remind students that the problems between new immigrants and Americans led to feelings of nativism, or a feeling of citizens against immigrants. Organize the students into three groups. Assign each group one of the following topics: *Chinese immigrants, Japanese immigrants,* or *Filipino immigrants.* You may wish to have students conduct further research on Asian immigration in the late 1800s for this project.

- Students take notes about their assigned group of immigrants. Notes should include where this group of immigrants settled, the types of jobs they held, how they lived, how they were treated by native-born Americans.
- Group members write a short paper that documents the above information. Have students think of an interesting title for their paper such as, "A Day in the Life of a Chinese Immigrant."
- Group members choose a spokesperson to present their paper to the class.

Customizing the Activity for Individual Needs

ESL To help students understand the concept of nativism, have ESL students share experiences they or people they know have faced when moving to a new country.

Learning Styles Students can:

 organize their notes by completing a KWL chart (Classroom Resource Binder, page GO 6) before and after they research their papers.

 sort index cards that include facts about each Asian immigrant group.

 work in pairs to discuss the different reasons immigrants from Asia came to the United States.

Enrichment Activity

Have students make a chart in which they identify the major immigrant groups from Asia. Under each immigrant group, have students list the problems that each group faced in the late 1800s to the early 1900s.

Alternative Assessment

Students can assume the role of new immigrants in the United States and write a letter to family members back home describing the immigrant's life and how it differs from life back home. Encourage students to include the section vocabulary words *nativism* and *exclusion* in their letters.

SECTION 3: African Americans Move North
Student Edition, pages 265–267

Section Objectives

- Explain the reasons why many African Americans left the South to move to the North.
- ★ Identify groups, such as the NAACP, that helped fight for African American rights and describe these rights.

Words to Know

migration, racism

Cooperative Group Activity

A Fight For Rights

Materials: reference materials (Unit 4 Bibliography and Internet sites, pages 236–240)

Procedure: Remind students that in 1909, a group of African Americans and white Americans formed the National Association for the Advancement of Colored People (NAACP), a group that advocated African American rights. You may want students to do additional research on this organization. Organize the students into groups and have them assume the roles of NAACP members attending an annual meeting.

- Students make a list of problems facing African Americans in the early 1900s, such as discrimination in the workplace, in housing, and in education.
- Group members recommend solutions to the problems African Americans face.
- Group members draft a mission statement that outlines the beliefs and goals of the NAACP, including basic beliefs and methods for fighting against racism and for achieving equal rights.
- Groups share their mission statements with the class.

Customizing the Activity for Individual Needs

ESL To help students understand the purpose of the NAACP, have them write important words, phrases, or people's names on index cards and work with a partner to relate the significance of each.

Learning Styles Students can:

 complete a Description Web (Classroom Resource Binder, page GO 3) about the NAACP.

 design a pamphlet that describes what the NAACP stands for.

 work in pairs to write and record a 30-second commercial or news bulletin that describes the NAACP.

Reteaching Activity

Have students make a chart that lists the ways in which the NAACP helped African Americans during the 1900s.

Alternative Assessment

Students can work in small groups to write a speech to increase NAACP membership. Have students include key facts about the NAACP, such as why it was established and methods for fighting against racism and for achieving equal rights. Encourage students to use persuasive language in their speeches in order to enlist the support of those listening. Group members choose a spokesperson to read their speech to the rest of the class.

Closing the Chapter
Student Edition, pages 268–269

Chapter Vocabulary

Review with students the Words to Know on page 253 of the Student Edition. Then have them complete the Vocabulary Review on page 268 of the Student Edition by answering each statement as *true* or *false*. If the statement is false, have students rewrite the statement to make it true.

For more vocabulary practice, have them complete the vocabulary exercise on page 89 of the Classroom Resource Binder.

Test Tip

Have students make a list of topics they need to review in order to prepare for taking the chapter test. Students should scan the boldfaced chapter headings to find information they need to review.

Learning Objectives

Have the students review their Chapter Goals and Self-Check worksheet found on page PA 6 of the Classroom Resource Binder. They can check off the goal they have reached. Note that each section of the quiz corresponds to a Learning Objective.

Group Activity

Summary: Students create a series of laws that will protect the health and safety of people living and working in cities today.

Procedure: Organize the students into small groups to brainstorm a list of health and safety issues of concern to people living and working in cities today. Group members rank these issues according to importance. Students then choose the top five issues and write a law for each that will help protect people in their homes and workplace environments in cities.

Assessment: Use the Group Activity Rubric found on page *xiii* of this guide. Fill in the rubric with the following additional information. For this activity, students should have

- brainstormed health and safety issues pertaining to people living and working in cities today.
- written five laws to help protect people in their homes and in their workplaces.

RELATED MATERIALS See the Unit Overview page for related Globe Fearon books that can be used to enrich and extend the chapter.

Traditional Assessment

Chapter Quiz
The Chapter Quiz on page 269 of the Student Edition can be used as an open-book test, a closed-book test, or a homework assignment. Use the quiz to identify concepts in the chapter that students need to review. Chapter Tests can be found in the Classroom Resource Binder on pages 93–94. Workbook pages 56–60 can be used for additional practice.

Chapter Tests
Use Chapter Tests A and B on pages 93–94 in the Classroom Resource Binder to further assess mastery of chapter concepts.

Additional Resources
Use the Resource Planner on page 97 of this guide to assign additional exercises from the Classroom Resource Binder and Workbook.

Alternative Assessment

Student Interview
Write the phrase *Coming to America* on the chalkboard. Ask:
- Where did immigrants come from in the late 1800s and early 1900s?
- What problems did immigrants face in the late 1800s and early 1900s?
- Did all American citizens accept new immigrants?

Presentation
Mention to students that the United States is sometimes called the land of opportunity.
- Students make a list of the reasons why immigrants of the late 1800s believed that the United States was the land of opportunity.
- Students use their lists to write statements, from the perspective of an immigrant that begin with the words *I believe . . .*
  Example: *I believe that the United States is a place where I can raise my children to become better-educated citizens.*
- Students present their statements to the class.

Unit Assessment

This is the last chapter in Unit 4: A Growing Nation. To assess cumulative knowledge and provide standardized-test practice, have students complete the Unit Review Test on page 270 of the Student Edition, and the Unit 4 Cumulative Test on pages 95–96 of the Classroom Resource Binder.

Unit 5 ▶ Becoming a World Leader

CHAPTER 15 The Reformers 1870–1920	PORTFOLIO PROJECT Essay	BUILDING YOUR SKILLS Identifying Cause and Effect	GROUP ACTIVITY Writing a List of Reforms	TIMELINE The Age of Reform
CHAPTER 16 Expansion Overseas 1890–1914	PORTFOLIO PROJECT Series of Headlines	VOICES FROM THE PAST José Martí	GROUP ACTIVITY Debating an Issue	TIMELINE United States Expansion
CHAPTER 17 World War I 1914–1920	PORTFOLIO PROJECT About World War I Chart	CONNECTING HISTORY AND... Language: Propaganda	GROUP ACTIVITY Making a Booklet	TIMELINE World War I

RELATED MATERIALS

These are some of the Globe Fearon books that can be used to enrich and extend the material in this unit.

Content ▶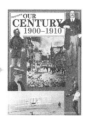

Fearon's Our Century 1900–1910 Explore the decade's history and provide in-depth content on President William H. Taft and Upton Sinclair.

Cultural Diversity ▶

Historical Case Studies: Somos Mexicanos; Mexican Americans in the United States Focus on Emiliano Zapata and the Mexican Revolution

Literature ▶

Pacemaker® Classics: All Quiet on the Western Front Written by Erich Maria Remarque. Explore World War I through the eyes of a German soldier.

Chapter 15 • **The Reformers** 1870–1920

Chapter at a Glance

SE page

272		*Opening the Chapter and Portfolio Project*
274	SECTION 1	Early Reforms
278		*Building Your Skills: Identifying Cause and Effect*
279	SECTION 2	The Progressives
283	SECTION 3	Reform Continues
288		*Chapter Review and Group Activity*

Learning Objectives

- Describe early reforms in business and government.
- Identify the goals of the Progressive movement.
- Explain how muckrakers brought change to government, business, and society.
- Describe reforms passed under Presidents Roosevelt, Taft, and Wilson.
- Discuss the struggle for women's suffrage.

Social Studies Skills

- Identify cause and effect.
- Use a timeline to identify events that occurred during the Age of Reform.

Writing Skills

- Write an essay explaining how some people worked to change the lives of other people during the Age of Reform.
- Write a paragraph discussing whether or not the Civil Service Act of 1883 is a fair law.
- Write a short essay about Theodore Roosevelt as the first Progressive President.
- Create a sign explaining why it is important to obey Prohibition laws.
- Write a list of reforms needed in school.

Map and Chart Skills

- Use a map to identify states that gave suffrage to women before the Nineteenth Amendment was adopted.

**Chapter 15
The Reformers**

Use the Program Resources below for reteaching, reinforcement, and enrichment. Additional activities for customizing the lessons can be found in this guide.

Key
Reteaching = ⌒   Reinforcement = ⇓   Enrichment = ⌒

Sections	Program Resources		
	Workbook Exercises	Teacher's Planning Guide	Classroom Resource Binder
Early Reforms	61	⇓ p. 106	
Building Your Skills: Identifying Cause and Effect		⇓ p. 107	⇓ Building Your Skills *Reading a Chart*, 99, 100
			⇓ Writing and Test-Taking Tip 5 *Organizing Information by Cause and Effect*
			⇓ Graphic Organizer 2 *Cause and Effect*
The Progressives	62	⌒ p. 108	
Reform Continues	63, 64	⌒ p. 108	⇓ Transparency 13 *United States: Political*
Chapter 15 Review		p. 109	⌒ Concept Builder 15 *The Reformers*
			⇓ Words to Know 97
			⌒ Challenge 101
			⇓ Chapter Tests A & B, 102, 103

Chapter
15

Customizing the Chapter

Opening the Chapter
Student Edition, pages 272–273

Photo Activity
Explain to students that by the 1870s, women were still not allowed to vote in the United States. Point out the two slogans in the photo and on the poster. Initiate a discussion about the effectiveness of these slogans. Then, have students create slogans that they think would sway the American public to support women's suffrage, or the right to vote.

Words to Know
Review the Words to Know on page 273 of the Student Edition. To help students remember the words, invite pairs of students to write what they believe to be the meaning of each vocabulary term.

Students can then verify their definitions in the Glossary in the Student Edition. Suggest that they use the following format:

I think that _____ means _____. The Glossary definition of _____ is _____.

The following words and definitions are covered in this chapter:

bribe money paid to get someone to do something against the law

civil service a system that includes most government workers who are appointed rather than elected

kickback an illegal payment made in return for a favor or service

capitalism a system in which private businesses, farms, and factories compete with one another to make a profit

muckraker a writer who brings attention to corruption

trust a giant corporation, or group of companies

income tax a tax paid on the money a person earns

Prohibition a time period when making, selling, and transporting alcohol was unlawful in the United States

Portfolio Project

Summary: Students write an essay about an important reformer who helped to change the lives of people in the United States.

Materials: reference materials (Internet sites, pages 236–240)

Procedure: Have students read the chapter to learn about the need for reform in the United States during the late 1800s and early 1900s. Then, have students choose one of the following reformers to research and write about: *Thomas Nast, Rutherford Hayes, Chester Arthur, Ida Tarbel, Lincoln Steffens, Upton Sinclair, Theodore Roosevelt, William Taft, Woodrow Wilson,* or *Carrie Chapman Catt.* Students take notes about the contributions that the reformer made to society and write an essay about the reformer. Student essays should contain information that explains how the reformer changed the lives of people in the United States.

Assessment: Use the Individual Activity Rubric on page *xii* of this guide. Fill in the rubric with the additional information below. For this project, students should have:

• written an essay about a U.S. reformer of the 1800s or early 1900s and what that person did.

Learning Objectives

Review the Learning Objectives on page 273 of the Student Edition before starting the chapter. Students can use the list as a learning guide. Suggest that they write the objectives in a journal or use the Chapter Goals and Self-Check worksheet found on page PA 6 of the Classroom Resource Binder.

After reading each section of the chapter, have students write an example of what they learned under the appropriate objective. Suggest that students use these worksheets as a practice guide to help them study for the chapter test.

Timeline

Use the timeline to discuss the sequence of events in this chapter. Point out the timeline's title, its time span, and the intervals. After students have read the chapter, have them review the timeline and suggest additional entries.

SECTION 1: Early Reforms
Student Edition, pages 274–277

Section Objectives

• Describe problems that occurred as big businesses grew rich and powerful.

• Explain the Civil Service Act and why it was put into effect as a result of the spoils system.

* Describe the corruption that occurred in government during the Gilded Age.

Words to Know

bribe, civil service, kickback

Cooperative Group Activity

Gilded People, Gilded Age

Materials: reference materials (Unit 5 Bibliography and Internet sites, pages 236–240), chart paper

Procedure: Explain to students that during the Gilded Age, from about 1870 to 1900, many government officials and some leaders of big business were dishonest and corrupt and tried to use the government for their own gain. Anger at business and government made many Americans call for reforms. Organize the students into three groups and have them assume the role of Americans who want to reform business and government during the Gilded Age. Students may wish to do additional research on the topic of reform.

- Group members brainstorm four reforms that they believe were needed to improve society. Groups then create a two-column chart. One column lists each reform. The other column explains how the reform would help eliminate corruption and the misuse of power.

- Group members choose a representative to present their chart to the class. After all charts have been presented, groups compare the charts to determine which five reforms were mentioned most and which would have been most effective in improving business and government.

Customizing the Activity for Individual Needs

ESL To help students understand the concept of reform, student pairs list the areas in their school that need reform and potential improvements for each area.

Learning Styles Students can:

 look at Thomas Nast's political cartoon on page 276 of the Student Edition and explain what it means.

 create a political cartoon that shows the corruption of business and government during the Gilded Age.

 explain their group's reform chart to the rest of the class.

Enrichment Activity

Explain to students that while there were many corrupt business leaders during the Gilded Age, other wealthy leaders used their money to create jobs, help the poor, and build museums and other public places. Have students list the ways wealthy leaders can help improve the lives of less-fortunate Americans and rank those improvements according to importance.

Alternative Assessment

Students can write a newspaper editorial from the perspective of a reformer wanting to make changes in business and government. Students explain why reform is necessary, suggest possible changes, and discuss ways that all Americans can get involved in the process of reform.

BUILDING YOUR SKILLS:
Identifying Cause and Effect
Student Edition, page 278

Objectives

- Social Studies Skill: Identify cause and effect statements in current newspaper articles.
- Social Studies Skill: Identify a series of cause and effect statements.
- Social Studies Skill: Identify cause and effect statements based on personal events.

Activities

In the News
Materials: current newspapers

Procedure: Have partners write four incomplete cause and effect statements based on current newspaper articles. Remind them that a *cause* is an action that leads to an event, and an *effect* is the outcome of the event. Partners complete each other's statement.

Chain Reaction
Materials: reference materials (Unit 5 Bibliography and Internet sites, pages 236–240)

Procedure: Explain that the relationship between cause and effect is similar to the way links in a chain combine. Each effect becomes a cause of something else. Have students research the life of William "Boss" Tweed. Based on the information they find, have students write a "chain" of five cause and effect statements.

My Own Cause and Effect
Procedure: Have students think of important events in their lives and list the causes and effects of these events. Invite students to write their own cause and effect statements based on these personal experiences.

Practice

Have students complete Building Your Skills: Identifying Cause and Effect on page 99 of the Classroom Resource Binder.

SECTION 2: The Progressives
Student Edition, pages 279–282

Section Objectives

- Explain President Roosevelt's plan to end the coal miners' strike of 1901.
- ✻ Identify Progressives and describe the changes they wanted to make.

Words to Know

capitalism, muckraker, trust

Cooperative Group Activity

Progressives Unite!

Materials: reference materials (Unit 5 Bibliography and Internet sites, pages 236–240)

Procedure: Remind students that muckrakers who called attention to corruption in business and government were an important part of the Progressive movement. Organize the class into four groups and have each group choose one of the following topics dating from the early 1900s to research: *poverty, unsafe working conditions, unclean food,* or *corruption in local government and industry.* You may want students to do additional research on the Progressive movement.

- Students work collaboratively to learn about their topic and about muckrakers who brought attention to the problem.
- Group members create a fictitious muckraker and write a speech from this person's point of view.
- Groups choose a spokesperson to give the speech to the class. After all speeches have been given, students can bind the written speeches together to form a "Muckracking Magazine."

Customizing the Activity for Individual Needs

ESL   To help students understand the roles of the Progressives, have ESL students work with English-proficient partners to sort index cards with important terms, phrases, or names related to the Progressive movement.

Learning Styles   Students can:

 complete a *Who, What, When, Where, Why, How* chart (Classroom Resource Binder, page GO 7) about important reforms of the Progressive movement.

 create a pamphlet about one of the reforms of the Progressive movement.

Enrichment Activity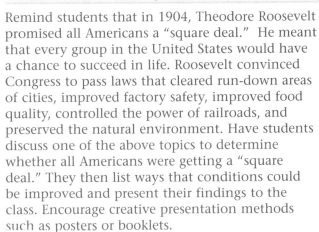

Remind students that in 1904, Theodore Roosevelt promised all Americans a "square deal." He meant that every group in the United States would have a chance to succeed in life. Roosevelt convinced Congress to pass laws that cleared run-down areas of cities, improved factory safety, improved food quality, controlled the power of railroads, and preserved the natural environment. Have students discuss one of the above topics to determine whether all Americans were getting a "square deal." They then list ways that conditions could be improved and present their findings to the class. Encourage creative presentation methods such as posters or booklets.

Alternative Assessment

Students can write one multiple choice, one true/false, and one fill-in-the-blank question about the Progressive movement. Each student then exchanges questions with a classmate, and answers the questions. Ask students to take turns reading and discussing their answers to the questions.

SECTION 3: Reform Continues
Student Edition, pages 283–287

Section Objectives

- Describe reforms initiated during President Taft's administration.
- Describe reforms under President Wilson.
- Explain why many women worked for Progressive reforms against alcohol.
- ✻ Describe the election of 1912.

Words to Know

income tax, Prohibition

Cooperative Group Activity

Campaign of 1912

Materials: reference materials (Unit 5 Bibliography and Internet sites, pages 236–240)

Procedure: Divide the class into groups of four. Each group represents the campaign team for one of the candidates in the 1912 election—Taft, Wilson, or Roosevelt.

- Groups research and take notes on their candidate and his issues.
- Each member of the group creates one of the following: position paper, sign, banner, or button for the candidate.
- Group members combine their efforts and make a class presentation. They can give speeches on the important issues of the campaign.

Customizing the Activity for Individual Needs

ESL To help students understand items associated with election campaigns, explain and show realia or photos of campaign buttons, banners, and signs.

Learning Styles Students can:

 complete a Comparison-Contrast chart (Classroom Resource Binder, page GO 4) comparing the positions of the three candidates.

 create posters supporting one of the candidates.

 hold a mock presidential debate.

Reteaching Activity

Review with students each of the candidate's positions in the election of 1912. Students can create a three-column chart listing each candidate and his ideas.

Alternative Assessment

Students can write a paragraph that identifies which candidate they would have voted for in 1912 and why they chose that candidate.

Closing the Chapter
Student Edition, pages 288–289

Chapter Vocabulary

Review with students the Words to Know on page 273 of the Student Edition. Then have them complete the Vocabulary Review on page 288 of the Student Edition, by answering each question as *true* or *false*. If a sentence is false, have students change the underlined term to make it true.

For more vocabulary practice, have them complete the vocabulary exercise on page 97 of the Classroom Resource Binder.

Test Tip

To help students prepare for the chapter test, have them scan the chapter for words or phrases that show a cause-and-effect relationship.

Example: Leaders of big business organized trusts. *(Cause)* Trusts forced smaller companies out of business. *(Effect)*

Learning Objectives

Have the students review their Chapter Goals Worksheet found on page PA 6 of the Classroom Resource Binder. They can check off the goal they have reached. Note that each section of the quiz corresponds to a Learning Objective.

Group Activity

Summary: Students brainstorm a list of reforms they think will help their school or community and debate pros and cons.

Procedure: Organize the students into groups of three or four to brainstorm a list of reforms they think would support and benefit members of the school or community. For example, a reform could be to raise the driving age to 21 to prevent the high numbers of accidents among young people. Group members rank the reforms according to importance and discuss the pros and cons of the top reform on their list. Students work to find a compromise to the issue. Groups then share their reforms with the class.

Assessment: Use the Group Activity Rubric found on page *xiii* of this guide. Fill in the rubric with the following additional information. For this activity, students should have

- written a list of reforms that are needed in their school or community.
- discussed one problem with the class and determined how it might be solved.

RELATED MATERIALS See the Unit Overview page for related Globe Fearon books that can be used to enrich and extend the materials in the chapter.

Chapter 15

Traditional Assessment

Chapter Quiz
The Chapter Quiz on page 289 of the Student Edition can be used as an open-book test, a closed-book test, or a homework assignment. Use the quiz to identify concepts in the chapter that students need to review. Chapter Tests can be found in the Classroom Resource Binder on pages 102–103. Workbook pages 61–64 can be used for additional practice.

Chapter Tests
Use Chapter Tests A and B on pages 102–103 in the Classroom Resource Binder to further assess mastery of chapter concepts.

Additional Resources
Use the Resource Planner on page 105 of this guide to assign additional exercises from the Classroom Resource Binder and Workbook.

Alternative Assessment

Student Interview
Give each student a sheet of paper with the names of reforms during the Progressive Movement. Ask:
- Who initiated this reform?
- When was it initiated?
- Why was this reform needed?
- What were the pros and cons of this reform?

Open-Ended
- Students scan the chapter to list important events and dates during the Age of Reform.
- Students create a timeline of events that occurred during the Age of Reform.

Chapter 16 · **Expansion Overseas** 1890–1914

Chapter at a Glance

SE page

290		*Opening the Chapter and Portfolio Project*
292	SECTION 1	Looking Toward Asia
297	SECTION 2	The Spanish-American War
301		*Voices From the Past: José Martí*
302	SECTION 3	The "Big Stick" and the Panama Canal
306		*Chapter Review and Group Activity*

Learning Objectives

- Describe how the growing United States became involved in Asia.
- Explain why the United States needed a port in the Pacific.
- Discuss the role of the United States in the Spanish-American War.
- Describe Theodore Roosevelt's foreign policy.
- Explain why the Panama Canal was built.

Social Studies Skills

- Explore the political views of José Martí.
- Use a timeline to identify events that cover the emergence of the United States as a world power between 1892 and 1914.
- Discuss isolationism and expansion by preparing arguments for a debate.

Writing Skills

- Write a headline for each main event that occurred during the expansion overseas.
- Write a dialogue comparing and contrasting the views of an isolationist and a supporter of expansion and what they might say about the Boxer Rebellion in China.
- Write a paragraph describing the views that people from Cuba, Puerto Rico, and the Philippines might hold about the Treaty of Paris.
- Write a report identifying the pros and cons of choosing the Isthmus of Panama as the place for a canal.

Map and Chart Skills

- Use a map to compare travel miles from New York City to San Francisco with and without the Panama Canal.

Chapter
16

Resource Planner

Chapter 16 Expansion Overseas	Use the Program Resources below for reteaching, reinforcement, and enrichment. Additional activities for customizing the lessons can be found in this guide.

Key
Reteaching = ⌢ Reinforcement = ⬇ Enrichment = ⌢⬎

Sections	Program Resources		
	Workbook Exercises	Teacher's Planning Guide	Classroom Resource Binder
Looking Toward Asia	65	⌢ p. 113	⌢⬎ Outline Map 8 *Asia*
The Spanish-American War	66	⬇ p. 114	
Voices From the Past: José Martí		⌢ p. 115	⌢ Feature Practice 106 *Voices From the Past: Theodore Roosevelt*
The "Big Stick" and The Panama Canal	67, 68	⬇ p. 115	⌢⬎ Outline Map 5, 6 *North America, South America*
Chapter 16 Review		p. 116	⌢⬎ Concept Builder 16 *Expansion Overseas* ⬇ Words to Know 104 ⌢ Challenge 107 ⬇ Chapter Tests A & B, 108, 109

Customizing the Chapter

Opening the Chapter
Student Edition, pages 290–291

Photo Activity

Ask students to look at the photo and postcard of the Panama Canal on page 290 of the Student Edition. Explain that it took ten years to build the Canal. Point out that President Roosevelt wanted the canal built because it would make trade and travel by ship faster and easier for the United States. Have students find the Panama Canal on a world map and describe its location. From the photo, have students describe the geography of the area and the location.

Words to Know

Review the Words to Know on page 291 of the Student Edition. To help students remember the words, have pairs of students write each vocabulary word on an index card. As students read the vocabulary words in each section, have them write at least one synonym or similar phrase on the back of the index card.

The following words and definitions are covered in this chapter:

isolationist a person or country that wants to stay out of political affairs of other countries

protectorate a country that is partly controlled or protected by a more powerful country

annex to add or take possession of a smaller country

yellow journalism the publishing of exaggerated or made-up news stories to attract readers and influence their ideas

imperialism the policy of one nation gaining control over other lands and using them to build an empire

foreign policy the way a country deals with other countries

isthmus a narrow strip of land that connects two large-sized lands

corollary an addition to a document

Portfolio Project

Summary: As students read the chapter, they write newspaper headlines describing each important event.

Procedure: Tell students that during the 1890s and early 1900s, most people received news from newspapers. As students read each section of the chapter, they write down each important event. Students use each event to write a newspaper headline describing it. Each headline should tell the story of an event in a few words that instantly capture the attention of readers. Students read their headlines to the class. For each event, students vote for the headline that most effectively describes the event and captures the interest of readers.

Assessment: Use the Individual Activity Rubric on page *xii* of this guide. Fill in the rubric with the additional information below. For this project, students should have

- listed major events of the chapter.
- written engaging headlines for each event.

Learning Objectives

Review the Learning Objectives on page 291 of the Student Edition before starting the chapter. Students can use the list as a learning guide. Suggest they write the objectives in a journal or use the Chapter Goals and Self-Check worksheet found on page PA 6 of the Classroom Resource Binder.

After reading each section of the chapter, have students write an example of what they learned under the appropriate objective. Suggest that students use these worksheets as a practice guide to help them study for the chapter test.

Timeline

Use the timeline to discuss the sequence of events in this chapter. Point out the timeline's title, its time span, and the intervals. After students have read the chapter, have them review the timeline and suggest additional entries.

SECTION 1: Looking Toward Asia
Student Edition, pages 292–296

Section Objectives

- Identify reasons why the United States needed a port in the Pacific Ocean.
- Explain what happened when the United States took control of Hawaii.
- Describe the relationship between the United States and China.
- Explain why President Roosevelt sent the Great White Fleet on tour.
- * Describe arguments for and against U.S. expansion.

Words to Know

isolationist, protectorate, annex

Cooperative Group Activity

To Expand or Not to Expand

Materials: reference materials (Unit 5 Bibliography and Internet sites, pages 236–240)

Procedure: Remind students that during the 1890s, there was a growing feeling that the United States needed to expand in order to increase its strength. However, not all Americans agreed with the need for expansion. Americans who wanted to stay out of the political affairs of other countries were called isolationists. Organize the students into two groups. One group represents the views of Americans in favor of U.S. expansion, and the second group takes the views of isolationists. Students may want to do additional research on American views of U.S. expansion during the 1890s in order to write an editorial.

- Group members discuss the following five topics: *reasons why they favor or disapprove of a policy that calls for U.S. expansion; their views about American businesses looking to Asia for trade; their views about the United States taking control of Hawaii; their views about the Open Door Policy with China;* and *their views concerning the Boxer Rebellion.*

- Students in both groups write editorials for a newspaper expressing their views.
- Groups choose a spokesperson to read each editorial to the class.

Customizing the Activity for Individual Needs

ESL To help students understand the meaning of the term *isolationist*, explain that it is easier to try to guess a word's meaning by removing the "ist" ending. Ask students for other words that end in "ist," such as extremist or Communist.

Learning Styles Students can:

 locate the countries that the United States developed relationships with during the early expansion movement on the world map in the Atlas of the Student Edition.

 design one bumper sticker that promotes U.S. expansion and another that takes an isolationist stance.

 work with a partner to debate the topic of U.S. expansion, with each student taking a different point of view.

Reteaching Activity

Organize the students into two groups and distribute a Description Web (Classroom Resource Binder, page GO 3) to each group. Instruct one group to write "For Expansion" in the middle circle, and the other group to write "Against Expansion" in the middle circle. Have students in each group write words or phrases about their topic. Then have both groups share their Description Webs.

Alternative Assessment

I Believe . . .

Students can assume the role of either a supporter of expansion or an isolationist. Students write down three statements that reflect their position and begin with the words "I believe." For example, a student assuming the role of an isolationist might write, *I believe that it is wrong to control other countries.* Students share their statements with the class. After each statement has been read, ask for a volunteer to guess the position represented. Volunteers then explain why the statement reflects that position.

SECTION 2: The Spanish-American War
Student Edition, pages 297–300

Section Objectives

- Explain why many Americans sided with Cubans in their revolt against Spain.
- Explain why U.S. newspapers printed the headline "Remember the Maine!"
- Identify areas the United States gained in the war against Spain.
- Describe how the United States became a world power.
- Discuss how newspapers used yellow journalism to influence readers.

Words to Know

yellow journalism, imperialism

Cooperative Group Activity

Special Edition

Materials: reference materials (Unit 5 Bibliography and Internet sites, pages 236–240)

Procedure: Remind students that some newspapers practiced yellow journalism, exaggerating news stories to attract readers and sway their opinions. To build up anger against Spain, many newspapers printed shocking stories about events in Cuba. Eventually, Americans were ready to fight, and on April 25, 1898, the United States declared war on Spain. Organize students into small groups and have them write sensational articles that would increase Americans' support of the Spanish-American War. Students may want to do additional research for this project.

- Group members review information about the Spanish-American War and take notes on important events and issues.
- Students use their notes to write a newspaper article that will build American support for the war. Students should include a sensational headline to accompany their article and answers to the questions *who, what, where, why, when,* and *how.*
- Group members choose a spokesperson to read their article to the class.
- After the articles are read aloud, students decide which articles are most persuasive.

Customizing the Activity for Individual Needs

ESL To help students understand yellow journalism, have them discuss the role of the media in their native country. ESL students can share their information with the class.

Learning Styles Students can:

 complete a Cause and Effect chart (Classroom Resource Binder, page GO 2) with information about yellow journalism and its effects.

 create a crossword puzzle using key words about the Spanish-American War.

 record the articles on a tape recorder.

Reinforcement Activity

Ask students if they think yellow journalism is still practiced today. Organize the students into groups and provide each with copies of newspapers and tabloids. Ask students to find and list examples. Students should decide whether the stories are exaggerated or completely false, and what their purpose is. Ask students to write a one-page essay that describes the practice of yellow journalism, and how it differs from standard journalism.

Alternative Assessment

Students can complete a Description Web (Classroom Resource Binder, page GO 3) with the term "yellow journalism" in the center circle. In the surrounding circles, have them write down examples of exaggerated news reports that occurred during the Spanish-American War.

VOICES FROM THE PAST: José Martí
Student Edition, page 301

Objectives

- Social Studies Skill: Describe the life of Cuban freedom fighter José Martí by writing a biographical account of his life.
- Social Studies Skill: Compare and contrast two newspaper articles that are written on the same topic—one relaying the facts and the other employing exaggerations, or yellow journalism.
- Social Studies Skill: Describe the struggle for Cuban independence by writing an inspirational poem.

Activities

Biography of a Freedom Fighter

Materials: reference materials (Unit 5 Bibliography and Internet sites, pages 236–240); colored markers

Procedure: Organize students into three groups and assign each group one of the following topics: *José Martí at age 16, fighting against Spanish forces; Martí living in New York from 1881–1895 as poet and writer;* or *Martí in later years during the Spanish-American War.* Have each group write and illustrate a chapter on the topic, to be included in a children's book about José Martí. Invite a spokesperson from each group to read its chapter to the class. Students can bind their chapters together to make a book.

Reporting the News

Procedure: Remind students that José Martí's poems and news articles were so powerful that people began to support Cuba's fight for freedom by giving money to the cause. Mention that his writing was inspirational and factual, not exaggerated or made-up as in the style of yellow journalism. Form two groups and ask each group to write a brief news article supporting Cuba's fight for freedom. Ask one group to report the news in a factual manner, while the other group reports it in an exaggerated way. Have each group read its articles aloud and discuss the similarities and differences.

For the Good of All

Procedure: Have students work in small groups to write a short poem that reflects José Martí's beliefs. Encourage them to use phrases such as *rise up, freedom, hard work, new flag,* and *for the good of all.*

Practice

Have students complete Voices From the Past: Theodore Roosevelt on page 106 of the Classroom Resource Binder.

SECTION 3: The "Big Stick" and the Panama Canal
Student Edition, pages 302–305

Section Objectives

- Explain the Roosevelt Corollary.
- Describe President Roosevelt's plan to build the Panama Canal.

* Describe the work involved in building the Panama Canal.
* Describe the opening of the Panama Canal and how it affected the United States.

Words to Know

foreign policy, isthmus, corollary

Cooperative Group Activity

The Building of a Canal

Materials: reference materials (Unit 5 Bibliography and Internet sites, pages 236–240)

Procedure: Organize the class into six groups and assign each group one of the following topics about the Panama Canal: *reasons for building the canal, events that led to the building of the canal, how the United States controlled disease in Panama, how the canal was built, when the first ship passed through the canal,* and *how the opening of the Panama Canal affected the United States.* Students may want to do additional research on their topic for this activity.

- Group members research and take notes on their topic.
- Each student in a group writes one paragraph about the topic. Groups also include an introductory paragraph and a brief summary.
- Group members choose a spokesperson to read their paper to the class.
- Groups arrange their papers in chronological order and bind them together to create a book on the Panama Canal.

Customizing the Activity for Individual Needs

ESL To help students understand the importance of a Canal, have them look at the map on page 304 of the Student Edition, which shows how the Panama Canal shortened the trip between New York City and San Francisco.

Learning Styles Students can:

 look at the photograph of the Panama Canal on page 290 of the Student Edition and write a brief description of it.

 create illustrations to supplement the text in their Panama Canal book.

 work with a partner to assume the roles of an interviewer and a construction worker on the Panama Canal and record an interview about the building process.

Reinforcement Activity

Have students work with partners and interview each other about the Panama Canal. Explain that each student has two minutes to provide as much information about the Panama Canal as possible. As one student relays facts, the other records the information on paper or on an audiotape. Have students switch roles and repeat the activity. When both students have had a turn, ask them to compare their information.

Alternative Assessment

Students can compose a short poem that provides information about the Panama Canal. Example:

It took seven years to build the canal. There were many ditches to dig.

It took thousands of men to do the work, for the project was so big!

The canal was built with sturdy locks to raise or lower each ship.

Now ships could sail from ocean to ocean and be guaranteed a short trip.

Closing the Chapter
Student Edition, pages 306–307

Chapter Vocabulary

Review with students the Words to Know on page 291 of the Student Edition. Then have them complete the Vocabulary Review on page 306 of the Student Edition, by answering each statement as *true* or *false*. If the sentence is false, students change the underlined term to make it true.

For more vocabulary practice, have them complete the vocabulary exercise on page 104 of the Classroom Resource Binder.

Test Tip

To help students prepare for the chapter test, have them reread each section of the chapter and then write a short summary that describes the key points of the section.

Learning Objectives

Have students review their Chapter Goals and Self-Check worksheet found on page PA 6 of the Classroom Resource Binder. They can check off the goal they have reached. Note that each section of the quiz corresponds to a Learning Objective.

Group Activity

Summary: Students debate the issue of whether the United States should take action in other countries today.

Materials: current newspaper articles

Procedure: Divide the class into groups of four students each. Have groups review current newspaper articles that pertain to U.S. involvement in other countries, such as sending soldiers, weapons, or aid in the form of supplies or money. Group members discuss reasons why the United States has taken action in these countries. Students debate the following question: *Should the United States take action in other countries today?* Two students in a group prepare to answer *yes* to the question while two students should prepare to answer *no.*

• Students have 15 minutes to complete their debate.

Assessment: Use the Group Activity Rubric found on page *xiii* of this guide. Fill in the rubric with the following additional information. For this activity, students should have

• listed reasons why the United States has been involved in the affairs of other countries.
• participated in a debate about U.S. involvement in other countries.

RELATED MATERIALS   See the Unit Overview page for related Globe Fearon books that can be used to enrich and extend the materials in the chapter.

Assessing the Chapter

Traditional Assessment

Chapter Quiz
The Chapter Quiz on page 307 of the Student Edition can be used as an open-book test, a closed-book test, or a homework assignment. Use the quiz to identify concepts in the chapter that students need to review. Chapter Tests can be found in the Classroom Resource Binder on pages 108–109. Workbook pages 65–68 can be used for additional practice.

Chapter Tests
Use Chapter Tests A and B on pages 108–109 in the Classroom Resource Binder to further assess mastery of chapter concepts.

Additional Resources
Use the Resource Planner on page 112 of this guide to assign additional exercises from the Classroom Resource Binder and Workbook.

Alternative Assessment

Student Interview
Ask students the following questions about the chapter:

• What time period or years do the events in this chapter span?
• What are three main events that are covered in this chapter?
• What was the outcome of the Spanish-American War?
• Which U.S. president was primarily responsible for building the Panama Canal?

Open-Ended
Ask students to choose one section of the chapter to write the following:

• Students prepare a true/false test by writing four statements from their section of the chapter, and by answering each question.
• Students write a critical thinking question for their section of the chapter, and write an answer to the question.
• Students write two multiple-choice questions for their section of the chapter, and answer the questions.

Chapter 16

Chapter 17 • World War I 1914–1920

Chapter at a Glance

SE page

308   *Opening the Chapter and Portfolio Project*

310   SECTION 1   A World War Begins

315   SECTION 2   From Neutral to Declaration of War

318   *Connecting History and Language: Propaganda*

319   SECTION 3   The Home Front

322   SECTION 4   The War to End All Wars

328   *Chapter Review and Group Activity*

Learning Objectives

- Describe the causes of World War I.
- Identify the events that led the United States to enter the war.
- Discuss how the war changed the lives of Americans at home.
- Explain how the United States helped the Allies win the war.
- Describe the Treaty of Versailles.

Social Studies Skills

- Explore how propaganda is used.
- Use a timeline to identify events that happened during and after World War I.

Writing Skills

- Describe what occurred during World War I by making a chart.
- Write a letter to explain fears that someone living in Europe during the outbreak of World War I in 1914 might feel.

- Describe in an essay how European Americans might have felt if they had family members still living in Europe when the United States took a neutral position regarding the war.
- Describe the feelings of an American soldier as he left home to fight in World War I.
- Explain some lessons the world has learned from World War I by preparing a speech in favor of the League of Nations.
- Write a booklet about World War I.

Map and Chart Skills

- Use a map to identify the Allied nations, Central Powers, and neutral nations.
- Use a chart to identify the number of soldiers wounded or killed in World War I.
- Use a map to identify new independent nations.

Resource Planner

**Chapter 17
World War I**

Use the Program Resources below for reteaching, reinforcement, and enrichment. Additional activities for customizing the lessons can be found in this guide.

Key
Reteaching = ⤺   Reinforcement = ⤓   Enrichment = ⤴

Sections	Program Resources		
	⤓ **Workbook Exercises**	**Teacher's Planning Guide**	**Classroom Resource Binder**
A World War Begins	69	⤓ p. 121	⤴ Concept Builder 17 *World War I* ⤓ Transparency 7 *Europe During World War I, 1913*
From Neutral to Declaration of War	70	⤺ p. 121	⤴ Concept Builder 17 *World War I*
Connecting History and Language: Propaganda		p. 122	⤴ Feature Practice 112 *Connecting History and Language: Hooverizing*
The Home Front	71	⤓ p. 123	⤴ Concept Builder 17 *World War I*
The War to End All Wars	72, 73	⤴ p. 123	⤴ Graphic Organizer 5 *Main Idea and Supporting Details* ⤓ Transparency 7 *Europe After World War I*
Chapter 17 Review		p. 124	⤓ Words to Know 110 ⤴ Challenge 113 ⤓ Chapter Tests A & B, 114, 115 ⤓ Unit Test Parts I & II, 116, 117

Opening the Chapter
Student Edition, pages 308–309

Photo Activity

Explain to students that the photo shows the destruction of the town of Ipres, Belgium, by German bombers. Mention that the destruction was characteristic of the devastation that occurred in Europe throughout World War I. Then point out the newspaper headline that announced the United States' declaration of war on Germany. Explain that the Allies were heartened when they learned that the United States would join their fight in 1917, since they had been left to fight Germany on their own since the start of the war in 1914.

From the perspective of a news editor in the United States, ask students to write two newspaper headlines: one that describes the bombing in Belgium, and another about the U.S. decision to join the war effort.

Words to Know

Review the Words to Know on page 309 of the Student Edition. To help students remember the words, invite pairs of students to write each word on one index card, and its definition on another. Have students take turns matching the word with its definition. Remind them to look up each word in the Glossary in the Student Edition to check for accuracy.

The following words and definitions are covered in this chapter:

arms race a contest to build weapons and military power

terrorist a person who uses violence for a political cause

stalemate a situation in which neither side wins or loses

propaganda the spreading of ideas, information, and beliefs to help or hurt a cause

ambassador a person sent to another country to speak for the government of his or her own country

victory garden a garden in which citizens raised their own food during World War I

bond a paper showing debt, or money owed

communism an economic system in which the government owns all property and businesses

armistice an agreement to stop fighting

Portfolio Project

Summary: Students create a chart about World War I and then write questions about the war that can be answered using information in the chart.

Procedure: Have students create a chart containing facts about World War I. Students choose headings for their charts, such as: *Causes of World War I, Nations involved, Events of the war, Weapons used, Casualty figures, Cost of the war,* or *Making peace.* Students then list facts to support the heading topics of their charts. When students have completed their charts, they write five questions based on information found on their charts. Pairs of students exchange charts and questions. Students answer each other's questions.

Assessment: Use the Individual Activity Rubric on page *xii* of this guide. Fill in the rubric with the additional information below. For this project, students should have

- created a chart about World War I.
- written five questions based on information from the chart.

Learning Objectives

Review the Learning Objectives on page 309 of the Student Edition before starting the chapter. Students can use the list as a learning guide. Suggest they write the objectives in a journal or use the Chapter Goals and Self-Check worksheet found on page PA 6 of the Classroom Resource Binder.

After reading each section of the chapter, have students write an example of what they learned under the appropriate objective. Suggest that students use these worksheets as a practice guide to help them study for the chapter test.

Timeline

Use the timeline to discuss the sequence of events in this chapter. Point out the timeline's title, its time span, and the intervals. After students have read the chapter, have them review the timeline and suggest additional entries.

SECTION 1: A World War Begins
Student Edition, pages 310–314

Section Objectives
- Identify the causes of war in Europe.
- Explain how Austria-Hungary's declaration of war on Serbia caused other countries to declare war.
- Identify the countries of the Central Powers and of the Allied Nations.
- Describe the first years of the war and attacks along the Western Front.
- * Describe new weapons used in World War I.

Words to Know
arms race, terrorist, stalemate

Cooperative Group Activity

The Weapons of War
Materials: reference materials (Unit 5 Bibliography and Internet sites, pages 236–240), construction paper; markers

Procedure: Remind students that World War I was different from earlier wars because it involved several nations and affected people all over the world. The two sides in the war were the Central Powers (Germany, Austria-Hungary, and the Ottoman Empire) and the Allied Nations (Great Britain, France, and Russia). Organize the class into small groups. Each group researches and discusses fighting techniques and weapons used in World War I. Students may want to do additional research on World War I for this activity.

- Group members research and take notes about the topic.
- Students use their notes to write and illustrate a short picture dictionary of fighting techniques and weapons.
- Group members choose a spokesperson to present their dictionary to the class.

Customizing the Activity for Individual Needs
ESL   To help students understand the weapons of war, review with them the weapons used during the Civil War in the United States.

Learning Styles   Students can:

 look up photographs of World War I weapons in reference materials such as encyclopedias and other books.

 draw pictures that depict a weapon used during World War I and write captions that describe them.

 explain to a small group how each weapon in the picture dictionary is used.

Reinforcement Activity
Have students assume the role of World War I soldiers and write letters to a family member that includes the following information: *feelings about fighting in the war, the side they are fighting for and who they are fighting against,* or *the types of weapons used.* Have students share their letters by reading them to the class.

Alternative Assessment
Students can complete KWL charts (Classroom Resource Binder, page GO 6) about World War I. Have students write what they know about World War I under the *K* (Known) category. They then write what they want to know about the war under the *W* (Want to know) category. Finally, they review the section as well as other resource materials to write what they have learned about the war under the *L* (Learned) category.

SECTION 2: From Neutral to Declaration of War
Student Edition, pages 315–317

Section Objectives
- Describe President Wilson's policy about United States neutrality.
- * Explain what happened to the ship *Lusitania*.
- * Identify the purpose of the Zimmermann telegram.

Words to Know
propaganda, ambassador

Cooperative Group Activity

We Declare War!
Materials: reference materials (Unit 5 Bibliography and Internet sites, pages 236–240)

Procedure: Remind students that when the war began, President Wilson wanted the country to remain neutral so that the United States could help bring the Allies and the Central Powers together. However, with the sinking of the *Lusitania* and the

Zimmermann telegram, President Wilson asked Congress to declare war on Germany and the Central Powers. Organize students into two groups to write magazine articles.

- One group assumes the role of journalists covering the story on the sinking of the ship *Lusitania*. The second group assumes the role of journalists covering the story of the Zimmermann telegram.
- Group members research and review information to write an article pertaining to their topic. Articles should include specific details about the incident, public reaction and opinion, and how the event could affect the decision of the United States to remain neutral.
- Students write the article and a headline.
- Group members choose a spokesperson to present their article to the class.

Customizing the Activity for Individual Needs

ESL To help students understand what events might cause a country to enter into war, help them create a list of events that have caused this country, and others around the world, to enter into war.

Learning Styles Students can:

 complete a Cause and Effect chart (Classroom Resource Binder, page GO 2) about the events that led to the United States declaring war.

 design posters that are meant to influence Americans to support U.S. involvement in the war.

 assume the role of President Wilson addressing the nation and explain why he chose to enter World War I.

Reteaching Activity

Organize students into two groups and assign each group one of the following topics: *the sinking of the* Lusitania, or *the Zimmermann telegram*. Distribute the Description Web (Classroom Resource Binder, page GO 3) to each group and have them complete the web on their topic. Have students include as many details about their topic as possible.

Alternative Assessment

Students can write five true/false, multiple-choice, and fill-in-the-blank questions and answers about events that caused the United States to enter World War I. Students can work with a partner to take turns quizzing each other using both sets of questions.

Objectives

- Social Studies Skill: Describe reasons to join the war effort by preparing a speech that contains propaganda.
- Social Studies Skill: Identify and write statements containing propaganda that focus on opinions rather than facts.
- Social Studies Skill: Identify reasons why Americans should help support the war by creating a brochure that contains propaganda.

Activities

The United States Wants You!

Procedure: Have students assume the role of military recruiters, trying to promote support for the war and enlist soldiers. Remind students that they will be using propaganda to persuade Americans to sign up and fight against Germany and the Central Powers. Have students work in groups to prepare a poster to be given to prospective volunteers.

It's Only My Opinion

Procedure: Have students write three facts and three opinions on index cards about the sinking of the *Lusitania* and the Zimmermann telegram. Encourage students to ask partners which are facts and which are opinions and why.

Example: More ocean liners will be attacked unless the United States joins in the fight! (opinion: because _____)

Help Our Cause

Materials: colored markers

Procedure: Have students design a pamphlet aimed at promoting U.S. involvement in the war and recruiting soldiers. Have them think of important information, phrases, and pictures to include in their pamphlets that would help influence Americans, increase support, and enlist soldiers. Ask students to present their pamphlets to the class, and have the students vote on the pamphlet that is most effective.

Practice

Have students complete Connecting History and Language: Hooverizing on page 112 of the Classroom Resource Binder.

SECTION 3: The Home Front
Student Edition, pages 319–321

Section Objectives
- Describe how the United States raised troops in 1917.
- Explain how the war changed the United States economy.
- Discuss how Americans helped to pay for World War I.
- ∗ Explain how Americans at home supported the war effort.

Words to Know
victory garden, bond

Cooperative Group Activity

Americans Unite!

Materials: reference materials (Unit 5 Bibliography and Internet sites, pages 236–240); cardboard; markers; ribbon; scissors; glue; tape; safety pins

Procedure: Remind students that as the United States prepared to enter World War I, men left their jobs and families to fight the war overseas. Americans at home helped to support the war effort in many ways. Students may want to do additional research on how all Americans helped to support the war effort. Organize students into groups of three American volunteers who are educating the public about ways in which they can help support the war at home.

- Group members use a variety of materials to create a poster, a flyer, and a button that provide information about the ways Americans can support the war effort at home. For example, students could design a poster that shows families planting a victory garden with a slogan that reads *Support for our troops is growing!*

- Have groups display their items to the rest of the class.

Customizing the Activity for Individual Needs

ESL To help students understand the importance of supporting the war effort, pair ESL students with English-proficient students to complete a *Who, What, Where, When, Why, How* chart (Classroom Resource Binder, page GO 7) with information about the home front. Have students present their charts to the class, and tell how they might have helped support the war during that time.

Learning Styles Students can:

 look at the recruitment poster from World War I on page 318 of the Student Edition and explain why people might have enlisted after seeing them.

 mime different actions that helped support the war, such as a woman working in a factory or a boy planting a victory garden.

 prepare a 30-second radio commercial that tells Americans how they can help the troops and support the war effort.

Reinforcement Activity

Explain to students that women and children at home often wrote letters and gathered books to send to soldiers overseas. Have students write supportive letters to soldiers fighting in the war. In their letters, students should describe their war efforts at home, the sentiments of people in the community about the war, and their feelings of pride about the United States fighting the war.

Alternative Assessment

Students can complete Description Webs (Classroom Resource Binder, page GO 3) about the home front. Have students write *Ways to Support the War Effort* in the center circle. In the remaining circles they write the ways in which Americans helped to support the war effort.

SECTION 4: The War to End All Wars
Student Edition, pages 322–327

Section Objectives
- Explain why a revolt took place in Russia in 1917.
- Identify ways in which U.S. troops arrived in Europe.
- Describe the Allies' plan for peace in 1919.
- ∗ Describe how the United States helped the Allies win the war.

Words to Know
communism, armistice

Chapter 17

Cooperative Group Activity

We Interrupt This Broadcast

Materials: reference materials (Unit 5 Bibliography and Internet sites, pages 236–240)

Procedure: Students assume the role of broadcasters who present brief, but critical, reports to the American people about the war. Students may wish to conduct additional research for this activity. Organize students into five groups. Assign each group one of the following topics: *U.S. troops arrive in Europe, Communists take control of the government in Russia, U.S. participates in key battles that help end the war, war causes mass destruction,* or *a peace plan.*

- Group members research and take notes on their topic.
- Students prepare a broadcast report that states the critical nature of their topic as well as providing an informative update to share with the American people.
- Students read their broadcast script aloud several times to make changes.
- Group members select a spokesperson to deliver their broadcast to the class.

Customizing the Activity for Individual Needs

ESL   To help students understand the meaning of key events during the fighting of the war, pair ESL students with English-proficient students to arrange index cards with events about the war written on them in the order in which they occurred. *Example:* Treaty of Versailles; revolt in Russia; Belleau Wood; battles of western front.

Learning Styles   Students can:

 look at photographs of key World War I battles in reference materials and describe what they see.

 design a memorial for the soldiers who died during World War I.

 work in a small group to tell each other facts about the Allies' plan for peace.

Enrichment Activity

Have students work in small groups to write a poem that expresses what soldiers fighting in the battles of Belleau Wood and in the Argonne Forest might have seen and heard. Encourage students to use descriptive phrases, such as *thick forest, barbed wire, big cannons, attack at dawn, wounded in battle,* and *thick fog.*

Alternative Assessment

Students can write a journal entry that describes the events of the war once U.S. troops arrived in Europe. Student entries should include information about the methods U.S. troops used to reach Europe; the battles in Belleau Wood and the Argonne Forest; casualties of the war; and the Allies' plan for peace.

Closing the Chapter
Student Edition, pages 328–329

Chapter Vocabulary

Review with students the Words to Know on page 309 of the Student Edition. Then have them complete the Vocabulary Review on page 328 of the Student Edition, by answering each statement as *true* or *false.* If the sentence is false, have students change the underlined term to make it true.

For more vocabulary practice, have students complete the vocabulary exercise on page 110 of the Classroom Resource Binder.

Test Tip

Have students scan the chapter to find key words, written in boldfaced type. Ask students to list each key word and then work with a partner to quiz each other about the words' meanings.

Learning Objectives

Have students review their Chapter Goals and Self-Check worksheet found on page PA 6 of the Classroom Resource Binder. They can check off the goal they have reached. Note that each section of the quiz corresponds to a Learning Objective.

Group Activity

Materials: colored markers; construction paper; stapler

Summary: Working in groups, students create a booklet about World War I.

Procedure: Organize the students into four or five groups to create booklets about World War I. Group members divide the tasks of creating a booklet about World War I, such as writing the text, drawing illustrations, and designing a cover page. Students may divide the task of writing the booklet among several group members. Students should include key events and people in their booklet, and make certain that events are presented in the order in which they occurred. Students can bind their different pages together and present their booklets to the class.

Assessment: Use the Group Activity Rubric found on page *xiii* of this guide. Fill in the rubric with the following additional information. For this activity, students should have

• participated in creating part of a booklet about World War I.

• worked together to combine the information into a coherent booklet.

RELATED MATERIALS   See the Unit Overview page for related Globe Fearon books that can be used to enrich and extend the materials in the chapter.

Assessing the Chapter

Traditional Assessment

Chapter Quiz
The Chapter Quiz on page 329 of the Student Edition can be used as an open-book test, a closed-book test, or a homework assignment. Use the quiz to identify concepts in the chapter that students need to review. Chapter Tests can be found in the Classroom Resource Binder on pages 114–115. Workbook pages 69–74 can be used for additional practice.

Chapter Tests
Use Chapter Tests A and B on pages 114–115 in the Classroom Resource Binder to further assess mastery of chapter concepts.

Additional Resources
Use the Resource Planner on page 119 of this guide to assign additional exercises from the Classroom Resource Binder and Workbook.

Alternative Assessment

Student Interview
Give each student a sheet of paper on which is written the following topics: *Sinking of the Lusitania, United States enters war, Americans work at home, battle at Belleau Wood,* and *President Wilson's Fourteen Points/Treaty of Versailles.* Ask:

• What is important about this event?
• Who took part in this event?
• What was the outcome of this event?
• When did this event occur?

Open-Ended
• Students scan the chapter to list eight important events that took place between 1914 and 1919 that are not listed on the chapter timeline.
• Students draw a timeline that identifies these important events in the order in which they occurred.

Unit Assessment
This is the last chapter in Unit 5: Becoming a World Leader. To review and assess cumulative understanding and provide standardized-test practice, have students complete the Unit Review Test on page 330 of the Student Edition, and the Unit 5 Cumulative Test on pages 116–117 of the Classroom Resource Binder.

Unit 6 ▶ Years of Uncertainty

CHAPTER 18

The Roaring Twenties
1920–1929

PORTFOLIO PROJECT	BUILDING YOUR SKILLS	GROUP ACTIVITY	TIMELINE
"Top 10" List	A Comparison Chart	Creating a Poster	The Roaring Twenties

CHAPTER 19

The Great Depression
1929–1934

PORTFOLIO PROJECT	CONNECTING HISTORY AND . . .	GROUP ACTIVITY	TIMELINE
Television Documentary	Environment: The Dust Bowl	Listing Ideas	The Great Depression

CHAPTER 20

The New Deal
1933–1941

PORTFOLIO PROJECT	VOICES FROM THE PAST	GROUP ACTIVITY	TIMELINE
Poster, Song, or Poem	Franklin D. Roosevelt	Writing a Compromise	The New Deal Brings Hope

RELATED MATERIALS

These are some of the Globe Fearon books that can be used to enrich and extend the material in this unit.

Content ▶

Skills ▶

Literature ▶

Fearon's Our Century 1920–1930
Explore the decade's history. Enrich content on the Scopes trial, Prohibition, the Jazz Age, Charles Lindbergh, and Sacco and Vanzetti.

Writing Across the Curriculum: Writing in Social Studies
Develop skills for writing reports and essays.

Pacemaker® Classics: The Grapes of Wrath
Written by John Steinbeck. A story about the struggles of farmers during the Great Depression.

Chapter 18 • The Roaring Twenties 1920–1929

Chapter at a Glance

SE page

332		*Opening the Chapter and Portfolio Project*
332	SECTION 1	A Time of Prosperity
338		*Building Your Skills: Comparing on a Chart*
339	SECTION 2	Good Times for Many
344	SECTION 3	A Time of Change
348		*Chapter Review and Group Activity*

Learning Objectives

- Describe the U.S. economy after World War I.
- Discuss how cars affected American life.
- Describe how culture changed during the 1920s.
- Explain why immigration was limited after World War I.
- Identify the causes of the Great Migration.

Social Studies Skills

- Compare ideas on a chart.
- Use a timeline to identify events that occurred during the Roaring Twenties.
- Identify ten people who lived during the 1920s who helped to change the way Americans viewed the world.

Writing Skills

- Explain the installment plan by writing an advertisement.
- Explain in a paragraph reasons why it would or would not have been interesting to live during the 1920s.
- Explain in a paragraph views about the immigration law passed in 1921.
- Create a poster about a movie, musical, or sports event in the 1920s or 1930s.

Map and Chart Skills

- Use a chart to compare and contrast automobiles of the 1920s with automobiles today.

Resource Planner

Chapter 18
Roaring Twenties

Use the Program Resources below for reteaching, reinforcement, and enrichment. Additional activities for customizing the lessons can be found in this guide.

Key
Reteaching = ⤺   Reinforcement = ⬇   Enrichment = ⤴

Sections	Program Resources		
	Workbook Exercises ⬇	Teacher's Planning Guide	Classroom Resource Binder
A Time of Prosperity	75	⤴ p. 129	⤴ Concept Builder 18 *The Roaring Twenties*
Building Your Skills: Comparing on a Chart		⤺ p. 130	⬇ Building Your Skills: ⤺ *Comparing and Contrasting* 120, 121 Writing and Test-Taking Tip 3 *Comparing and Contrasting* Graphic Organizer 4 *Comparison-Contrast*
Good Times for Many	76	⬇ p. 131	⤴ Concept Builder 18 *The Roaring Twenties*
A Time of Change	77, 78	⤴ p. 131	⤴ Outline Map 1 *United States: Political* Transparency 12 *United States: Political*
Chapter 18 Review		p. 132	⬇ Words to Know 118 ⤴ Challenge 122 ⬇ Chapter Tests A & B, 123, 124

Customizing the Chapter

Opening the Chapter
Student Edition, pages 332–333

Photo Activity

Direct students' attention to the photos of the jazz musicians and the sheet music. Explain that music, especially jazz, became an important part of people's lives in the 1920s. Have students look at the large photo and name the instruments played by jazz musicians (trombone, trumpet, drums, piano, banjo, and clarinet). If available, have students listen to recordings of jazz. Students can create a chart of music styles by listening to other styles of music that developed over time, such as rock 'n' roll, rhythm and blues, and rap. Next to each style, have them write words or phrases to describe the style as well as list the instruments used in performing this type of music.

Words to Know

Review with students the Words to Know on page 333 of the Student Edition. To help students remember the words, invite pairs to find the words in the Glossary in the Student Edition. Have them take turns giving clues that tell about each vocabulary word without using any part of the word. Ask each pair of students to keep track of the number of clues it takes to guess each word.

The following words and definitions are covered in this chapter:

assembly line a system in which each worker does a different job in putting together a product

installment plan the payment of money over time toward the total cost of an item

mass media the communications that reach large numbers of people

jazz a kind of music created by African Americans in the South in the early 1900s.

renaissance a time of new interest and activity in the arts

inflation a steep rise in the price of goods

deport to force a person who is not a citizen to leave the country by government order

Portfolio Project

Summary: Students create a list of 10 people who changed the way Americans viewed the world in the 1920s.

Materials: chart paper; markers

Procedure: Have students review information in the chapter and list the names of talented individuals, such as musicians, writers, and sports stars, who impacted American society in the 1920s. Students cite reasons why each person is on their list.

Assessment: Use the Individual Activity Rubric on page *xii* of this guide. Fill in the rubric with the additional information below. For this project, students should have

• listed 10 outstanding Americans of the 1920s.

• cited reasons to support their choices.

Learning Objectives

Review the Learning Objectives on page 333 of the Student Edition before starting the chapter. Students can use the list as a learning guide. Suggest that they write the objectives in a journal or use the Chapter Goals and Self-Check worksheet found on page PA 6 of the Classroom Resource Binder.

After reading each section of the chapter, have students write an example of what they learned under the appropriate objective. Suggest that students use these worksheets as a practice guide to help them study for the chapter test.

Timeline

Use the timeline to discuss the sequence of events in this chapter. Point out the timeline's title, its time span, and the intervals. After students have read the chapter, have them review the timeline and suggest additional entries.

SECTION 1: A Time of Prosperity
Student Edition, pages 334–337

Section Objectives

• Explain why Americans elected Warren Harding as President.

• Explain increased spending by Americans in the 1920s.

* Describe how the automobile industry changed the American economy.

Words to Know

assembly line, installment plan, mass media

Cooperative Group Activity

It's the Rage

Materials: reference materials (Unit 6 Bibliography, pages 236–240); markers; posterboard

Procedure: Remind students that as Americans spent more of their money during the 1920s, the advertising industry grew. Advertisements tried to convince people that they needed certain products, and that these products would make them happier and smarter. One item that many Americans wanted to buy was the Model T Ford. Place the students into groups of three or four to write ads for the Model T.

- Group members design magazine ads that will help promote and sell the Model T Ford. Ads should include reasons why the Model T Ford will improve the lives of Americans and how the purchase will benefit the American economy.
- One group member writes the copy for the ads.
- A second group member draws illustrations.
- A third group member writes slogans or phrases to make the ads convincing.
- Each group presents its ad to the class.

Customizing the Activity for Individual Needs

ESL To help students understand the role of advertisements and how they affect sales, have pairs of students look for ads in a newspaper or magazine. They should discuss the pictures and words in each ad to see how they persuade people to buy.

Learning Styles Students can:

 complete a Cause and Effects chart (Classroom Resource Binder, G0 2) to show the effect of the Model T on the American economy.

 design a pamphlet that explains how the Model T had a positive effect on the American economy.

 work with a partner to write and record a radio ad that promotes the Model T Ford.

Enrichment Activity

Invite students to look at automobile advertisements found in current magazines and newspapers. Have students choose one ad to analyze. Students can write how the ad promotes the product and how it influences consumers to buy the product. Have students look for information in their ads suggesting that people would be happier or smarter if they had this product.

Alternative Assessment

Ask students to make a flow chart for one of the following topics: the growth of the automobile industry or the growth of the advertising industry. Students can explain which event occurred first and why they think so.

Objectives
- Social Studies Skill: Describe how music has changed by comparing and contrasting jazz from the 1920s with popular music today.
- Social Studies Skill: Use a chart to compare and contrast sports statistics of popular athletes from the 1920s and today.
- Social Studies Skill: Describe the similarities and differences of clothing styles from the 1920s and today.

Activities

All That Jazz
Materials: reference materials (Unit 6 Bibliography and Internet sites, pages 236–240)

Procedure: Have students use a variety of sources to learn more about jazz from the 1920s. Then, have students work in pairs to write a brief paragraph comparing jazz of the 1920s to popular music today. Remind them to use phrases such as *also, in addition, likewise,* and *in the same way* when describing similarities. When describing differences, remind them to use the terms *but, however,* and *on the other hand.*

Sports Statistics
Materials: reference materials (Unit 6 Bibliography and Internet sites, pages 236–240)

Procedure: Have students make a chart to compare the sports statistics of baseball hero Babe Ruth with a popular baseball player of today. Or, have students choose two other sports heroes to analyze.

Change of Clothes
Materials: reference materials (Unit 6 Bibliography and Internet sites, pages 236–240)

Procedure: Divide students into groups of three or four. Have them research clothing styles of the 1920s. Ask students to make a chart that compares and contrasts clothing of the 1920s to clothing styles today.

Practice

Have students complete Building Your Skills: Comparing a Chart on page 120 of the Classroom Resource Binder.

SECTION 2: Good Times For Many
Student Edition, pages 339–343

Section Objectives
- Describe the Harlem Renaissance.
- Explain why the 1920s was a time of change for women.
- * Explain why the 1920s were called the Roaring Twenties.

Words to Know
jazz, renaissance

Cooperative Group Activity

Reporting for a Magazine

Materials: reference materials (Unit 6 Bibliography and Internet sites, pages 236–240), recent weekly news magazine.

Procedure: Remind students that for many people, the 1920s, or Roaring Twenties, was a time to be entertained and to enjoy life. During this era, many famous magazines were first published. Place students in three or four groups. Assign one of the following topics to each group: *Music of the 1920s, Movies and radio, Sports, the Harlem Renaissance,* or *Women in the 1920s.* Give each student a copy of a recent weekly news magazine. You may wish to have students conduct further research on their assigned topic.

- Group members research and take notes on their topic using a variety of resources.
- Group members look through a current issue of a magazine to see how articles are written.
- Group members work cooperatively to write a one- or two-page article about their assigned topic. Students then agree on a title and an illustration for their article.
- Group members choose a spokesperson to present their article to the class.
- If appropriate, students create a class magazine.

Customizing the Activity for Individual Needs
ESL To help students understand the concept of the Roaring Twenties, explain that one meaning of *roaring* is "laughing loudly in a rowdy way." During the "twenties," people had such a good time they were "roaring" with laughter.

Learning Styles Students can:

 look at paintings from the Roaring Twenties, in particular from the Harlem Renaissance, and describe the types of colors used and the scenes depicted.

 play a matching game about the 1920s by writing the names of famous people on one set of index cards and their occupations on another set of cards. Students then work in pairs to match the famous people with their occupation.

 give an oral report about the life of a musician, sports figure, or magazine writer from the 1920s to the class.

Reinforcement Activity

Organize students into small groups and have them compose a short poem or song about life during the Roaring Twenties. Students may wish to focus on a particular topic, such as sports, or include many topics within their poem or song.

Alternative Assessment

Students can review information about the Roaring Twenties to write questions that begin with *who, what, when, where, why,* and *how. Example:* Who was the greatest hero of the 1920s? Students then exchange their paper with a classmate to answer each other's questions.

SECTION 3: A Time of Change
Student Edition, pages 344–347

Section Objectives
- Explain why the government passed the immigration law in 1921.
- Describe the Great Migration.
- * Describe economic problems of the 1920s.

Words to Know
inflation, deport

Cooperative Group Activity

Problems and Change: Illustrated Book
Materials: reference materials (Unit 6 Bibliography and Internet sites, pages 236–240)

Procedure: Remind students that during the 1920s, Americans faced a growing concern over joblessness, and inflated prices. Have students form three groups to research and take notes on the problems that existed in the 1920s. African Americans began to move north to start new lives.

- Some group members use their notes to create illustrations that reflect the issues and problems of the 1920s.
- Other group members write captions for the pictures that briefly describe each scene and its significance.
- Still other group members design a cover page that includes a title. They combine the pages to make a book.
- Each group presents its book to the class.

Customizing the Activity for Individual Needs
ESL To help students understand the problems that new Americans faced in the 1920s, have partners discuss fears that people face when they move to a new country.

Learning Styles Students can:

 work with a partner to complete a KWL chart (Classroom Resource Binder, G0 5) about problems people faced during the 1920s.

 bind the book their group has written.

 present their group's book aloud to the class.

Enrichment Activity 🔎

Have a group of students prepare a skit that presents a problem, issue, or event of the 1920s. Group members write the dialogue, rehearse, and then perform their skit for the rest of the class.

Alternative Assessment

Students can write three journal entries that deal with the problems of the 1920s from the perspective of the following: *an American returning home from the war and facing unemployment, an immigrant facing prejudice,* and *an African American living in the South and wanting to migrate to the North.*

Closing the Chapter
Student Edition, pages 348–349

Chapter Vocabulary
Review with students the Words to Know on page 333 of the Student Edition. Then have them complete the Vocabulary Review on page 348 of the Student Edition by matching each definition with a term from the list.

For more vocabulary practice, have them complete the vocabulary exercise on page 118 of the Classroom Resource Binder.

Test Tips
Working in pairs, have students take turns asking and answering the review questions for each section of the chapter. As one student answers a question, the other scans the section to verify the answer.

Learning Objectives
Have the students review their Chapter Goals and Self-Check worksheet found on page PA 6 in the Classroom Resource Binder. They can check off the goal they have reached. Note that each section of the quiz corresponds to a Learning Objective.

Group Activity
Summary: Students create posters advertising a movie, sports event, or a musician from the 1920s.

Materials: colored markers; posterboard

Procedure: Have students work in small groups to create posters about an entertainment event of the 1920s. Groups decide what movie, sports event, or musician to create an advertisement for. Groups create an illustrated poster advertising their event or person.

Assessment: Use the Group Activity Rubric found on page *xiii* of this guide. Fill in the rubric with the following additional information. For this activity, students should have

- participated in brainstorming a list of events from the 1920s.
- created a poster advertising a movie, sports event, or musician from the 1920s.

RELATED MATERIALS See the Unit Overview page for related Globe Fearon books that can be used to enrich and extend the materials in the chapter.

Traditional Assessment

Chapter Quiz

The Chapter Quiz on page 349 of the Student Edition can be used as an open-book test, a closed-book test, or a homework assignment. Use the quiz to identify concepts in the chapter that students need to review. Chapter Tests can be found in the Classroom Resource Binder on pages 123–124. Workbook pages 75–78 can be used for additional practice.

Chapter Tests

Use Chapter Tests A and B on pages 123–124 in the Classroom Resource Binder to further assess mastery of chapter concepts.

Additional Resources

Use the Resource Planner on page 128 in this guide to assign additional exercises from the Classroom Resource Binder and Workbook.

Alternative Assessment

Presentation

Have students design a catalog from the 1920s, listing a variety of products for purchase. Students scan the chapter to list products that could be included in the catalog. They write descriptive text for each item in their catalog, and provide illustrations and prices. Students present their catalogs and leave them on display for the rest of the class to review.

Student Interview

Write the following head on the chalkboard: *The Roaring Twenties.* Ask:

- What effect did the automobile industry have on the economy in the 1920s?
- What were some things Americans did for entertainment in the 1920s?
- What were some fears Americans had in the 1920s?

Chapter
18

Chapter 19 · **The Great Depression** 1929–1934

Chapter at a Glance

SE page

350		*Opening the Chapter and Portfolio Project*
352	SECTION 1	The Nation's Troubled Economy
357	SECTION 2	Hard Times for Americans
362		*Connecting History and the Environment: The Dust Bowl*
363	SECTION 3	The U.S. Government and the Great Depression
366		*Chapter Review and Group Activity*

Learning Objectives

- Explain the causes of the Great Depression.
- Describe how the Great Depression changed the lives of Americans.
- Discuss the hardships suffered by farmers, African Americans, and Mexican Americans during the Great Depression.
- Explain President Hoover's approach to helping Americans during the Great Depression.

Social Studies Skills

- Explore how the Dust Bowl affected Americans.
- Use a timeline to identify events that occurred during the Great Depression.
- Describe how a particular group of people were affected by the Great Depression.

Writing Skills

- Describe in a newspaper article one change the Great Depression caused in people's lives.
- Write a paragraph describing a farm located on the Great Plains from the perspective of someone leaving his or her home during the Great Depression.
- Explain in a persuasive radio commercial why Americans should vote for Franklin Roosevelt in 1932.

Map and Chart Skills

- Use a map to identify the states that were affected by the Dust Bowl.

Resource Planner

Chapter 19
The Great Depression

Use the Program Resources below for reteaching, reinforcement, and enrichment. Additional activities for customizing the lessons can be found in this guide.

Key
Reteaching = ⌒   Reinforcement = ⬇   Enrichment = ⌒

Sections	Program Resources		
	Workbook Exercises	Teacher's Planning Guide	Classroom Resource Binder
The Nation's Troubled Economy	79	⬇ p. 136	
Hard Times for Americans	80, 81	⌒ p. 137	⌒ Outline Map 2 *United States: Physical* Geography and Economics 6 *Effects of the Great Depression* Transparency 14 *United States: Physical*
Connecting History and the Environment: The Dust Bowl		p. 138	Feature Practice 127 Connecting History and the Environment: *Flood*
The U.S. Government and the Great Depression	82	⌒ p. 138	
Chapter 19 Review		p. 139	⬇ Words to Know 125 ⌒ Challenge 128 ⬇ Chapter Tests A & B, 129, 130

Customizing the Chapter

Opening the Chapter
Student Edition, pages 350–351

Photo Activity
Explain to students that as a result of hard economic times, many Americans lost all of their money and their homes. Because of this, many people were forced to live in shacks made of wood and tin. Direct students' attention to the photo of tin shacks. Have students brainstorm a list of hardships people living in these makeshift dwellings experienced. Ask students to think of newspaper headlines that could describe the suffering and hardship of Americans who lived in communities of shacks across the nation, such as "Stock Market Takes All" and "Americans Lose Everything."

Words to Know

Review the Words to Know on page 351 of the Student Edition. To help students remember the words, have one student read a definition for a word in the Glossary in the Student Edition while another student guesses the word. Have students switch roles often until all words have been defined.

The following words and definitions are covered in this chapter:

stock market a place where stocks, or shares in businesses, are bought and sold

depression a time when the economy of a nation falls sharply

default to fail to pay a loan when it is due

foreclose to take the property of someone who has failed to pay back a loan

bonus money given in addition to what is owed

drought a long period of very dry weather

migrant worker a worker who travels from place to place to harvest crops

public works construction projects paid for by the government, such as building roads

relief help given to poor people

Portfolio Project

Summary: Students write the script for a TV documentary about a group of people affected by the Great Depression.

Materials: reference materials (Unit 6 Bibliography and Internet sites, pages 236–240)

Procedure: As they read the chapter, have students take notes about the people and regions of the United States that were affected by the Great Depression. Students choose a group of people who were deeply affected during the Depression and conduct further research on these people by accessing a variety of reference materials and Internet sites.

Students use their research to write a script for a TV documentary that discusses how the lives of people changed during the Great Depression. Students write suggestions for visuals and music that will enhance their presentation.

Assessment: Use the Individual Activity Rubric on page *xii* of this guide. Fill in the rubric with the additional information below. For this project, students should have

- chosen a group of people who were greatly affected by the Great Depression.

- written an article for a TV documentary about their topic.

Learning Objectives

Review the Learning Objectives on page 351 of the Student Edition before starting the chapter. Students can use the list as a learning guide. Suggest that they write the objectives in a journal or use the Chapter Goals and Self-Check worksheet found on page PA 6 of the Classroom Resource Binder.

After reading each section of the chapter, have students write an example of what they learned under the appropriate objective. Suggest that students use these worksheets as a practice guide to help them study for the chapter test.

Timeline

Use the timeline to discuss the sequence of events in this chapter. Point out the timeline's title, its time span, and the intervals. After students have read the chapter, have them review the timeline and suggest additional entries.

SECTION 1: The Nation's Troubled Economy
Student Edition, pages 352–356

Section Objectives

- Explain why the stock market crashed in 1929.
- Identify the groups of people who were most affected by the Great Depression.
- Describe why people protested President Hoover's policies.
- Describe hardships people living in the United States suffered during the Great Depression.

Words to Know

stock market, depression, default, foreclose, bonus

Cooperative Group Activity

"Vital Statistics" Skit

Materials: reference materials (Unit 6 Bibliography and Internet sites, pages 236–240)

Procedure: Remind students that by the end of the 1920s, thousands of people were jobless and homeless as the country entered a severe depression. Organize students into three groups.

- One member of the group assumes the role of a research analyst who interviews Americans during the Great Depression. This student develops a list of five interview questions, such as *How has the Great Depression affected your life? Are you out of work? Where do you live? Did you lose money when the stock market crashed in 1929? Do you agree with President Hoover's view that Americans must help themselves and not rely on government charity?*

- Other members of the group assume the roles of Americans living during the Great Depression. They will prepare answers for the research analyst's questions.

- Group members perform a skit for the class in which a research analyst asks questions and the others answer the questions.

Customizing the Activity for Individual Needs

ESL To help students understand how Americans' lives were affected during the Great Depression, have ESL students work with English-proficient students to write a story about the experiences of a family living during the Great Depression. Encourage students to include as much factual information about the Great Depression as they can.

Learning Styles Students can:

 can complete a Description Web (Classroom Resource Binder, page G0 3) on the Great Depression.

 list on index cards items that Americans needed during the Depression years. They then sort the cards into categories.

 work with a partner to practice their part aloud for the skit.

Reinforcement Activity

Distribute Cause and Effects charts (Classroom Resource Binder, page G0 2) about the Great Depression. Students should brainstorm and list as many effects of the Great Depression as they can.

Alternative Assessment

Students can write a poem or a first-person narrative about the Great Depression from the perspective of an American teenager. Encourage students to use the words *boxcar, disease, burden, adventure,* and *railroad* in their writing. Students may wish to illustrate their work.

Section Objectives

- Explain how the Great Depression changed American families.
- Describe the Dust Bowl and the effect it had on farmers on the Great Plains.
- Explain how the Great Depression affected African Americans and Mexican Americans.

Words to Know

drought, migrant worker

Cooperative Group Activity

Tell Me a Story

Materials: reference materials (Unit 6 Bibliography and Internet sites, pages 236–240), tape recorder

Procedure: Remind students that farmers, Mexican Americans, and African Americans were affected most by the Great Depression. Farmers were forced to leave their homes, African Americans and Mexican Americans faced discrimination, and many families became migrant workers to survive. Place students into three groups and have them conduct research on the Great Depression and its effects on farmers, Mexican Americans, or African Americans.

- Students use their research to outline a short story about the lives of the group they were assigned. Using a tape recorder, groups will record their story.

- One group member begins to tell a story using the research. After a few minutes, the storyteller introduces another person in the group, who will continue the story.

- Groups continue to tell a story until all members have had a chance to contribute.

- Groups play their recordings for the class.

Customizing the Activity for Individual Needs

ESL To help students understand the effects the Great Depression had on farmers, Mexican Americans, and African Americans, have partners sort index cards that list facts about each of these groups, such as *had to leave their homes on the Great Plains,* or *were ordered to leave the country.*

Learning Styles Students can:

 look at photographs from the Great Depression and tell a story based on the photographs.

 draw pictures that depict the Dust Bowl or hardships Mexican Americans or African Americans experienced during the Great Depression. Then write captions for the pictures.

 work with a partner to act out a scene in which a family of migrant workers living in the Dust Bowl packs up their home to go to California to look for work.

Reteaching Activity

Organize students into two groups, and have each group develop ten questions about farmers, migrant workers, African Americans, and Mexican immigrants/Mexican Americans during the Great Depression. Tell students that their questions can be true/false, multiple-choice, sentence completion, or fill-in-the-blank. Then, have groups take turns asking each other questions. Have a volunteer assign points for correctly answered questions, and tally the points at the end of the game.

Alternative Assessment

Students can complete a *Who, What, When, Where, Why, How* chart (Classroom Resource Binder, page G0 7) with information about how Mexican Americans, African Americans, and farmers were affected by the Great Depression.

CONNECTING HISTORY AND THE ENVIRONMENT: The Dust Bowl
Student Edition, page 362

Objectives
- Social Studies Skill: Describe life in the Great Plains during the time of the Dust Bowl.
- Social Studies Skill: Identify ways to protect the environment and prevent drought from occurring.
- Social Studies Skill: Explain why planting trees on farms might help prevent the Dust Bowl.

Activities
Dust Bowl Blues
Procedure: Have students write a poem or rap song describing what life must have been like living on the Great Plains during the Dust Bowl. Encourage them to use descriptive words or phrases, such as *sun-baked fields, huge mounds of dust, strong winds blew, dry, bare fields, dust curtain,* and *windbreaks.*

Help Prevent Dust Bowls
Materials: colored markers; construction paper

Procedure: Review how drought conditions of the 1930s caused the Dust Bowl. Have students brainstorm a list of ways that people might prevent drought from occurring today. Students use their list to create a flyer to be distributed to farming communities throughout the Great Plains region. Encourage them to draw illustrations that accompany each suggestion for preventing drought.

Plant a Tree
Materials: colored markers; drawing paper

Procedure: Invite students to make a poster encouraging farmers on the Great Plains to plant trees on their farms during the time of the Dust Bowl. Students should include reasons why having trees on their farms will help farmers.

Practice
Have students complete Connecting History and the Environment: Floods on page 127 of the Classroom Resource Binder.

SECTION 3: The U.S. Government and the Great Depression
Student Edition, pages 363–365

Section Objectives
- Explain the actions of President Hoover in battling the Great Depression.
- Explain why Franklin D. Roosevelt won the election of 1932.

Words to Know
public works, relief

Cooperative Group Activity

Vote for President!

Materials: reference materials (Unit 6 Bibliography and Internet sites, pages 236–240)

Procedure: Remind students that 1932 was an election year. President Hoover and Franklin Roosevelt were the candidates. Organize students into groups of three to create campaign materials for the candidate of their choice. Students may wish to conduct additional research to complete this activity.

* Group members brainstorm a list of reasons why Americans should vote for their candidate in the upcoming presidential election.
* Each group member creates a campaign flyer.
* A second member writes a campaign speech.
* A third member designs and creates a campaign slogan for buttons and bumper stickers.
* Groups then present their campaign materials to the class.

Customizing the Activity for Individual Needs

ESL To help students understand the concept of a political campaign, organize students into two groups. Tell each group that it is a political party. Each group chooses a candidate for class president and then develops a party platform. Each candidate gives a speech to the class. A class election is held.

Learning Styles Students can:

 complete a Main Idea and Details chart (Classroom Resource Binder, page GO 5) with information about Franklin Roosevelt's ideas about the Great Depression.

 create a flyer advocating the election of their candidate, and explaining why his presidency would be good for the nation.

 assume the role of Franklin Roosevelt and explain to Americans the reasons why they can count on him to end the Great Depression.

Enrichment Activity

Explain to students that President Hoover felt the government should not be responsible for solving the problems of the economy, while Franklin Roosevelt believed that a strong government was needed to care for suffering families. Organize students into small groups and have them discuss the following question: *Should the United States have a strong central government that has a powerful role in taking care of Americans?* Have students write an essay describing their views on the subject.

Alternative Assessment

Students can write about President Hoover and Franklin Roosevelt on chart paper. Have students share and discuss their charts with classmates.

Closing the Chapter
Student Edition, pages 366–367

Chapter Vocabulary

Review with students the Words to Know on page 351 of the Student Edition. Then have them complete the Vocabulary Review on page 366 of the Student Edition, by completing each sentence with a term from the list.

For more vocabulary practice, have them complete the vocabulary exercise on page 125 in the Classroom Resource Binder.

Test Tip

Divide the class into three groups. Assign each group one of the sections in the chapter. Have group members read their section and then create questions based on the section content. Have groups exchange papers to answer each other's questions.

Learning Objectives

Have students review their Chapter Goals and Self-Check worksheet found on page PA 6 of the Classroom Resource Binder. They can check off the goal they have reached. Note that each section of the quiz corresponds to a Learning Objective.

Group Activity

Summary: Students make a list of the steps they think President Roosevelt should take to help Americans recover from the Great Depression.

Procedure: Divide the class into three or four groups. Have each group list the steps it thinks newly elected President Franklin D. Roosevelt should take to help Americans recover from the Great Depression. After students have completed their list, have them read the next chapter to learn how President Roosevelt helped Americans and the nation recover from the Great Depression.

Assessment: Use the Group Activity Rubric found on page *xiii* of this guide. Fill in the Rubric with the following additional information. For this activity, students should have

- participated in the discussion.
- participated in making a list of steps President Roosevelt and the government should take.

RELATED MATERIALS See the Unit Overview page for related Globe Fearon books that can be used to enrich and extend the materials in the chapter.

Assessing the Chapter

Traditional Assessment

Chapter Quiz
The Chapter Quiz on page 367 of the Student Edition can be used as an open-book test, a closed-book test, or a homework assignment. Use the quiz to identify concepts in the chapter that students need to review. Chapter Tests can be found in the Classroom Resource Binder on pages 129–130. Workbook pages 79–82 can be used for additional practice.

Chapter Tests
Use Chapter Tests A and B on pages 129–130 in the Classroom Resource Binder to further assess mastery of chapter concepts.

Additional Resources
Use the Resource Planner on page 135 of this guide to assign additional exercises from the Classroom Resource Binder and Workbook.

Alternative Assessment

Student Interview
Write the following heading on the chalkboard: *The Dust Bowl.* Ask:
- What caused the Dust Bowl?
- Which region of the United States was most affected by the Dust Bowl?
- What happened to farmers as a result of the Dust Bowl?
- What other groups of people were affected by the Dust Bowl? How were these groups affected?

Presentation
Have students write the script for a TV talk show in which the host discusses the stock market crash of 1929 with an "expert." Students create questions and answers, and perform the interview for the class. If appropriate, students can include props and visual aids, such as charts and graphs of the economy in 1929.

Chapter 20 · **The New Deal** 1933–1941

Chapter at a Glance

SE page

368	*Opening the Chapter and Portfolio Project*
370	SECTION 1 The New Deal Begins
374	*Voices From the Past: Franklin D. Roosevelt*
375	SECTION 2 Social Reform and the New Deal
380	SECTION 3 Americans at Leisure
384	*Chapter Review and Group Activity*

Chapter
20

Learning Objectives

- Describe the steps that Franklin D. Roosevelt took to end the Great Depression.
- Identify the programs developed during the New Deal.
- Explain why some people were against the New Deal.
- Describe how the New Deal affected the lives of Americans.
- Identify how Americans spent their free time during the 1930s.

Social Studies Skills

- Explain how Franklin D. Roosevelt's speeches brought hope to a nation.
- Use a timeline to identify events that occurred during the New Deal.
- Describe feelings about the Great Depression by creating a song, poem, or poster.

Writing Skills

- Identify one member of the Brain Trust and his or her field of knowledge by writing an interview.
- Explain in a newspaper column what people have thought about the "alphabet" of names in the Roosevelt program.
- Write a fan letter to a star or athlete of the 1930s.
- Describe the difference between conservatives and liberals by writing a compromise that pleases both groups.

Map and Chart Skills

- Use a chart to identify early New Deal programs and their purposes.
- Use a chart to identify New Deal agencies and their purposes.

Resource Planner

**Chapter 20
The New Deal**

Use the Program Resources below for reteaching, reinforcement, and enrichment. Additional activities for customizing the lessons can be found in this guide.

Key
Reteaching = ⤴   Reinforcement = ⬇   Enrichment = ⤴

Sections	Program Resources		
	⬇ Workbook Exercises	Teacher's Planning Guide	Classroom Resource Binder
The New Deal Begins	83, 84	⤴ p. 143	⤴ Concept Builder 20 *The New Deal*
Voices From the Past: Franklin D. Roosevelt		p. 144	⤴ Feature Practice 133 Voices From the Past *Mary McLeod Bethune*
Social Reform and the New Deal	85	⤴ p. 144	⤴ Concept Builder 20 ⤴ The New Deal, Transparency 13 *United States: Political*
Americans at Leisure	86	⤴ p. 145	⤴ Concept Builder 20 *The New Deal*
Chapter 20 Review		p. 146	⬇ Words to Know 131 ⤴ Challenge 134 ⬇ Chapter Tests A & B, 135, 136 ⬇ Unit Tests Part I & II, 137, 138

Customizing the Chapter

Opening the Chapter
Student Edition, pages 368–369

Photo Activity

Explain to students that President Roosevelt's programs provided jobs for many people. Ask them to look at the photo of the men working and describe the job these men are doing. Next, direct their attention to the poster and have students think about the types of jobs being advertised. Ask students to brainstorm a list of other jobs that the U.S. government could provide to help Americans recover from the Great Depression, such as planting trees and public works projects. Chart their responses and have students review their list after reading the chapter.

Words to Know

Review the Words to Know on page 369 of the Student Edition. To help students remember the words, invite them to scan the chapter for words, and define each word using context clues. Then have volunteers write sentences on the chalkboard using the words.

The following words and definitions are covered in this chapter:

New Deal Franklin D. Roosevelt's plan for helping the U.S. economy during the Great Depression

fireside chat a radio speech to Americans given by President Franklin Roosevelt

conservative a person who wants the government to do less for its citizens

liberal a person who wants the government to do more for its citizens

soap opera a daytime radio show that was paid for by soap companies

anti-Semitism the practice of hating Jewish people simply because they are Jewish

Portfolio Project

Summary: Students create posters, poems, and songs describing the Great Depression and the changes it brought to the United States.

Materials: colored markers; posterboard

Procedure: Students review the Student Edition or other resources and take notes about how musicians, writers, and artists who lived during the Great Depression expressed themselves. Students then create their poems, songs, or posters and include information about changes in the United States during the Great Depression. Students share their projects with the class.

Assessment: Use the Individual Activity Rubric on page *xii* of this guide. Fill in the rubric with the additional information below. For this project, students should have

- reviewed information about musicians, poets, and artists of the Great Depression.
- created a poem, song, or poster about changes that the Great Depression brought.

Learning Objectives

Review the Learning Objectives on page 369 of the Student Edition before starting the chapter. Students can use the list as a learning guide. Suggest they write the objectives in a journal or use the Chapter Goals and Self-Check worksheet found on page PA 6 of the Classroom Resource Binder.

After reading each section of the chapter, have students write an example of what they learned about under the appropriate objective. Suggest that students use these worksheets as a practice guide to help them study for the chapter test.

Timeline

Use the timeline to discuss the sequence of events in this chapter. Point out the timeline's title, its time span, and the intervals. After students have read the chapter, have them review the timeline and suggest additional entries.

SECTION 1: The New Deal Begins
Student Edition, pages 370–373

Section Objectives

- Explain Franklin Roosevelt's huge victory in the election of 1932.
- Describe the role of the Brain Trust.
- Describe the Hundred Days and why Roosevelt used the radio to speak to the nation.
- Discuss the New Deal and what it meant for Americans.

Words to Know

New Deal, fireside chat

Cooperative Group Activity

It's a Deal

Materials: reference materials (Unit 6 Bibliography and Internet sites, pages 236–240)

Procedure: Remind students that Americans elected Franklin D. Roosevelt in 1932 because he gave Americans hope with his plans to end the Great Depression. The New Deal was the name of Roosevelt's plan for helping the U.S. economy. Organize students into seven groups and have them create storyboards that reflect the following topics and events: *the election of Roosevelt in 1932; Roosevelt's first speech; the New Deal; Roosevelt's Three R's plan; the Brain Trust;* and *fireside chats.*

- Group members research the topics for their storyboard.
- Different group members then sketch the storyboard, draw and color the backgrounds, write captions, and write dialogue balloons to accompany the illustrations.
- Groups share their storyboards with the class.

Customizing the Activity for Individual Needs

ESL To help students understand the concept of the New Deal, ask partners to think of other words that mean "deal," such as *agreement* or *bargain*. Point out that Roosevelt's New Deal was intended to be a new, big agreement that would help Americans get out of the depression.

Learning Styles Students can:

 complete a Description Web (Classroom Resource Binder, page GO 3) with information about the New Deal.

 design postage stamps that symbolize President Roosevelt's New Deal ideas.

 assume the role of President Roosevelt giving one of his famous fireside chats.

Enrichment Activity

Have students research the early New Deal programs President Roosevelt established during the Hundred Days. Are any of these programs still used today? What is their role today? Have students complete a Comparison-Contrast chart (Classroom Resource Binder, page GO 4) comparing the role of these programs during the New Deal and their role today.

Alternative Assessment

Students can make a Cause and Effect chart (Classroom Resource Binder, page GO 2) about each of the following topics: *the New Deal, the Three R's plan, the Brain Trust,* and *fireside chats.*

VOICES FROM THE PAST: Franklin D. Roosevelt
Student Edition, page 374

Objectives
• Social Studies Skill: Describe the life and work of Franklin D. Roosevelt by writing a biography.

• Social Studies Skill: Examine quotes made by Franklin D. Roosevelt, and draft a speech Roosevelt might have given.

• Social Studies Skill: Describe a personal struggle and how it can provide inspiration to others.

Activities
Biography of a Leader
Materials: reference materials (Unit 6 Bibliography and Internet sites, pages 236–240)

Procedure: Have students research and take notes about the life of Franklin D. Roosevelt. They then create a picture book biography for young children. Ask them to include illustrations.

It's a Quote
Materials: reference materials (Unit 6 Bibliography and Internet sites, pages 236–240)

Procedure: Working in pairs, ask students to write an inspirational speech that Roosevelt might have delivered to the American people. Have students research some of President Roosevelt's speeches before they write their own.

A Source of Hope
Procedure: Discuss Roosevelt's struggle with polio. Ask students to think about a personal struggle they have had to overcome. Students write a journal entry that describes the struggle, how they worked through the struggle, and how it might provide hope or a source of inspiration to others.

Practice
Have students complete Voices From the Past: Mary McLeod Bethune from page 133 of the Classroom Resource Binder.

SECTION 2: Social Reform and the New Deal
Student Edition, pages 375–379

Section Objectives
• Identify some of the New Deal agencies and their purposes.

• Describe some of the reforms that Eleanor Roosevelt supported.

* Explain how conservatives and liberals disagreed over the New Deal, and how the Supreme Court regarded Roosevelt's plans.

Words to Know
conservative, liberal

Cooperative Group Activity

Conservative vs. Liberal Debate

Materials: reference materials (Unit 6 Bibliography and Internet sites, pages 236–240)

Procedure: Remind students that conservatives and liberals disagreed over the New Deal and how the country should be run. Organize students into two groups. Assign each group the role of conservatives or liberals to prepare a debate. You may wish to have students conduct additional research for this activity.

- Group members research and review information about the New Deal.
- Students write their views on how the country should be run.
- Students list ways in which their plan for the country differs from that of Roosevelt's.
- Each group member writes one statement that best expresses his or her views.
- Groups then hold a debate, with each student having one minute to read his or her statement to the opposing team. Students on the opposing team have one minute each to respond to the statement.
- Continue the debate until all students have given their statements and rebuttals. Then, invite the students to vote on the statement that was most compelling.

Customizing the Activity for Individual Needs

ESL To help students understand how much involvement a government should have in the lives of its citizens, have them discuss the role that government plays in the lives of citizens of their native country.

Learning Styles Students can:

 complete a Comparison-Contrast chart (Classroom Resource Binder, page G0 4) comparing the views of conservatives and liberals during the New Deal.

 design posters that reflect the views of conservatives and liberals to hang during the debate.

 explain to a partner the ways in which liberals and conservatives have similar and dissimilar views about the New Deal.

Enrichment Activity

Explain to students that the terms *conservative* and *liberal* are still used in politics today. Organize students into pairs and have them look through current magazines and newspapers to find articles about conservatives and liberals. Have students make a Comparison-Contrast chart (Classroom Resource Binder, page G0 4) comparing present-day conservative and liberal views.

Alternative Assessment

Students can write a letter to President Roosevelt explaining why they are not happy with the New Deal. Encourage them to include their ideas about the way in which the country should be governed.

SECTION 3: Americans at Leisure
Student Edition, pages 380–383

Section Objectives

- Explain the role of books during the 1930s.
- Explain how people treated athletes in the 1930s.
- ∗ Explain reasons why people went to the movies and listened to the radio.

Words to Know

soap opera, anti-Semitism

Cooperative Group Activity

That's Entertainment Radio Show

Materials: reference materials (Unit 6 Bibliography and Internet sites, pages 236–240)

Procedure: Explain to students that during the 1930s, Americans turned to radio shows for entertainment. Organize students into small groups to create a radio show. You may wish to have them conduct further research for this activity.

- Group members brainstorm ideas for a radio show that Americans living during the 1930s would find both funny and entertaining.
- Students write a summary of the radio show, briefly explaining the story and its characters.
- Group members work together to write a script. There should be the same number of characters in the radio show as there are group members.

- Each member of the group assumes the role of one of the characters in the radio show. Groups practice performing the radio show.
- Students then present their radio show to the class.

Customizing the Activity for Individual Needs

ESL   To help students understand the different forms of entertainment people used to escape their problems during the Great Depression, ask students what forms of entertainment are popular in their native country.

Learning Styles   Students can:

 complete a *Who, What, When, Where, Why, How* chart (Classroom Resource Binder, page GO 7) with information about the plot their radio show.

 illustrate scenes from their radio show.

 read dialogue from the radio show aloud with a partner.

Reinforcement Activity

Have students think about activities that help people get through hard or stressful times. Offer some examples to students, such as playing baseball or singing. Ask students to write a journal entry that explains why leisure activities are important to people.

Alternative Assessment

Students can write a paragraph describing a leisure activity that people from the 1930s enjoyed and the reasons why. Have them choose between going to the movies, listening to the radio, or reading books.

Closing the Chapter
Student Edition, pages 384–385

Chapter Vocabulary

Review with students the Words to Know on page 369 of the Student Edition. Then have them complete the Vocabulary Review on page 384 of the Student Edition, by completing each sentence with a term from the list.

For more vocabulary practice, have them complete the vocabulary exercise on page 131 of the Classroom Resource Binder.

Test Tip

Have students write vocabulary words from this chapter on an index card. On the other side of the index card, students should write a sentence for each vocabulary word. Remind students that they can do this in other content areas.

Learning Objectives

Have students review their Chapter Goals and Self-Check worksheet found on page PA 6 of the Classroom Resource Binder. They can check off the goal they have reached. Note that each section of the quiz corresponds to a Learning Objective.

Group Activity

Summary: Students assume the roles of liberals and conservatives as they try to find a compromise on New Deal issues.

Procedure: Divide the class into two groups, liberals and conservatives. Have them review information about different views held by liberals and conservatives concerning the New Deal. As either conservatives or liberals, group members list the reasons why they disagree with the New Deal. Both groups hold a meeting in which they voice their disagreements and try to find a compromise on issues. Students list their compromises on the chalkboard to review after the meeting.

Assessment: Use the Group Activity Rubric found on page *xiii* of this guide. Fill in the rubric with the following additional information. For this activity, students should have

- listed reasons why they disagree with the New Deal from the perspective of either a conservative or liberal.
- participated in a meeting in which both groups tried to work out a compromise.

RELATED MATERIALS   See the Unit Overview page for related Globe Fearon books that can be used to enrich and extend the materials in the chapter.

Traditional Assessment

Chapter Quiz

The Chapter Quiz on page 385 of the Student Edition can be used as an open-book test, a closed-book test, or a homework assignment. Use the quiz to identify concepts in the chapter that students need to review. Chapter Tests can be found in the Classroom Resource Binder on pages 135–136. Workbook pages 83–87 can be used for additional practice.

Chapter Tests

Use Chapter Tests A and B on pages 135–136 in the Classroom Resource Binder to further assess mastery of chapter concepts.

Additional Resources

Use the Resource Planner on page 142 of this guide to assign additional exercises from the Classroom Resource Binder and Workbook.

Alternative Assessment

Student Interview

Discuss the New Deal. Ask:
- What was the New Deal?
- What were some steps that President Roosevelt took to end the Great Depression?
- Why were conservatives against the New Deal?
- Why were some liberals against the New Deal?
- Why was free time important to Americans during the Great Depression?

Presentation

- Students choose one of the following topics: *the Brain Trust, the Hundred Days, Eleanor Roosevelt,* or *American writers of the 1930s.*
- Students write an essay about the significance of this topic as it relates to improvements or change in American society and government.
- Students present their essays to the class.

Chapter
20

Unit Assessment

This is the last chapter in Unit 6, *Years of Uncertainty.* To review and assess cumulative understanding and provide standardized-test practice, have students complete the Unit Review Test on page 386 of the Student Edition, and the Unit 6 Cumulative Test on pages 137–138 of the Classroom Resource Binder.

Unit 7 ▷ The United States in Crisis

CHAPTER 21	PORTFOLIO PROJECT	BUILDING YOUR SKILLS	GROUP ACTIVITY	TIMELINE
Leading Up to War 1922–1941	A Dialogue	Recognizing a Point of View	Writing a Paragraph	The Road to War

CHAPTER 22	PORTFOLIO PROJECT	VOICES FROM THE PAST	GROUP ACTIVITY	TIMELINE
A World at War 1941–1945	Time Capsule	Yuri Tateshi	Making a Storyboard	A Second World War

CHAPTER 23	PORTFOLIO PROJECT	CONNECTING HISTORY AND...	GROUP ACTIVITY	TIMELINE
The Cold War 1945–1960	News Broadcast	Government: The United Nations	Listing Questions	The Cold War

RELATED MATERIALS

These are some of the Globe Fearon books that can be used to enrich and extend the material in this unit.

Content ▷

Fearon's Our Century 1930–1940
Explore the decade's history. Trace world events leading to World War II with "Around the World."

Literature ▷

Pacemaker® Classics: Anne Frank: The Diary of a Young Girl
Provides a personal view of the Holocaust.

Skills ▷

Exercises in Critical Thinking: Issues in U.S. History
Use Unit 4 to help students understand the issues leading to Japanese American internment.

Chapter 21 • **Leading Up to War** 1922–1941

Chapter at a Glance

SE page

388		*Opening the Chapter and Portfolio Project*
390	SECTION 1	Dictators in Europe
395		*Building Your Skills: Recognizing a Point of View*
396	SECTION 2	Japan Rises to Power
398	SECTION 3	From Isolation to Pearl Harbor
402		*Chapter Review and Group Activity*

Chapter
21

Learning Objectives

- Discuss the rise of dictators in Europe.
- Describe how Japan expanded during the 1930s.
- Explain how Americans felt about becoming involved in another world war.
- Describe why the United States was drawn into war.

Social Studies Skills

- Identify ways to recognize a point of view.
- Use a timeline to identify events that led the United States into another world war.
- Explain why the United States should either enter or stay out of the war in Europe in 1939.

Writing Skills

- Describe the meeting in Munich held in 1938 by writing headlines for a German newspaper and a British newspaper.
- Describe in a paragraph how Japan's goal of changing its economy led to the use of force in Manchuria and other regions of China.
- Write a paragraph describing the attack on Peal Harbor from an isolationist's point of view.
- Write a paragraph discussing whether or not the United States should adopt a policy of isolation.

Map and Chart Skills

- Use a map to identify European countries that were controlled by Germany.
- Use a chart to identify events that led up to World War II.

Resource Planner

Chapter 21
Leading Up to War

Use the Program Resources below for reteaching, reinforcement, and enrichment. Additional activities for customizing the lessons can be found in this guide.

Key
Reteaching = ⌒   Reinforcement = ↓   Enrichment = ⌒

Sections	Program Resources		
	Workbook Exercises	Teacher's Planning Guide	Classroom Resource Binder
Dictators in Europe	88, 89	⌒ p. 151	⌒ Concept Builder 21 *Leading Up to War*
Building Your Skills: Recognizing a Point of View		⌒ p. 152	↓ *Recognizing a Point of View* 141, 142
Japan Rises to Power	90	⌒ p. 153	⌒ Concept Builder 21 *Leading Up to War* ⌒ Transparency 8, *World War II: The Pacific and East Asia, 1941-1945*
From Isolation to Pearl Harbor	91	⌒ p. 153	⌒ Concept Builder 21 *Leading Up to War*
Chapter 21 Review		p. 154	↓ Words to Know 139 ⌒ Challenge 143 ↓ Chapter Tests A & B, 144, 145

Customizing the Chapter

Opening the Chapter
Student Edition, pages 388–389

Photo Activity

Have students look at the photograph and poster. Explain that Adolf Hitler, who is depicted in the poster, was the leader of the Nazi party in Germany. He rallied the support of many Germans, both young and old. Ask students if they have ever attended a rally, such as a pep rally, and what the purpose of the rally was. Then, have them discuss why a rally may be an effective way to arouse enthusiasm in people.

Words to Know

Review the Words to Know on page 389 of the Student Edition. To help the students remember the words, have pairs of students discuss and write what they think each word means. Then, have them look up the definition of each word in the Glossary in the Student Edition. Ask students to write the definitions in their notebooks.

The following words and definitions are covered in this chapter:

dictator a ruler with complete power in a country

Fascist a member of a political party who supports extreme nationalism and a dictator

Nazi a member of a political party in Germany led by Adolf Hitler

appeasement the policy of giving in to someone's demands in order to keep peace

militarism the policy of strong military actions taken by the leaders of a country

puppet state a government under the control of another, stronger power

cash-and-carry policy a plan that lets nations at war buy goods that they could pay cash for and then carry home

lend-lease plan to lend or lease supplies to a country whose defense is needed to protect the United States

Portfolio Project

Summary: Students write a dialogue between two groups of Americans taking sides on the question of whether the United States should enter or stay out of the war in Europe in 1939.

Materials: chart paper; markers

Procedure: Have students begin this project after they have read and reviewed information about America's decision to enter the war in Europe. Students divide a sheet of chart paper into two columns. In one column, they list reasons why some Americans wanted to keep the United States out of war. In the other column, they list reasons why some Americans believed that the United States should join in the war in Europe. Students use their lists to write a dialogue between two groups of Americans, taking sides on the question of whether the United States should enter or stay out of the war. The dialogue should include facts to support their point of view.

Assessment: Use the Individual Activity Rubric on page *xii* of this guide. Fill in the rubric with the additional information below. For this project, students should have

- created a chart listing reasons for and against the United States entering the war.

- written a dialogue between two groups of Americans.

Learning Objectives

Review the Learning Objectives on page 389 of the Student Edition before starting the chapter. Students can use the list as a learning guide. Suggest they write the objectives in a journal or use the Chapter Goals and Self-Check worksheet found on page PA 6 of the Classroom Resource Binder.

After reading each section of the chapter, have students write an example of what they learned under the appropriate objective. Suggest that students use these worksheets as a practice guide to help them study for the chapter test.

Timeline

Use the timeline to discuss the sequence of events in this chapter. Point out the timeline's title, its time span, and the intervals. After students have read the chapter, have them review the timeline and suggest additional entries.

SECTION **1: Dictators in Europe**
Student Edition, pages 390–394

Section Objectives

- Describe the events leading up to the signing of the pact in Munich in 1939.
- Explain why Great Britain and France declared war on Germany.
* Identify the dictators in Europe after World War I and explain how they came to power.

Words to Know

dictator, Fascist, Nazi, appeasement

Cooperative Group Activity

A Game About Power

Materials: reference materials (Unit 7 Bibliography and Internet sites, pages 236–240); index cards

Procedure: Remind students that a dictator is a ruler with complete power in a country. Joseph Stalin, Benito Mussolini, and Adolf Hitler were three very powerful dictators who gained power after World War I. Organize students into two teams to create questions for a quiz game about dictators from this time period. Give each team member two index cards.

- Team members review information about dictators in Europe.
- On index cards, members write two questions that begin with *Who, What, When, Where, Why,* and *How* on the following topics: *communism in the Soviet Union, Fascism in Italy,* or *Nazism in Germany.* They write the answers on the back.
- One student from each team collects the cards and moderates the game.
- Students take turns answering the other team's questions.
- Students receive one point for each correct answer. The team with the higher score at the end of the game wins.

Customizing the Activity for Individual Needs

ESL To help students understand the rise of dictators in Europe after World War I, have them write the names of European dictators on index cards. On the back of each index card, have students write a brief description of the dictator and how he rose to power. Have students read their cards to an English-proficient partner.

Learning Styles Students can:

 highlight the "question word" and the answer on each index card.

 work with a partner to write World War II events on index cards, shuffle them, and then put them in chronological order.

 read the questions aloud and answer them.

Enrichment Activity

Have groups of students scan newspapers or conduct research on the Internet to create a list of dictators and their countries since 1939, such as Saddam Hussein in Iraq and Fidel Castro in Cuba. Have each group choose one dictator to write about. Students should include biographical information as well as the individual's political beliefs.

Alternative Assessment

Students can write three important events that led to war in Europe on separate index cards. Then, have students turn each card over and list important facts about the event.

BUILDING YOUR SKILLS:
Recognizing a Point of View
Student Edition, page 395

Objectives
- Social Studies Skill: Explain the importance of respecting differences.
- Social Studies Skill: Explain in a flyer why Hitler's beliefs and actions were unsound.
- Social Studies Skill: Examine quotes about democracy and determine possible points of view regarding Nazi Germany.

Activities
The Importance of Being Tolerant
Procedure: Initiate a discussion about the meaning of tolerance toward groups of people in our everyday lives. For example, point out that some people with disabilities are not treated fairly. Ask students to think of current incidents when people did not respect others because of differences. Then, have students discuss how Adolf Hitler's opinions about Jews were intolerant and prejudiced. Ask students to write a letter to a friend explaining why they feel it is important to be tolerant.

Against a Dictatorship
Materials: colored markers; construction paper

Procedure: Point out that many people in Germany, and in the rest of the world, were against the Nazis. Invite students to create a flyer, from the perspective of an anti–Nazi, explaining why Adolf Hitler's beliefs and actions were wrong and should be stopped. Have them draw charts or graphs, that support their opinion.

Quotes About Democracy
Procedure: Read the following quotes about democracy to students, and ask them to explain what each quote means. Then ask students to consider how the author of each quote would regard Hitler's beliefs about Germany and the master race.

"It has been said that Democracy is the worst form of government except all those other forms that have been tried from time to time." (Winston Churchill)

"It is the greatest good to the greatest number which is the measure of right and wrong." (Jeremy Bentham)

"As I would not be a slave, so I would not be a master. This expresses my idea of democracy." (Abraham Lincoln)

Practice

Have students complete Building Your Skills: Recognizing a Point of View on page 141 of Classroom Resource Binder.

SECTION 2: Japan Rises to Power
Student Edition, pages 396–397

Section Objectives

* Explain why Japan decided to expand its empire and attack China.
* Explain why Japan allied with Germany and Italy.

Words to Know

militarism, puppet state

Cooperative Group Activity

Japan's Rise to Power

Materials: reference materials (Unit 7 Bibliography and Internet sites, pages 236–240); colored markers; hole punch; ribbon or cord

Procedure: Remind students that in the 1930s, military leaders attempted to make Japan the most feared country in Asia. Organize students into three groups to create picture books about Japan as a rising military power in the 1930s. Students should do additional research for this activity.

• Group members decide on how many illustrations and maps to include in their books. Illustrations can depict battles, military leaders, life in Japan in the 1930s, and what the land looked like.

• Students create illustrations and maps, labeling each to provide information about Japan's rise to power.

• One group member assembles the pages and creates a book using a hole punch and ribbon or cord.

• Groups choose a spokesperson to share their books with the class.

Customizing the Activity for Individual Needs

ESL To help students understand Japan's reasons for expanding its empire, review the terms *military, militarism, puppet state, natural resource,* and *anti-Communist.* Then, have ESL students and English–proficient students ask each other questions about Japan's rise to power and the ways in which it accomplished this goal.

Learning Styles Students can:

 locate Japan and the countries it attacked on a map. Students can then locate on the map the countries that Japan became allies with.

 match index cards with terms, such as *militarism* and *puppet state,* with index cards that contain their definitions.

 assume the role of a military leader in Japan in the 1930s and explain to a partner the leader's plan of militarism and how they can increase their country's power.

Reinforcement Activity ⬇

Organize the students into pairs and have them assume the role of television anchors. Have each team prepare an in-depth news brief of Japan's rise to power. Students should discuss the following in their news reports: *Japan's plan of militarism, Japan's attack on Manchuria, Japan's full-scale attack on China,* and *Japan's plan to become a world power with Germany and Italy.*

Alternative Assessment

Students can write ten true/false questions about Japan's rise to power on index cards. They write the answers on the backs of the cards.

SECTION 3: From Isolation to Pearl Harbor
Student Edition, pages 398–401

Section Objectives

• Describe how the presidential election of 1940 differed from past elections.
• Identify events that ended isolationism in the United States.
• Describe the event that took place at Pearl Harbor.
* Explain why American isolationists wanted to stay out of the war.

Words to Know

cash-and-carry policy, lend-lease plan

Cooperative Group Activity

Debating Isolationism

Procedure: Remind students that some Americans favored a policy of isolationism. Yet, many Americans could see the growing signs of war in Europe and Asia. Organize students into two groups. Have one group assume the role of isolationists. Students in the second group assume the role of Americans in favor of going to war.

- The isolationist group brainstorms and lists reasons why the United States should not go to war. The other group lists reasons for entering the war.

- Students incorporate the following information in their lists: *the election of 1940, the lend-lease plan, the peacetime draft, the sinking of the U.S. Navy ship in 1941 by German submarines,* and *the attack on Pearl Harbor by Japan.*

- Groups hold a debate over the question of the United States going to war or remaining isolationist. Students will switch places frequently so that all students will get a chance to debate.

Customizing the Activity for Individual Needs

ESL To help students understand the meaning of isolationism, discuss the role their native country takes in the affairs of other countries today. Does the country take an active role, or does it remain neutral? Have ESL students continue the discussion with English-proficient students. Encourage them to use the term *isolationism.*

Learning Styles Students can:

 create a timeline (Classroom Resource Binder, page G0 8) with the important events leading up to U.S. involvement in World War II.

 work in groups to create banners with slogans that promote an isolationist stance or banners promoting American involvement in the war.

 summarize the high points of the debate aloud for the class.

Enrichment Activity

Ask students to bring in newspaper and magazine articles about countries that have recently been involved in war or serious political struggles. Have them look for examples of U.S. involvement in these countries. Students divide a piece of paper into two sections and label one section *For U.S. Involvement* and the other section *Against U.S. Involvement.* Ask students to write reasons for and against the United States getting involved in the problems of other countries.

Alternative Assessment

Students can create a Sequence of Events chart (Classroom Resource Binder, page G0 1) that lists four events and dates leading to the U.S. involvement in the war.

Closing the Chapter
Student Edition, pages 402–403

Chapter Vocabulary

Review with students the Words to Know on page 389 of the Student Edition. Then have them complete the Vocabulary Review on page 402 of the Student Edition, by answering each statement as *true* or *false.* If the statement is false, have them change the underlined word to make it true.

For more vocabulary practice, have them complete the vocabulary exercise on page 139 of the Classroom Resource Binder.

Test Tip

Have students scan the chapter for key words and phrases and write them on index cards. On the reverse side of each card, have students write the meaning of the word or phrase. When studying for a test, have pairs of students use the cards to quiz one another.

Learning Objectives

Have students review their Chapter Goals and Self-Check worksheet found on page PA 6 of the Classroom Resource Binder. They can check off the goal they have reached. Note that each section of the quiz corresponds to a Learning Objective.

Group Activity

Summary: Students discuss positive aspects of isolationism and whether it is possible for a powerful country such as the United States to remain isolated.

Materials: newspaper and magazine articles

Procedure: Have the students form small groups of three or four to review information about isolationism. Students take notes about isolationism and discuss its good points. They discuss if it is possible for a powerful country such as the United States to remain isolated. Group members may read newspaper and magazine articles that contain information about recent U.S. involvement in other countries to substantiate their discussion. Each group writes a group paragraph composed of all the members' ideas. A spokesperson reads the paragraph to the class.

Assessment: Use the Group Activity Rubric found on page *xiii* of this guide. Fill in the rubric with the following additional information. For this activity, students should have

- participated in a group discussion about isolationism.
- participated in creating a paragraph to support their opinion.

RELATED MATERIALS   See the Unit Overview page for related Globe Fearon books that can be used to enrich and extend the materials in the chapter.

Assessing the Chapter

Traditional Assessment

Chapter Quiz
The Chapter Quiz on page 403 of the Student Edition can be used as an open-book test, a closed-book test, or a homework assignment. Use the quiz to identify concepts in the chapter that students need to review. Chapter Tests can be found in the Classroom Resource Binder on pages 144–145. Workbook pages 88–91 can be used for additional practice.

Chapter Tests
Use Chapter Tests A and B on pages 144–145 in the Classroom Resource Binder to further assess mastery of chapter concepts.

Additional Resources
Use the Resource Planner on page 150 of this guide to assign additional exercises from the Classroom Resource Binder and Workbook.

Alternative Assessment

Student Interview
Write the following topics on index cards: *Adolf Hitler leads the Nazi Party, War breaks out in 1939,* and *Japan attacks Pearl Harbor.* Students select one card. Ask:

- What is important about this event?
- Who was involved?
- How did this event impact the United States?
- What happened as a result of this event?

Open-Ended
Have students use the timeline on pages 388–389 of the Student Edition as a basis for creating their own timelines that list events leading to World War II. Have students scan the chapter to search for at least eight additional events to add to the chapter timeline.

Chapter 22 · A World at War 1941–1945

Chapter at a Glance

SE page

404   *Opening the Chapter and Portfolio Project*

406   SECTION 1   A World at War Again

409   SECTION 2   The Allies Strike Back

413   SECTION 3   The War at Home

419   *Voices From the Past: Yuri Tateshi*

420   SECTION 4   Winning the War

424   *Chapter Review and Group Activity*

Learning Objectives

- Explain the Allies' plan for winning World War II.
- Discuss ways in which the U.S. government controlled the economy during the war.
- Describe how the war affected women, African Americans, and Latinos.
- Discuss the treatment of Japanese Americans during the war.
- Describe the effect of the Holocaust.
- Explain how the United States forced Japan to surrender.

Social Studies Skills

- Explore the life of a Japanese family during the war.
- Use a timeline to identify events that occurred during World War II.
- Create a time capsule to document what life was like during World War II.

Writing Skills

- Write a news article to describe the attack on Pearl Harbor from the perspective of an American reporter.
- Write the opening scene for a movie, describing the Battle of Midway.
- Explain in a news report the role of the 332nd Fighter Group in protecting U.S. bombers.
- Write a radio script describing the Allied victory over Japan.
- Write a storyboard about the contributions of a famous American during World War II.

Map and Chart Skills

- Use a map to locate battles that occurred between the Allied forces and Japan.

Resource Planner

Use the Program Resources below for reteaching, reinforcement, and enrichment. Additional activities for customizing the lessons can be found in this guide.

Key
Reteaching = ⌒   Reinforcement = ⬇   Enrichment = ⌒

Sections	Program Resources		
	⬇ Workbook Exercises	Teacher's Planning Guide	Classroom Resource Binder
A World at War Again	92	⬇ p. 158	
The Allies Strike Back	93, 94	⌒ p. 159	⌒ Transparency 9 *World War II: Europe and North Africa, 1942–1945*
The War at Home	95	⌒ p. 160	⌒ Document-Based Question 7 *World War II Poster* ⌒ Geography and Economics 7 *African Americans Move North*
Voices From the Past: Yuri Tateshi		⌒ p. 161	⌒ Feature Practice 148 *Voices From the Past: Ernie Pyle*
Winning the War	96	⌒ p. 161	
Chapter 22 Review		p. 162	⬇ Words to Know 146 ⬇ Challenge 149 ⬇ Chapter Tests A & B, 150, 151

Customizing the Chapter

Opening the Chapter
Student Edition, pages 404–405

Photo Activity
Have students study the photo of allied soldiers landing in Normandy, France. Explain that this was the largest land and sea attack in history.

Discuss the difficulties American soldiers might have encountered in preparing for this attack. Then list on the chalkboard the difficulties the soldiers might have encountered once they landed on the beach. Point out the "dog" tags in the lower right corner of the photo, and explain that tags such as these were worn by every American soldier. Ask students to think of what important information might be written on the tags. (Name, birth date, social security number.) Ask students why they think these tags would be important for soldiers to wear. (In case they were killed or wounded, soldiers could be identified by their tags.)

Words to Know

Introduce the Words to Know on page 405 of the Student Edition. To help the students remember the words, invite pairs of students to predict what each word means, then look each word up in the Glossary in the Student Edition. Encourage them to write the words and the definitions in their notebooks.

The following words and definitions are covered in this chapter:

Axis Powers the countries that fought the Allies in World War II

mobilize to get ready for war

siege a military blockade of a city to force its surrender

partisan a person who strongly believes in a cause

amphibious landing a planned movement of troops from the sea

rationing limiting the amount of something that each person can buy

internment camp a prisonlike place in which people are held during a war

Holocaust the mass murder of millions of Jews by the Nazis

genocide the planned murder of an entire people

atomic bomb a nuclear bomb with enormous power to harm

Portfolio Project

Summary: Students prepare time capsules that hold items relating to World War II, such as newspaper headlines, maps, and a rationing book.

Materials: colored markers; scissors; stapler; rubber bands; and a cardboard-box time capsule

Procedure: Students take notes about items to include in their capsules as they read the chapter. Students then create items for their capsule, such as newspaper headlines, a rationing book, and maps. Students can roll up the items and use rubber bands to secure them. Students place their items in cardboard boxes. They then make a list of items in the time capsule and tape it to the top of their boxes.

Assessment: Use the Individual Activity Rubric on page *xii* of this guide. Fill in the rubric with the additional information below. For this project, students should have

- created at least three pertinent time capsule items.
- listed the items in their time capsule.

Learning Objectives

Review the Learning Objectives on page 405 of the Student Edition before starting the chapter. Students can use the list as a learning guide. Suggest that they write the objectives in a journal or use the Chapter Goals and Self-Check worksheet found on page PA 6 of the Classroom Resource Binder.

After reading each section of the chapter, have students write an example of what they learned under the appropriate objective. Suggest that students use these worksheets as a practice guide to help them study for the chapter test.

Timeline

Use the timeline to discuss the sequence of events in this chapter. Point out the timeline's title, its time span, and the intervals. After students have read the chapter, have them review the timeline and suggest additional entries.

SECTION 1: A World at War Again
Student Edition, pages 406–408

Section Objectives

- Explain why the United States declared war on Japan and entered World War II on the side of Great Britain and the Soviet Union.
- Identify areas that Japan controlled after December 1941.
- Describe the Allies' plan to defeat the Axis powers and Japan.

Words to Know

Axis Powers, mobilize, siege

Cooperative Group Activity

Mapping a World at War

Materials: reference materials (Unit 7 Bibliography, pages 236–240, and Internet sites); atlas; markers

Procedure: Divide the students into groups and have them review information about the Axis Powers, the Allied forces, and Japanese invasions. Have students create a map showing what the world looked like in 1941. You may wish to have students use reference materials and other resources to help them complete their maps.

- Group members draw an outline map of the world and color code the countries that formed the Allied and the Axis Powers.
- Students should include the following labels on their maps: *attack on Pearl Harbor, Japanese takeover of the Philippines, major Allied forces,* and *Axis Powers.*
- Group members create a map key that identifies each event.
- Have groups choose a spokesperson to present their maps to the class.

Customizing the Activity for Individual Needs

ESL To help students understand the forces at war, have them write a short paragraph about which side their native country was on during World War II. Have them include the reasons for their country's position in World War II. Then have ESL students read their paragraphs to an English-proficient student.

Learning Styles Students can:

 work with a partner to locate on a map the countries of the Allied forces and those of the Axis Powers.

 sort index cards with the names of counties belonging to the Allied forces and the Axis Powers.

 develop a radio news bulletin that informs listeners about the U.S. decision to join forces with Great Britain and the Soviet Union.

Reinforcement Activity

Remind students that the United States drafted more than 10 million men to fight in the war. Another 6 million American men and women volunteered for the armed forces. Ask students to assume the role of Americans who have just been drafted to serve in World War II. Have them write a journal entry expressing their feelings about going off to war.

Alternative Assessment

Students can assume the role of American soldiers in World War II. Ask them to write letters home to their families and provide information about where they will be sent to fight, Allied soldiers who will help them fight the war, and the country they will be fighting against.

Section Objectives

- Explain the importance of the Battle of Midway.
- Describe the plan that the Allies used to fight the Axis powers, beginning with an attack in North Africa.
- ⋆ Describe how the Allied forces defeated Erwin Rommel in North Africa.
- ⋆ Explain why island-hopping was a good plan for the Allies.

Words to Know

partisan, amphibious landing

Cooperative Group Activity

We Interrupt This Program

Materials: tape recorder and cassette tape

Procedure: Place students in two groups and assign each group one of the following topics: *the fighting in North Africa* or *the war in the Pacific.* Each group will create a radio report on its topic. Remind students to answer the questions *who, what, where, when,* and *why.*

- Group members assume the role of radio news announcers who will update Americans on the status of the war. Students choose a name for the radio station they report for and the name of the news show.
- Group members review information about their assigned topic, and take notes about facts they wish to include in their news report.
- Group members write their news report together. Each member takes part in the radio newscast. One member introduces the news segment by giving the date and the name of the radio station that they work for. The report should be about one minute in length.
- Students then record their news report on tape for the class to hear.

Customizing the Activity for Individual Needs

ESL To help students understand the concept of island-hopping, ask them to think about places that are close enough for them to get there by taking one hop. Ask students to sketch several islands on the chalkboard that are near one another. Have them use chalk to demonstrate "island hopping."

Chapter
22

Learning Styles Students can:

 work in groups to complete a Description Web (Classroom Resource Binder, page G0 3) about their topic.

 classify index cards of battles and people into three groups: *fighting in North Africa, war in the Pacific,* and *island-hopping.*

 practice their part of the news report aloud and summarize each of the other members' parts.

Enrichment Activity

Remind students that navy code experts were able to figure out the secret messages being sent between Japanese ships. This meant that the U.S. Navy knew the location of enemy ships. Have students create a system of coding that allows them to send secret messages. Invite students to write messages about the fighting in North Africa, the war in the Pacific, or island-hopping. Then, have students exchange messages and try to break the code to read the message.

Alternative Assessment

Students can write ten questions on separate index cards about the fighting in North Africa, the war in the Pacific, or island-hopping, using a variety of formats, such as multiple choice, true/false, and fill-in-the-blank. Students answer their questions on the backs of the cards.

SECTION 3: The War at Home
Student Edition, pages 413–418

Section Objectives
- Describe how Americans helped on the home front during the war.
- Describe how the U.S. government mobilized the economy during wartime.
- ★ Explain how the roles of women and African Americans changed during the war and how Latinos helped the war effort.
- ★ Describe what happened to Japanese Americans during the war.

Words to Know
rationing, internment camp

Cooperative Group Activity

"The War at Home" Scene
Procedure: Explain to students that to defeat the Axis Powers, the United States needed the help of all Americans at home. Divide the class into four groups. Each group will show the struggles and triumphs of African Americans, Latinos, women, or Japanese Americans during World War II by creating storyboards.

- Group members review information and take notes about the ways in which the group of Americans they have chosen aided the war effort and the difficulties they faced at home.
- Group members work together to develop a plot and create characters and draw pictures for their storyboards. The scene can be based on either how their group helped the war effort or how their group faced discrimination during World War II.
- Students then write a brief scene for their storyboards.
- Some group members can announce the scene.
- Other group members read the storyboards to the class.

Customizing the Activity for Individual Needs
ESL To help students understand the ways in which different groups of Americans contributed to the war effort at home, have small groups complete a *Who, What, Where, When, Why, How* chart (Classroom Resource Binder, page G0 7) about the roles women, African Americans, and Latinos played in the war effort at home.

Learning Styles Students can:

 locate photos in reference books of Japanese Americans in internment camps and write captions.

 design posters encouraging Americans at home to get involved in the war effort.

 work with a partner to role-play a factory worker who is being interviewed about the job of making bombs for use in the war.

Reteaching Activity

Have students create a chart that lists the ways the United States mobilized its economy during World War II. The chart should compare and contrast the experiences of African Americans, Latinos, women, and Japanese Americans during the war.

Alternative Assessment

Students can make an outline that includes the following information: *War Effort at Home, Mobilizing the Economy, Opportunities for Women, African Americans During the War, Latinos During the War,* and *Japanese Americans During the War.* Have students review the Student Edition to write facts about each of the above headings.

VOICES FROM THE PAST:
Yuri Tateshi
Student Edition, page 419

Objectives
- Social Studies Skill: Create a flyer explaining why internment camps for Japanese American citizens were unjust.
- Social Studies Skill: Write a journal entry describing daily life in an internment camp.
- Social Studies Skill: Describe differing views of internment camps.

Activities
Protesting Internment
Materials: colored markers

Procedure: From the perspective of someone living in 1942, have students create a flyer announcing a protest march against internment camps to be held in Washington, D.C. Students should include reasons why internment camps were unjust, as Japanese Americans were serving in the armed forces and fighting for their country.

Daily Life in the Camp
Procedure: Ask students to write a journal entry in the style of Yuri Tateshi, describing what daily life was like living at Manzanar. Have them draw a black-and-white sketch of what her family's room might have looked like or the dining hall where she had her daily meals.

Differing Views
Procedure: Invite students to write a series of interview questions they would ask government officials and Japanese American citizens at Manzanar. Then, form groups of three or four students and have them assume the roles of interviewers, government officials at the camp, and Japanese American citizens to role-play a scene using the interview questions.

Practice
Have students complete Voices From the Past: Ernie Pyle on page 148 of the Classroom Resource Binder.

Section 4: Winning the War
Student Edition, pages 420–423

Section Objectives
- Describe how D-day was planned and the outcome of the invasion.
- Describe the Allies' victory over Japan.
- Describe the new weapon used to end the war.
- * Explain what the Holocaust was.

Words to Know
Holocaust, genocide, atomic bomb

Cooperative Group Activity

D-Day Scramble
Materials: markers; 12 index cards

Procedure: Explain to students that D-day was the largest land and sea attack in history. Organize the class into two groups to play a game of D-day Scramble.

- Group members write facts about D-day on the index cards. Students can use the following facts: *June 6, 1944; D-day; Normandy; General Dwight D. Eisenhower; Allies; English channel; France; land mines; barbed wire; Britain; Hitler;* and *over 170,000 Allied soldiers.* Students divide the cards into two piles. Each group takes a pile of cards.
- Each member of the group takes a turn drawing a card from the pile. Students then make up a sentence using the fact on their card.
- After the game, the class discusses the information they learned from the game.

Customizing the Activity for Individual Needs
ESL To help students understand the concept of D-day, point out that many organizations use letters to represent ideas such as *G.I.* for *government issue.* Have students work with English-proficient students to create ideas of their own.

Learning Styles Students can:

 look at the landing photo on page 404 in the Student Edition to help them create a sentence.

 move their finger under the word as they read the fact.

 say the fact before they give their sentence.

Reteaching Activity

Have students write letters based on the sentence they created. Letters can include the sights soldiers might have seen, and the feelings that soldiers might have had.

Alternative Assessment

Students can create a *Who, What, Where, When, Why,* and *How* chart about the D-day invasion.

Closing the Chapter
Student Edition, pages 424–425

Chapter Vocabulary

Review with students the Words to Know on page 405 of the Student Edition. Then have them complete the Vocabulary Review on page 424 of the Student Edition, by answering each statement as *true* or *false*. If the statement is false, have them change the underlined word to make it true.

For more vocabulary practice, have them complete the vocabulary exercise on page 146 of the Classroom Resource Binder.

Test Tip

Have students practice scanning each section of the chapter. Ask partners to discuss what they think each section is about based on the photos, charts, maps, and captions.

Learning Objectives

Have students review their Chapter Goals and Self-Check worksheet found on page PA 6 of the Classroom Resource Binder. They can check off the goal they have reached. Note that each section of the quiz corresponds to a Learning Objective.

Group Activity

Summary: Students develop a storyboard about a person in the chapter who contributed to the war effort. They list what the person did and why the person is remembered.

Materials: posterboard; markers

Procedure: Organize students into four groups. Group members choose a person who contributed to the war effort. Students list the individual's contributions to the war and reasons why this person should be remembered. Group members create a storyboard of at least four panels about the individual, including illustrations or maps. Each group member can present a part of the storyboard to the class.

Assessment: Use the Group Activity Rubric found on page *xiii* of this guide. Fill in the rubric with the following additional information. For this activity, students should have

- taken notes about an individual who contributed to the war effort.
- participated in developing a storyboard about the person.

RELATED MATERIALS See the Unit Overview page for related Globe Fearon books that can be used to enrich and extend the materials in the chapter.

Traditional Assessment

Chapter Quiz

The Chapter Quiz on page 425 of the Student Edition can be used as an open-book test, a closed-book test, or a homework assignment. Use the quiz to identify concepts in the chapter that students need to review. Chapter Tests can be found in the Classroom Resource Binder on pages 150–151. Workbook pages 92–96 can be used for additional practice.

Chapter Tests

Use Chapter Tests A and B on pages 150–151 in the Classroom Resource Binder to further assess mastery of chapter concepts.

Additional Resources

Use the Resource Planner on page 157 of this guide to assign additional exercises from the Classroom Resource Binder and Workbook.

Alternative Assessment

Student Interview

Write the following topic on the chalkboard: *World War II*. Ask:

- Which countries were allies of the United States? Which were not?
- What happened on D-day?
- What events led to Japan's surrender?
- What was the Holocaust?

Open-Ended

- Students scan the chapter to list important events in World War II.
- Students use those events to create a timeline about World War II.

Chapter
22

Chapter 23 • The Cold War 1945–1960

Chapter at a Glance

SE page

426   *Opening the Chapter and Portfolio Project*

428   SECTION 1   The Cold War Begins

434   *Connecting History and Government:*
       The United Nations

435   SECTION 2   Communism in Asia

438   SECTION 3   The Cold War at Home

442   *Chapter Review and Group Activity*

Learning Objectives

- Describe how communism spread in Eastern Europe.
- Explain attempts to stop the spread of communism.
- Explain how communism spread in Asia.
- Describe the reasons why the United States was drawn into the arms race.

Social Studies Skills

- Explore how the United Nations began.
- Use a timeline to explore events in the United States and the international community during the cold war.
- Describe events that took place during the cold war by developing a news broadcast.

Writing Skills

- Describe in a paragraph the reasons why it was important to the United States for Canada to join NATO.
- Explain in a paragraph how communism affected Asia after World War II.
- Describe reactions to the news that the Soviet Union has sent *Sputnik* into space from the perspective of a group of students.
- Discuss a world problem that the United Nations should address.

Map and Chart Skills

- Use a map to identify countries that were part of NATO, the Warsaw Pact, and non-member nations of Europe.

Resource Planner

| Chapter 23 | Use the Program Resources below for reteaching, reinforcement, and |
| The Cold War | enrichment. Additional activities for customizing the lessons can be found in this guide. |

Key
Reteaching = ⤴ Reinforcement = ⤓ Enrichment = ⤴

Sections	Program Resources		
	Workbook Exercises	Teacher's Planning Guide	Classroom Resource Binder
The Cold War Begins	97, 98	⤴ p. 166	⤴ Concept Builder 23 *The Cold War* Outline Map 3 *Europe*
Connecting History and Government: The United Nations		⤴ p. 167	⤴ Feature Practice *Connecting History and World Government: UNICEF* 154
Communism in Asia	99	⤓ p. 168	⤴ Concept Builder 23 *The Cold War* Outline Map 8 *Asia*
The Cold War at Home	100	⤴ p. 168	⤴ Concept Builder 23 *The Cold War*
Chapter 23 Review		p. 169	⤓ Words to Know 152 ⤓ Challenge 155 ⤓ Chapter Tests A & B, 156, 157 ⤓ Unit Test Parts I & II, 158, 159

Chapter
23

Customizing the Chapter

Opening the Chapter
Student Edition, pages 426–427

Photo Activity

Direct students' attention to the photograph showing an atomic bomb being tested. Based on the photo, ask students to describe the force of an atomic explosion and what might happen if it exploded in a heavily populated area. Have them recall learning about the devastating effects of the U.S. bombing of Hiroshima and Nagasaki during World War II. Tell students that the United States built underground fallout shelters after World War II, when other world powers were developing atomic bombs. Have students look at the picture of the fallout shelter sign. Explain that a fallout shelter is safe from radioactive waste. Have students make a list of what they and their family would need to survive for a month living in a fallout shelter.

Words to Know

Review the Words to Know on page 427 of the Student Edition. To help students remember the words, have pairs of students write each word on an index card and the definitions on other index cards. Then have them take turns matching the word to the correct definition. Encourage students to look up each term in the Glossary in the Student Edition to check its meaning.

The following words and definitions are covered in this chapter:

satellite a country controlled by a more powerful country

iron curtain an imaginary wall, or dividing line, separating the Soviet nations from the rest of Europe

cold war a sharp conflict between countries without actual war

containment a policy of preventing the expansion of power of one country over another country

superpower a country that is a top world power

demilitarized zone an area where no military forces are allowed

blacklist a list of people who are not approved for employment

McCarthyism a term named for Senator Joseph McCarthy's campaign of accusing people of being Communists

fallout the radioactive waste from a nuclear blast

space race the competition among countries to be first in exploring space

Portfolio Project

Summary: Students develop news broadcasts that tell the story of the cold war. They use pictures from the chapter to explain the events.

Procedure: As students read the chapter, ask them to make a list of the pictures that tell the story of the cold war. After reading the chapter, students write news broadcasts that explain the events that occurred during the cold war. Point out that newscasts give facts rather than opinions and that the most important news is presented first. Encourage students to practice and then present their news broadcast, pointing to the pictures to help tell the cold war story.

Assessment: Use the Individual Activity Rubric on page *xii* of this guide. Fill in the rubric with the additional information below. For this project students should have:

- made a list of pictures that tell the cold war story.

- written a news broadcast about the cold war.

Learning Objectives

Review the Learning Objectives on page 427 of the Student Edition before starting the chapter. Students can use the list as a learning guide. Suggest they write the objectives in a journal or use the Chapter Goals and Self-Check worksheet found on page PA 6 of the Classroom Resource Binder.

After reading each section of the chapter, have students write an example of what they learned under the appropriate objective. Suggest that students use these worksheets as a practice guide to help them study for the chapter test.

Timeline

Use the timeline to discuss the sequence of events in this chapter. Point out the timeline's title, its time span, and the intervals. After students have read the chapter, have them review the timeline and suggest additional entries.

SECTION 1: The Cold War Begins
Student Edition, pages 428–433

Section Objectives

- Describe the effects of communism on Eastern European countries.
- Describe the Truman Doctrine.
- Explain how the Marshall Plan helped the United States.
- Explain the purpose of NATO.
- * Describe the cold war between the United States and the Soviet Union.

Words to Know

satellite, iron curtain, cold war, containment

Cooperative Group Activity

Class News Magazine

Materials: reference materials (Unit 7 Bibliography and Internet sites, pages 236–240); news magazines; computer

Procedure: Remind students that after World War II ended, the spread of communism led to conflicts between the United States and the Soviet Union. Divide the class into six groups and have them write magazine articles on the post-war era and the rising conflict between the United States and the Soviet Union. Distribute current news magazines to show how articles are written. Students may want to do additional research on this rising conflict.

- Each group reviews information and conducts research on one of the following topics: *communism in Eastern Europe, the cold war, the Truman Doctrine, the Marshall Plan, the Berlin Airlift,* or *the North Atlantic Treaty Organization.*
- Each member provides at least two facts for the article.
- Some group members provide art or photos for the article.
- Each group chooses a member to input the article on the computer. Then, students bind the articles together to form a news magazine.

Customizing the Activity for Individual Needs

ESL To help students understand the idea of *cold war,* have ESL students work with English-proficient students to discuss ways a cold war is different from a military or "hot" war.

Learning Styles Students can:

 locate on a map the countries that were part of the Warsaw Pact and the countries that were part of NATO.

 sort index cards with names of countries into two piles: those that were satellites of the Soviet Union and those that were not.

 assume the role of Winston Churchill and explain the meaning of the iron curtain.

Enrichment Activity

Remind students that the iron curtain was an imaginary wall, or dividing line, separating the Soviet Union and the nations under its control from the rest of Europe. Have students imagine that the classroom is cut off from contact with the rest of the school and the outside world. Have students describe the problems or difficulties they might encounter, and the types of information that would be inaccessible to them.

Alternative Assessment

Students can review the section to create a simple crossword puzzle using words from the section. Then have students trade puzzles with classmates, and invite them to complete the puzzles.

CONNECTING HISTORY AND GOVERNMENT:
The United Nations
Student Edition, page 434

Objectives

- Social Studies Skill: Explain why countries belonging to NATO should be member nations of the United Nations.
- Social Studies Skill: Identify rules and laws for a charter or constitution.

Activities

Quiz Show
Procedure: Have students work in three teams to create questions for a television quiz show about the United Nations. Students list their questions on a set of index cards. They write the answers on the back. Then have a representative from each team serve as the game show host. The host will ask the other two teams the questions on the cards. When a team gets an answer right, they get a point. The team with the highest number of points at the end of the game wins.

NATO
Procedure: Have students review information about the North Atlantic Treaty Organization. They will then prepare a speech to be given to the UN Security Council, recommending that all NATO nations be allowed to join the United Nations.

Mock United Nations
Procedure: Ask students to assume the role of representatives forming the United Nations in 1945. Tell them that their job is to create a set of rules and laws for the UN. Encourage them to think about what issues might be important to address, including recommendations on ways in which opposing nations could work cooperatively.

Practice

Have students complete Connecting History and World Government: UNICEF on page 154 of the Classroom Resource Binder.

Chapter
23

SECTION 2: Communism in Asia
Student Edition, pages 435–437

Section Objectives
* Describe the changes that took place in Japan and China after World War II.
* * Explain how the Korean War became an American war.

Words to Know
superpower, demilitarized zone

Cooperative Group Activity

Debate For or Against Involvement
Materials: reference materials (Unit 7 Bibliography and Internet sites, pages 236–240)

Procedure: Discuss the Truman Doctrine, and how it related to the conflict in Korea. You may wish to have students conduct further research on the Korean War. Then divide the class into two teams to debate U.S. involvement in the Korean War.

* Students on one team assume the role of Americans who are in favor of U.S. involvement in the Korean War. Team members discuss and list reasons why the United States was justified in sending troops to help South Korea fight against communism.
* Students on the other team assume the role of American isolationists who believe that the United States should stay out of the affairs of other countries. Team members discuss and list reasons against U.S. involvement in the Korean War.
* Each team chooses a spokesperson to debate its side of the issue in a classroom debate.
* Team members are then encouraged to ask questions of the opposing team. Questions are answered by all team members.

Customizing the Activity for Individual Needs
ESL To help students understand the ramifications of a country divided by war, have students recall the U.S. Civil War or a civil war in another nation.

Learning Styles Students can:

 complete a Sequence of Events chart (Classroom Resource Binder, page G0 1) with information about the events leading up to U.S. involvement in the Korean War.

 create a poster showing opposition to the Korean War.

 explain the main points of the debate to a partner.

Reinforcement Activity

Provide students with a Comparison-Contrast chart (Classroom Resource Binder, page G0 4) to use to reinforce the difference between isolationists and Americans favoring involvement in the Korean War.

Alternative Assessment

Students can write news bulletins about the changes in Japan and China after World War II and after the Korean War. They can then deliver their news bulletins to the class. Each bulletin should contain answers to the questions *who, what, where, when,* and *why.*

SECTION 3: The Cold War at Home
Student Edition, pages 438–441

Section Objectives
* Explain the formation of the House Un-American Activities Committee.
* * Describe the events that took place during the McCarthy era.
* * Describe the race for arms and the space race between the United States and the Soviet Union.

Words to Know
blacklist, McCarthyism, fallout, space race

Cooperative Group Activity

Cold War "Jeopardy"
Materials: index cards

Procedure: Divide the class into three teams and assign each team one of the following categories: *The Hunt for Spies, the Arms Race,* or *the Space Race.*

* Each team writes five Jeopardy-style answers for their category on index cards.
* Team members then assign a point value to each question: 100, 200, 300, 400, or 500.
* On the back of the cards, team members write a question to the answer.
* The class chooses someone to be the host. Each team gives that person its answer cards.

- The teams play Jeopardy against each other using the answers each team made. The team with the highest score at the end of the game wins.

Customizing the Activity for Individual Needs

ESL To help students understand the term *McCarthyism*, explain that the suffix *-ism* can mean "the conduct or ideas of someone." McCarthyism is the conduct of Senator McCarthy who claimed he had knowledge of Communists working in the U.S. government.

Learning Styles Students can:

 complete a Description Web (Classroom Resource Binder, page G0 3) with information about the space race or other categories from the Jeopardy game.

 draw a cartoon that attacks McCarthyism in this country in the 1950s.

 ask the questions on the index cards for the Jeopardy game.

Reteaching Activity

Have students list the major events that occurred in the United States during the cold war. Ask them to organize this information in chart form.

Alternative Assessment

Students can create a timeline (Classroom Resource Binder, page G0 8) of at least five important events that occurred in the United States between 1947 and 1957. Encourage them to include events about HUAC, the McCarthy Era, and the race for arms and space.

Closing the Chapter
Student Edition, pages 442–443

Chapter Vocabulary
Review with students the Words to Know on page 427 of the Student Edition. Then have them complete the Vocabulary Review on page 442 of the Student Edition, by matching each definition with a term from the list.

For more vocabulary practice, have them complete the vocabulary exercise on page 152 of the Classroom Resource Binder.

Test Tip
Have students find the main idea and details as they read each section of a chapter.

Learning Objectives
Have students review their Chapter Goals and Self-Check worksheet found on page PA 6 of the Classroom Resource Binder. They can check off the goal they have reached. Note that each section of the quiz corresponds to a Learning Objective.

Group Activity
Summary: Students discuss a world problem and ways to bring it to the attention of the United Nations, along with a list of questions for UN representatives.

Materials: newspaper and magazine articles

Procedure: Organize students into three groups. Have each group search newspapers or magazines for an article focusing on a world problem that the United Nations can act on. Students discuss how to bring the problem to the attention of the United Nations. Suggest that they consider writing a letter or holding a rally. Group members then write a list of questions to present to the United Nations. Some questions might be, *How do you intend to resolve this issue?* or *When will you take action?*

Assessment: Use the Group Activity Rubric found on page *xiii* of this guide. Fill in the rubric with the following additional information. For this activity, students should have

- participated in finding an article about a current world problem.
- helped to create a list of questions for the UN.

RELATED MATERIALS See the Unit Overview page for related Globe Fearon books that can be used to enrich and extend the materials in the chapter.

Traditional Assessment

Chapter Quiz

The Chapter Quiz on page 443 of the Student Edition can be used as an open-book test, a closed-book test, or a homework assignment. Use the quiz to identify concepts in the chapter that students need to review. Chapter Tests can be found in the Classroom Resource Binder on pages 156–157. Workbook pages 97–100 can be used for additional practice.

Chapter Test

Use Chapter Tests A and B on pages 156–157 in the Classroom Resource Binder to further assess mastery of chapter concepts.

Additional Resources

Use the Resource Planner on page 165 of this guide to assign additional exercises from the Classroom Resource Binder.

Alternative Assessment

Student Interview

Write the following topic on the chalkboard: *The Cold War.* Ask:

• What was the Truman Doctrine?
• What countries were involved in the Berlin Airlift?
• Who was Joseph McCarthy? What effect did he have on life in the United States?
• What was *Sputnik?* What affect did *Sputnik* have on the space race?

Performance

Have students write and act out a scene in which one person is Joseph McCarthy and another is an American filmmaker accused of being a Communist during the McCarthy era. The filmmaker denies the accusation and denounces McCarthyism.

Unit Assessment

This is the last chapter in Unit 7, *The United States in Crisis*. To assess cumulative knowledge and provide standardized-test practice, administer the practice test on page 444 of the Student Edition and Unit 7 Cumulative Test, pages 158–159 of the Classroom Resource Binder. These tests are in multiple-choice format.

Unit 8 ► A Changing Society

CHAPTER 24

Changing Ways of Life
1945–1960

PORTFOLIO PROJECT	BUILDING YOUR SKILLS	GROUP ACTIVITY	TIMELINE
Booklet of Information	Reading a Graph	Creating a TV Ad	The Years After World War II

CHAPTER 25

The Struggle for Equality
1947–1965

PORTFOLIO PROJECT	VOICES FROM THE PAST	GROUP ACTIVITY	TIMELINE
A List of Heroes	Dr. Martin Luther King, Jr.	TV News Report	Working for Equal Rights

CHAPTER 26

A New Frontier and a Great Society
1960–1968

PORTFOLIO PROJECT	CONNECTING HISTORY AND...	GROUP ACTIVITY	TIMELINE
Comparison Chart	Science: The Space Race	Creating a Poster	The 1960s

RELATED MATERIALS

These are some of the Globe Fearon books that can be used to enrich and extend the material in this unit.

 Skills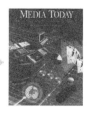

Media Today
Focus on evaluating print, audio, and visual media.

Cultural Diversity

Historical Case Studies: The Civil Rights Movement
Explore aspects of the civil rights movement in greater detail.

Skills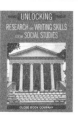

Unlocking Research and Writing Skills for Social Studies
Reinforce the writing process from choosing a topic to revising reports.

Chapter 24 • Changing Ways of Life 1945–1960

Chapter at a Glance

SE page

446   *Opening the Chapter and Portfolio Project*

448   SECTION 1   Progress and Change

454   *Building Your Skills: Reading a Graph*

455   SECTION 2   The Growth of Popular Culture

459   SECTION 3   Eisenhower as President

462   *Chapter Review and Group Activity*

Learning Objectives

- Explain how veterans were treated after World War II.
- Describe the economy after World War II.
- Describe how American life changed during the 1950s.
- Describe the growth of popular culture during the 1950s.
- Discuss the policies of President Eisenhower.

Social Studies Skills

- Identify how bar graphs give information.
- Use a timeline to identify events that occurred during the years after World War II.

Writing Skills

- Create a booklet that describes changes in the American lifestyle during the 1950s.
- Write a paragraph describing the streets, parks, and buildings that would make up a community.
- Explain in a paragraph why some people enjoy rock 'n' roll, while others do not.
- Write a paragraph about a world problem during the Eisenhower administration.
- Create a television ad to persuade viewers to buy a certain product.

Map and Chart Skills

- Use a chart to identify homes with television sets between 1950 and 1960.

**Chapter 24
Changing Ways of Life**

Use the Program Resources below for reteaching, reinforcement, and enrichment. Additional activities for customizing the lessons can be found in this guide.

Key
Reteaching = ⌢   Reinforcement = ↓   Enrichment = ⌢

Sections	Program Resources		
	Workbook Exercises	Teacher's Planning Guide	Classroom Resource Binder
Progress and Change	101	⌢ p. 174	
Building Your Skills: Reading a Graph		⌢ p. 175	⌢ Building Your Skills: *Reading Graphs,* 162, 163
The Growth of Popular Culture	102	⌢ p. 175	
Eisenhower as President	103, 104	⌢ p. 176	
Chapter 24 Review		p. 177	↓ Words to Know 160 ⌢ Challenge 164 ↓ Chapter Tests A & B, 165, 166

Chapter
24

Customizing the Chapter

Opening the Chapter
Student Edition, pages 446–447

Photo Activity
Discuss the photo of the frozen TV dinner first. Explain that in the postwar era, the American lifestyle began to change and people took advantage of time-saving conveniences, such as frozen TV dinners. Then direct students' attention to the photograph of Levittown, New York, a planned community that was built in the 1950s. Discuss the characteristics of this planned community and what life there might have been like. Have students brainstorm a list of advantages to living in a planned community. Then have them create a list of disadvantages.

Words to Know
Review the Words to Know on page 447 of the Student Edition. To help students remember the words, have pairs of students scan the chapter looking for the words. Ask them to draw a chart in their notebooks listing the words and their definitions.

The following words and definitions are covered in this chapter:

automation the use of machines to do jobs once done by people

service industry a business that provides a service for others

baby boom a large increase in births, especially in the United States after World War II

suburb a community at the edge of a city

consumer a person who buys and uses products

generation gap a large difference in taste and values between young people and their parents

recession a period of time when the economy slows down

interstate highway system a network of roads built and cared for by the U.S. government

Portfolio Project

Summary: Students create a booklet depicting what life was like during the 1950s.

Materials: posterboard; markers

Procedure: As students read the chapter, ask them to take notes about life during the 1950s. Students include in their notes information about television, music, advances in medicine, and changes in the way people worked and lived. Students make booklets that provide information about lifestyle changes in the 1950s.

Assessment: Use the Individual Activity Rubric on page *xii* of this guide. Fill in the rubric with the additional information below. For this project students should have

• made a booklet of scenes of life in the 1950s.

• written accurate information for the booklet.

Learning Objectives

Review the Learning Objectives on page 447 of the Student Edition before starting the chapter. Students can use the list as a learning guide. Suggest that they write the objectives in a journal or use the Chapter Goals and Self-Check worksheet found on page PA 6 of the Classroom Resource Binder.

After reading each section of the chapter, have students write an example of what they learned under the appropriate objective. Suggest that students use these worksheets as a practice guide to help them study for the chapter test.

Timeline

Use the timeline to discuss the sequence of events in this chapter. Point out the timeline's title, its time span, and the intervals. After students have read the chapter, have them review the timeline and suggest additional entries.

SECTION 1: Progress and Change
Student Edition, pages 448–453

Section Objectives

* Explain how the GI Bill of Rights helped veterans.

* Describe how the economy grew after World War II.

* Describe changes in family life, health care, and work after World War II.

Words to Know

automation, service industry, baby boom, suburb

Cooperative Group Activity

Changing Times Outline

Materials: reference materials (Unit 8 Bibliography, pages 236–240); Main Idea and Details chart (Classroom Resource Binder, page GO 5); index cards

Procedure: Explain to students that after World War II, the United States changed in many ways. As the economy grew, Americans found new kinds of work, new places to live, and new ways of doing things. Organize students into five groups. Assign each group one of the following research topics: *how veterans were helped after the war; the growth of the U.S. economy; new kinds of jobs; changes in family life;* or *changes in health care.* Each group will create an outline for a report. Distribute a Main Ideas and Details chart to each group and review how an outline works.

• Each group member writes two statements on index cards that he or she thinks are the two most important facts that support the group's topic.

• Group members combine their ideas and decide which ones belong in the outline.

• One group member writes the outline.

• Another group member presents the outline to the class.

Customizing the Activity for Individual Needs

ESL To help students understand the changing ways of life in the United States after the war, have them write all words they did not understand on index cards. Students look up unfamiliar words in a dictionary and write the definitions next to the word. On the other side of the index card, students make up sentences containing their new vocabulary words.

Learning Styles Students can:

 complete a Description Web (Classroom Resource Binder, page GO 31) with information about the changes in American life during the 1950s.

 draw a labeled illustration showing how the United States changed after the war.

 work with a partner to perform a radio commercial from the 1950s encouraging families to buy a home in a new housing development in a suburb.

Reinforcement Activity

Distribute two index cards to all students. Students will write a question about changes in the United States after World War II on each card. Then have students exchange cards with a partner. Students answer the questions on the back of the index card.

Alternative Assessment

Students can create a chart that outlines the changes that occurred in the U.S. as the economy grew during the 1950s.

BUILDING YOUR SKILLS:
Reading a Graph
Student Edition, page 454

Objectives
- Social Studies Skill: Compare the number of passenger cars sold in 1940 with the number sold in 1950.
- Social Studies Skill: Compare the price of eggs in 1940 with the price of eggs in 1950.
- Social Studies Skill: Compare the population of the United States in 1930, 1940, and 1950.

Activities
Comparing Passenger Car Sales
Material: graph paper

Procedure: Have students make a bar graph comparing U.S. car sales in 1940 with car sale in 1950. Tell students that in 1940, more than 3.7 million passenger cars were sold in the United States. By 1950, the number of cars sold jumped to 6.6 million. Ask students to make a graph with two bars that reflects this information.

Graphing the Price of Eggs
Material: graph paper

Procedure: Have students make a bar graph comparing the price of eggs in 1940 with the price of eggs in 1950. Tell students that in 1940, a dozen eggs cost 33 cents. By 1950, the price of a dozen eggs had jumped to 72 cents. Ask them to make a graph with two bars that reflects this information.

Population Graph
Material: graph paper

Procedure: Have students make a bar graph comparing the population of the United States in 1930, 1940, and 1950. Tell students that in 1930, there were 123.1 million Americans. In 1940, there were 131.7 million Americans. By 1950, there were 151.3 million Americans. Ask them to make a graph with three bars that reflects this information.

Practice

Have students complete Building Your Skills: Reading A Graph on page 162 of the Classroom Resource Binder.

SECTION 2: The Growth of Popular Culture
Student Edition, pages 455–458

Section Objectives
- Describe how the United States became a society of consumers and how this affected the media.
- Explain how rock 'n' roll helped to create a generation gap.
- Identify ways in which television changed Americans' lives.

Words to Know
consumer, generation gap

Cooperative Group Activity

A Documentary About TV
Materials: video recorder; photos; colored markers; construction paper

Procedure: Explain to students that during the 1950s, television began to change the lives of Americans, affecting family life, politics, and the economy of the nation. Organize students into three groups to write a TV documentary that outlines how television affected the American family, the nation's economy, and politics during the 1950s.

- Group members review information and take notes about ways in which TV affected family life, politics, and the American economy.
- Students write a script of their documentary and provide photos and illustrations for the TV audience.
- The TV script should be well-organized so that the TV audience's attention is captured. Students decide how to make it interesting and where to use photos to illustrate a point.
- Students determine where and when to "zoom" in with the camera.
- One group member, a teacher, or other adult, tapes the TV documentary after group members practice their presentation. Group members take turns reading, or speaking their memorized script, to the class.

Customizing the Activity for Individual Needs

ESL To help students understand how television affected American life discuss how families spent more of their leisure time around the television. Ask students how their families spend their leisure time.

Learning Styles Students can:

 look at advertisements for a 1950s television set and a present-day television set and compare the differences between them.

 create an advertisement for a 1950s television set.

 work with a partner to discuss how TV affected the way Americans viewed candidates for political office.

Enrichment Activity

Remind students that during the 1950s, adults and children spent many hours watching television. Television is still very much a part of American life today. Have students list the pros and cons of television viewing. Have students create a chart using their information.

Alternative Assessment

Students can write two journal entries to discuss how television affects people's lives. One entry will be written from the perspective of an American teenager from the 1950s, and another from the perspective of a political candidate.

Section Objectives

- Explain how the interstate highway system changed the way people lived.
- Describe President Eisenhower's foreign and domestic policies for the United States in the 1950s.

Words to Know

recession, interstate highway system

Cooperative Group Activity

Polling the Population

Materials: reference materials (Unit 8 Bibliography, and Internet sites, pages 236–240)

Procedure: Review that in 1952, Dwight D. Eisenhower was elected President of the United States. Organize students into three groups. Each group creates a questionnaire to find out how Americans feel about Dwight D. Eisenhower in the year 1955. Point out that polls ask for people's opinions.

- Group members create five questions about each of the following topics: *Eisenhower's policies at home, the interstate highway system,* and *Eisenhower's foreign policy.*
- Group members write their questions on a separate sheet of paper and ask at least five class members to answer their questions. They share the results.

Customizing the Activity for Individual Needs

ESL To help students understand the difference between domestic and foreign policy, have ESL students work with English-proficient students to complete a *Who, What, Where, When, Why, How* chart (Classroom Resource Binder, Page GO 7) about events at home and in the world during the Eisenhower administration.

Learning Styles Students can:

 complete a Cause and Effect chart (Classroom Resource Binder, page GO 2) about the effect the interstate highway system had on the U.S. economy.

work in groups to cast ballots for or against the following Eisenhower issues: *controlling government spending; building public housing;* and *creating the interstate highway system.* Have students collect, tally, and analyze the votes.

 explain to a partner President Eisenhower's plan to end the U.S. recession during his second term in office.

Enrichment Activity

Have students examine current magazines and newspapers to find articles focusing on issues that are of concern to our national leaders, such as the national tax reform issue. Have students make a list of issues or actions that fall under U.S. domestic policy and those that can be categorized as U.S. foreign policy. Have students share their lists with the class.

Alternative Assessment

Students can write five true/false questions about changes in the United States after World War II. Students then exchange papers and answer each other's questions.

Closing the Chapter
Student Edition, pages 462–463

Chapter Vocabulary

Review with students the Words to Know on page 447 of the Student Edition. Then have them complete the Vocabulary Review on page 462 of the Student Edition by completing each sentence with a term from the list.

For more vocabulary practice, have them complete the vocabulary exercise on page 160 of the Classroom Resource Binder.

Test Tip

Have students scan the chapter to find words or phrases that contrast ideas, such as *although,* *however, while,* and *but.* Encourage students to list contrasting ideas or information they find in the chapter, and review these for the test.

Learning Objectives

Have the students review their Chapter Goals and Self-Check worksheet found on page PA 6 of the Classroom Resource Binder. They can check off the goal they have reached. Note that each section of the quiz corresponds to a Learning Objective.

Group Activity

Summary: Students analyze current TV ads, then create an ad based on a favorite product and present the ad to the class.

Materials: colored markers; construction paper

Procedure: Organize students into four groups to discuss some ways in which television ads influence consumers to buy a product. Group members list their ideas on paper and discuss whether these ads accurately reflect the value or purpose of products. Groups then create an advertisement of their own, based on a current product they like. Students write the copy for the ad and provide visuals to accompany the text. Groups present their ads to the class.

Assessment: Use the Group Activity Rubric found on page *xiii* of this guide. Fill in the rubric with the following additional information. For this activity, students should have

- participated in analyzing TV ads.
- developed a TV advertisement for a current product.

RELATED MATERIALS   See the Unit Overview page for related Globe Fearon books that can be used to enrich and extend the materials in the chapter.

Chapter 24

Traditional Assessment

Chapter Quiz

The Chapter Quiz on page 463 of the Student Edition can be used as an open-book test, a closed-book test, or a homework assignment. Use the quiz to identify concepts in the chapter that students need to review. Chapter Tests can be found in the Classroom Resource Binder on pages 165–166. Workbook pages 101–104 can be used for additional practice.

Chapter Tests

Use Chapter Tests A and B on pages 165–166 in the Classroom Resource Binder to further assess mastery of chapter concepts.

Additional Resources

Use the Resource Planner on page 173 of this guide to assign additional exercises from the Classroom Resource Binder.

Alternative Assessment

Presentation

Students scan the chapter and list changes in American family life, in the American economy, and in American society/culture between 1945 and 1960. Students use this information to create a three-column chart listing each change. They present their charts to the class and explain what the charts mean.

Student Interview

Write the following on the chalkboard: *Television Changes American Life.* Ask:

- What did Americans do for entertainment before television?
- How did television change American politics?
- How did television change they way Americans spent their leisure time?

Chapter 25 · **The Struggle for Equality** 1947–1965

Chapter at a Glance

SE page

464   *Opening the Chapter and Portfolio Project*

466   SECTION 1   Early Gains for Equal Rights

469   SECTION 2   Fighting for an Equal Education

474   SECTION 3   Protests and Marches for Equality

481   *Voices From the Past: Dr. Martin Luther King, Jr.*

482   *Chapter Review and Group Activity*

Learning Objectives

- Explain the importance of the integration of the armed forces.
- Discuss the Supreme Court decision in *Brown* vs. *Board of Education of Topeka*.
- Discuss the ways in which the federal government took steps to integrate southern schools.
- Identify the events that led to the passing of the Civil Rights Act of 1964.
- Explain how Americans used nonviolence to end segregation.

Social Studies Skills

- Explore the views of Dr. Martin Luther King, Jr. on social protest.
- Use a timeline to identify events that occurred during the struggle for equal rights.

Writing Skills

- Make a list identifying the accomplishments of civil rights heroes.
- Describe in a paragraph how the Supreme Court supported Southern segregation.
- Write a thank-you note describing how an important American made a difference in the lives of others.
- Write a poem describing a personal dream for a better world.
- Write a TV news report describing one event of the civil rights movement.

Map and Chart Skills

- Use a map to identify states that allowed and did not allow segregated schools.

Chapter
25

Resource Planner

Chapter 25
The Struggle for Equality

Use the Program Resources below for reteaching, reinforcement, and enrichment. Additional activities for customizing the lessons can be found in this guide.

Key
Reteaching = ⤾   Reinforcement = ⬇   Enrichment = ⤿

Sections	Program Resources		
	⬇ **Workbook Exercises**	**Teacher's Planning Guide**	**Classroom Resource Binder**
Early Gains for Equal Rights	105	⬇ p. 181	⤿ Geography and Economics 8 *School Segregation and Integration*
Fighting for an Equal Education	106, 107	⤾ p. 182	
Protests and Marches for Equality	108	⤾ p. 183	⤿ Outline Map 1 *United States: Political* Transparency 12 *United States: Political*
Voices From the Past: Dr. Martin Luther King, Jr.		⤾ p. 184	⤾ Feature Practice *Voices From the Past: Rosa Parks* 169
Chapter 25 Review		p. 184	⬇ Words to Know 167 ⤾ Challenge 170 ⬇ Chapter Tests A & B, 171, 172

Customizing the Chapter

Opening the Chapter
Student Edition, pages 464–465

Photo Activity

Direct students' attention to the photo of Dr. Martin Luther King, Jr. at the civil rights march on Washington, D.C., in 1963. Mention that he gave his famous "I Have a Dream" speech during this march. Ask students to read the sign in the right corner that tells one goal of the march on Washington. Have students work in groups to complete a KWL chart (Classroom Resource Binder page GO 6) about the March on Washington and Dr. Martin Luther King, Jr. Students can complete the *Know* and *Want to Know* sections of the chart based on the photo. As they read the chapter, ask them to complete the last column of the chart.

Words to Know

Review the Words to Know on page 465 of the Student Edition. To help students remember the words, invite pairs to find the words in the Glossary in the Student Edition. Have them take turns giving clues that tell about a word, without using any part of the word itself. Ask each pair of students to keep track of the number of clues it takes to guess each key word.

The following words and definitions are covered in this chapter:

integrate to open to people of all backgrounds; to bring together

executive order a rule made by the President

appeal to ask a higher court to review the decision of a lower court

desegregate to end segregation, or separation of the races

boycott a nonviolent protest in which people refuse to buy products or use services

sit-in a nonviolent protest in which people sit down and refuse to get up

civil disobedience a nonviolent refusal to obey laws or government demands in order to cause change

Portfolio Project

Summary: Students make an alphabetical list of heroes in the civil rights movement and their accomplishments.

Procedure: As students read the chapter, ask them to write down the names of people who made a difference in the lives of others during the civil rights movement. Next to each name, students write at least one action or contribution of this individual to the struggle for equal rights. After compiling their lists, students arrange the entries in alphabetical order.

Assessment: Use the Individual Activity Rubric on page *xii* of this guide. Fill in the rubric with the additional information below. For this project, students should have

• made a list of heroes of the civil rights movement.

• arranged entries in alphabetical order.

Learning Objectives

Review the Learning Objectives on page 465 of the Student Edition before starting the chapter. Students can use the list as a learning guide. Suggest that they write the objectives in a journal or use the Chapter Goals and Self-Check worksheet found on page PA 6 of the Classroom Resource Binder.

After reading each section of the chapter, have students write an example of what they learned under the appropriate objective. Suggest that students use these worksheets as a practice guide to help them study for the chapter test.

Timeline

Use the timeline to discuss the sequence of events in this chapter. Point out the timeline's title, its time span, and the intervals. After students have read the chapter, have them review the timeline and suggest additional entries.

SECTION 1: Early Gains for Equal Rights *Student Edition, pages 466–468*

Section Objectives

• Describe the segregation that African Americans faced in the North and the South.

• Explain how President Truman's executive order integrated the armed forces.

* Explain how integration was accomplished in sports and entertainment.

Words to Know

integrate, executive order

Cooperative Group Activity

Breaking Through the Barrier

Materials: reference materials (Unit 8 Bibliography and Internet sites, pages 236–240)

Procedure: Organize students into groups to write biographical sketches. Have students do additional research on the early years of the civil rights movement.

• Group members research and take notes about African Americans who broke the barrier of segregation, such as Jackie Robinson and Benjamin Davis, Jr.

• Group members combine their notes to write a two- or three-page biographical sketch. The sketch should include basic information about the person plus the contribution he or she made.

• Group members choose a spokesperson to read the sketch to the class.

Customizing the Activity for Individual Needs

ESL To help students understand the concept of integration discuss what *color barrier* means. Have students describe the kinds of social barriers that may exist in their native countries.

Learning Styles   Students can:

 complete a Main Idea and Details chart (Classroom Resource Binder, page G0 5) with information about early gains for equal rights.

 create a postage stamp that shows the integration of the armed forces in 1948.

 prepare a short speech that Jackie Robinson might have given when he became the first African American elected to the Baseball Hall of Fame.

Reinforcement Activity

Have students assume the role of civil rights activists living during the post-war era. Invite them to brainstorm ways that they could promote equality and affect change. Using chart paper and markers, have them list their recommendations.

Alternative Assessment

Students can make a chart with the title: *Early Gains for Equal Rights*. They divide the chart into three sections: *Segregation in the North and the South; Integrating the Armed Forces;* and *Integrating Sports and Entertainment*. Students fill in the chart with facts about each topic.

SECTION 2: Fighting for an Equal Education
Student Edition, pages 469–473

Section Objectives
* Explain how the federal government helped desegregate Central High School, in Little Rock, Arkansas.
* Describe the *Brown* vs. *Board of Education of Topeka* decision in the Supreme Court.
* Explain how schools for African Americans and white Americans in the South were unequal.

Words to Know
appeal, desegregate

Cooperative Group Activity

Closing Arguments
Materials: reference materials (Unit 8 Bibliography and Internet sites, pages 236–240)

Procedure: Remind students that Thurgood Marshall led the legal fight to integrate schools. Organize students into groups of three or four to write closing arguments for Marshall's case to the Supreme Court. Students may wish to do additional research on Marshall and the fight to end segregation.

* Students review and research information about Thurgood Marshall's role in ending segregation in the schools.
* Using their information, students prepare a closing argument that Thurgood Marshall might have delivered to the Supreme Court for the *Brown* vs. *Board of Education of Topeka* case. Point out that a closing argument is a persuasive speech based on facts.
* Group members include the following topics in their closing arguments: *why the idea of "separate but equal" does not work* and *why schools must desegregate.*
* Group members write their closing arguments and choose a spokesperson to deliver it to the class.

Customizing the Activity for Individual Needs
ESL   To help students understand the meaning of closing arguments, explain how the legal system works in the courts of the United States. Ask about the courts in their native country.

Learning Styles   Students can:

 look at photos of the Little Rock Nine and tell a story about them based on the photos.

 sort index cards with facts about the fight for equal schools into chronological order.

 tell a partner why the idea of "separate but equal" is unfair to children.

Enrichment Activity

The African American students at Central High School, who were known as the Little Rock Nine, were considered heroes by may people. Have students consider how they would have felt and reacted if they were in the same situation as the Little Rock Nine. Have students write a rap or song about the Little Rock Nine that reflects their courageous efforts to integrate Central High School and set an example for all young people in the United States.

Alternative Assessment

Students can answer the following questions about African Americans' fight for equal education:

- What were some reasons why African American parents wanted their children to go to the same schools as white children?
- What happened in *Brown* vs. *the Board of Education of Topeka ?*

SECTION 3: Protests and Marches for Equality
Student Edition, pages 474–480

Section Objectives

- Describe the Montgomery bus boycott and Rosa Parks's role.
- Explain why sit-ins took place in the South.
- Describe what the Freedom Riders hoped to change by using civil disobedience.
- Describe the purpose of the march on Washington.
- Describe Freedom Summer and how it relates to the Voting Rights Act of 1965.
- * Explain how civil rights leaders used nonviolent forms of protest.

Words to Know

boycott, sit-in, civil disobedience

Cooperative Group Activity

Writing for a Cause

Materials: reference materials (Unit 8 Bibliography and Internet sites, pages 236–240)

Procedure: Explain to students that during the 1950s and 1960s, many African Americans and others took part in nonviolent, or peaceful, protests. They participated in these protests to change laws and gain equal rights for all Americans. Organize students into five groups to write news articles. Review the *who, what, where, when,* and *why* questions of a news article. Then assign one of the following topics to each group: *the Montgomery bus boycott, sit-ins across the South, the Freedom Riders, the march on Washington,* and *registering African Americans to vote.*

Students may wish to do additional research on their topic.

- Some group members write the articles.

- Other group members illustrate their newspaper article with political cartoons or sketches.
- Other members choose a headline for their article.
- One group member inputs the article on the computer.
- Group members choose a spokesperson to present their article to the class. Groups then compile their articles into a newspaper about civil rights.

Customizing the Activity for Individual Needs

ESL To help students understand the concept of nonviolent protest, have them write the terms *boycott, sit-in,* and *civil disobedience* on index cards. On the reverse side, have students list situations in which it would be appropriate to use that form of nonviolent protest.

Learning Styles Students can:

 highlight important words in the news article.

 design a poster that encourages people to use nonviolent means of protest in the civil rights movement.

 prepare a radio announcement that urges people to use nonviolent protests to gain equal rights.

Reteaching Activity

Have students reread the section and take notes on the Montgomery bus boycott, sit-ins across the South, the Freedom Riders, protests in Birmingham, the march on Washington, and Freedom Summer. Students then use their notes to complete a Sequence of Events chart (Classroom Resource Binder, page G0 1) about nonviolent protests during the civil rights movement in the 1950s and 1960s.

Alternative Assessment

Students can create 10 multiple-choice statements on index cards using pertinent information from the section. When they have completed the questions, have them write the answers on the reverse side.

**Chapter
25**

VOICES FROM THE PAST:
Dr. Martin Luther King, Jr.
Student Edition, page 481

Objectives
- Social Studies Skill: Discuss equal rights and describe a right that is worth fighting for.
- Social Studies Skill: Identify injustices that currently exist in the world today.
- Social Studies Skill: Analyze Dr. King's "I Have a Dream" speech in order to write a similar speech that promotes civil rights, equality, and justice.

Activities
Something Worth Fighting For
Procedure: Remind students that Dr. King devoted his life to fighting for civil rights. Pair students and have them take turns answering the following question: *What is a right that you would fight for if someone tried to take it away?* As one student is talking, have the other write down his or her response. Reconvene the class and invite volunteers to share their answers with the class.

If I Could Change the World
Materials: chart paper; marker

Procedure: Have students brainstorm a list of injustices that exist in today's society. Examples include discrimination in the workplace, racism, and religious intolerance. Pair students and have them write a poem or paragraph, beginning with the words, *"If I Could Change the World, I would..."*

I Have a Dream
Materials: copies of Dr. King's "I Have a Dream" speech

Procedure: Have students take turns reading aloud each section of Dr. King's "I Have a Dream" speech. After each section, invite volunteers to talk about what his words meant. Then, ask students to write their own speech that promotes civil rights, equality, and justice.

Practice
Have students complete Voices From the Past: Rosa Parks on page 169 of the Classroom Resource Binder.

Closing the Chapter
Student Edition, pages 482–483

Chapter Vocabulary
Review with students the Words to Know on page 465 of the Student Edition. Then have them complete the Vocabulary Review on page 482 of the Student Edition, by completing each sentence with a term from the list.

For more vocabulary practice, have them complete the vocabulary exercise on page 167 of the Classroom Resource Binder.

Test Tip
Have students review Chapter 25 and write out the names of people and events. Have them practice spelling these names several times. When they are done, give them a short spelling quiz, using the names in the chapter. Then have them look back through the chapter to see if they spelled the names correctly.

Learning Objectives
Have students review their Chapter Goals and Self-Check worksheet found on page PA 6 of the Classroom Resource Binder. They can check off the goal they have reached. Note that each section of the quiz corresponds to a Learning Objective.

Group Activity
Materials: index cards

Summary: Students prepare and present a TV news report based upon an important event described in this chapter.

Procedure: Organize students in pairs and have them reread information about the civil rights movement. Students then choose one event of the civil rights movement and prepare a TV news report about it. They write pertinent information about their event on index cards and deliver their TV reports orally to the class. One student in each pair acts as a reporter at the scene of the event, while the other student acts as a news commentator to deliver a summary of the report.

Assessment: Use the Group Activity Rubric found on page *xiii* of this guide. Fill in the rubric with the following additional information. For this activity, students should have

- prepared an accurate news report on the civil rights movement.
- presented the report orally to the class.

RELATED MATERIALS   See the Unit Overview page for related Globe Fearon books that can be used to enrich and extend the materials in the chapter.

Assessing the Chapter

Traditional Assessment

Chapter Quiz
The Chapter Quiz on page 483 of the Student Edition can be used as an open-book test, a closed-book test, or a homework assignment. Use the quiz to identify concepts in the chapter that students need to review. Chapter Tests can be found in the Classroom Resource Binder on pages 171–172. Workbook pages 105–108 can be used for additional practice.

Chapter Tests
Use Chapter Tests A and B on pages 171–172 in the Classroom Resource Binder to further assess mastery of chapter concepts.

Additional Resources
Use the Resource Planner on page 180 of this guide to assign additional exercises from the Classroom Resource Binder and Workbook.

Alternative Assessment

Real-Life Connection
- Students review events of the civil rights movement in the 1950s and 1960s.
- Students then create a list of modern-day civil rights concerns.

Performance
Have students review information about the 1963 march on Washington. Students then prepare a speech that highlights the reasons for the march and the expectations that resulted from it. Students present their speech to the class.

Chapter
25

Chapter 26 · A New Frontier and a Great Society 1960–1968

Chapter at a Glance

SE page

484   *Opening the Chapter and Portfolio Project*

486   SECTION 1   The New Frontier

491   *Connecting History and Science: The Space Race*

492   SECTION 2   Kennedy's Foreign Policy

496   SECTION 3   President Johnson and the Great Society

500   *Chapter Review and Group Activity*

Learning Objectives

- Describe the goals and programs of President Kennedy's New Frontier.
- Discuss U.S. relations with Cuba and the Soviet Union during the 1960s.
- Describe President Kennedy's assassination and the reactions of the American people.
- Describe the goals and programs of President Johnson's Great Society.

Social Studies Skills

- Explore the role of the United States in the space race.
- Use a timeline to identify events that occurred during the 1960s.
- Compare and contrast Kennedy's New Frontier and the programs of Johnson's Great Society.

Writing Skills

- Explain "what you can do for your country," based on Kennedy's speech to the American people.
- Write a paragraph describing feelings about the building of the Berlin Wall based on the perspective of someone living in East Berlin in 1961.
- Identify three things that you think government money should be used for today.
- Create a poster about the space program.

Map and Chart Skills

- Use a map to identify the states that voted for either Kennedy or Nixon during the 1960 presidential election.
- Use a chart to analyze federal funding for public schools between 1960 and 1970.

**Chapter 26
A New Frontier and
a Great Society**

Use the Program Resources below for reteaching, reinforcement, and enrichment. Additional activities for customizing the lessons can be found in this guide.

Key
Reteaching = ⌒   Reinforcement = ↓   Enrichment = ⌒

Sections	Program Resources		
	↓ Workbook Exercises	Teacher's Planning Guide	Classroom Resource Binder
The New Frontier	109, 110	↓ p. 188	
Connecting History and Science: The Space Race		⌒ p. 189	⌒ Feature Practice 175 Connecting History and Science: *John Glenn, Space Pioneer*
Kennedy's Foreign Policy	111	⌒ p. 190	⌒ Transparency 16 *Regions of the United States* Outline Map 4 *The World*
President Johnson and the Great Society	112	⌒ p. 190	
Chapter 26 Review		p. 191	↓ Words to Know 173 ⌒ Challenge 176 ↓ Chapter Tests A & B, 177, 178 ↓ Unit Test Parts I & II, 179, 180

Customizing the Chapter

Opening the Chapter
Student Edition, pages 484–485

Photo Activity

Discuss the photo of President Kennedy giving a speech to the American people as he took office in 1961. Also point out the campaign button featuring John F. Kennedy and his running mate, Lyndon B. Johnson. Ask students to observe the following: *who* was there (Vice President Johnson, Ladybird Johnson, Jacqueline Kennedy, various members of Congress, and other members of government); *what* was happening (President Kennedy was giving his inaugural address, the rest were listening); *when* it took place (in the winter of 1961, everyone is warmly dressed); *where* (Washington, D.C.); *why* (Kennedy was being sworn in as President of the United States). On the chalkboard, draw a chart with the five questions as headings. Ask individual students to come up and fill in the chart.

Chapter 26

Words to Know

Review the Words to Know on page 485 of the Student Edition. To help students remember the words, have each student create a chart with two headings: *Word and Meaning*. Have students scan the chapter to write each vocabulary word on their chart. Students can look up the definition in the Glossary in the Student Edition and write it on the chart.

The following words and definitions are covered in this chapter:

New Frontier President Kennedy's ideas, goals, and programs for America's future

urban renewal a program to rebuild run-down areas of cities

exile a person who lives away from his or her home country

quarantine to isolate, or cut off, from other countries

Great Society President Johnson's ideas, goals, and programs for America's future

Medicare medical insurance and hospital care for older Americans

Medicaid medical insurance for low-income people and people with disabilities

Portfolio Project

Summary: On a chart, students compare and contrast the programs that were initiated by Presidents Kennedy and Johnson.

Procedure: As students read the chapter, they take notes about the programs initiated by President Kennedy and President Johnson during their terms in office. After students have completed the chapter, they each create a chart comparing and contrasting the programs of both presidents.

Assessment: Use the Individual Activity Rubric on page *xii* of this guide. Fill in the rubric with the additional information below. For this project, students should have

- listed Kennedy's and Johnson's programs.
- made a comparison and contrast chart.

Learning Objectives

Review the Learning Objectives on page 485 of the Student Edition before starting the chapter. Students can use the list as a learning guide. Suggest that they write the objectives in a journal or use the Chapter Goals and Self-Check worksheet found on page PA 6 of the Classroom Resource Binder.

After reading each section of the chapter, have students write an example of what they learned under the appropriate objective. Suggest that students use these worksheets as a practice guide to help them study for the chapter test.

Timeline

Use the timeline to discuss the sequence of events in this chapter. Point out the timeline's title, its time span, and the intervals. After students have read the chapter, have them review the timeline and suggest additional entries.

SECTION 1: The New Frontier
Student Edition, pages 486–490

Section Objectives

- Identify presidential candidates in the election of 1960.
- Relate the campaign promises of 1960 to the American public.
- Discuss the television debates in 1960.
- Describe the accomplishments of President Kennedy.

Words to Know

New Frontier, urban renewal

Cooperative Group Activity

Making Headlines

Materials: reference materials (Unit 8 Bibliography and Internet sites, pages 236–240)

Procedure: Remind students that Kennedy's vision of America as a New Frontier included support for civil rights, laws to protect the environment, and programs to help urban areas. Have students form groups of three or four to write newspaper headlines. You may wish to have students conduct further research on the Kennedy presidency for this activity.

- Group members brainstorm a list of ten newspaper headlines from the 1960s about Kennedy's campaign and his subsequent actions as U.S. President. Examples: *Kennedy Debates His Way to Victory! Kennedy and Congress Don't See Eye to Eye.*

- Group members choose their top ten headlines and share them with the class. If appropriate, they display them on a bulletin board.

- Students discuss how each headline relates to Kennedy's vision of the United States as a New Frontier.

Customizing the Activity for Individual Needs

ESL To help students understand the vocabulary term *New Frontier,* have ESL students work with English-proficient students to discuss some new frontiers that they have experienced in their own lives, such as coming to a new country. Then have students share some of their hopes about the new frontiers they faced.

Learning Styles Students can:

 look at photos from the 1960 presidential debates and describe why more people liked Kennedy after watching the debate.

 write simple questions on index cards that begin with *Who, What, When, Where, Why,* and *How.* They sort the cards and ask classmates to answer the questions.

 explain the meaning of each headline to a partner.

Reinforcement Activity ⇓

Have students create a Description Web (Classroom Resource Binder, page G0 3) that lists information about the Kennedy years, including accomplishments and disappointments that Kennedy experienced during his term in office. Have students title their Description Web *The Kennedy Years.*

Alternative Assessment

Students can answer the following question: *What were Kennedy's and Johnson's ideas, goals, and plans for the country?*

Answer: Kennedy and Johnson both supported urban renewal, civil rights, and volunteer programs.

CONNECTING HISTORY AND SCIENCE: The Space Race
Student Edition, page 491

Objectives
- Social Studies Skill: Describe Neil Armstrong's quote as he took his first step on the moon.
- Social Studies Skill: Draw a diagram of a space station where Americans might live and work.

- Social Studies Skill: Write a short illustrated biography that identifies astronauts in the U.S. space program.

Activities
One Small Step
Material: journal

Procedure: Have students write in their journals the following quote by Neil Armstrong: "That's one small step for a man, one giant leap for mankind." Then, ask students to write a journal entry that describes what Armstrong might have seen, felt, and thought as he took his first step onto the moon. Have students explain why the quote has had such a lasting impact.

A Space Station
Materials: construction paper; colored pencils or markers

Procedure: Explain to students that the U.S. government continues to support funding of the space program with the hopes that at some time in the future, American citizens might be able to live on the moon and elsewhere in space. Ask students to draw a diagram of what a futuristic space station might look like, including work stations, leisure areas, science labs, and equipment areas, as well as living quarters. Have students label their diagrams.

Astronauts in Space
Materials: markers

Procedure: Have students research three astronauts who participated in the U.S. space program. Then, have students work on illustrated entries for *Who's Who in America* that includes information about the astronauts' lives and accomplishments.

Practice
Have students complete Connecting History and Science: John Glenn, Space Pioneer on page 175 of the Classroom Resource Binder.

SECTION 2: Kennedy's Foreign Policy
Student Edition, pages 492–495

Section Objectives
* Describe the Bay of Pigs crisis.
* Explain why the Berlin Wall was built.
* Describe the Cuban Missile Crisis.
* Describe events in Dallas that led to President Kennedy's death.
* Describe the relationship between the United States and the Soviet Union during the Kennedy administration.

Words to Know
exile, quarantine

Cooperative Group Activity

"Years of Peril" Panel Discussion

Materials: reference materials (Unit 8 Bibliography and Internet sites, pages 236–240)

Procedure: Remind students that during the 1960s there were many problems between the Soviet Union and the United States. You may wish to have students conduct additional research on the topic of Kennedy's foreign policy for this activity. Divide the class into two groups to prepare for a panel discussion. On the chalkboard list the following issues: *the growth of communism, the Bay of Pigs crisis, Nikita Khrushchev's demand that the Communists control all of Berlin,* and *the Soviet Union's decision to send missiles to Cuba.*

* Group members discuss and then list other ways in which the United States could have handled the above incidents.
* Both groups hold a panel discussion about the above issues. They select a moderator and determine the length of time each panelist may speak. It may be helpful if students assume the roles of cabinet advisers to President Kennedy during the panel discussion.
* One student on each panel lists its recommendations for handling each of the issues.

Customizing the Activity for Individual Needs
ESL To help students understand the spread of communism during Kennedy's administration, have partners complete a Cause and Effect chart (Classroom Resource Binder, page G0 2) with information about the Bay of Pigs invasion, the building of the Berlin Wall, and the Cuban Missile Crisis.

Learning Styles Students can:

 locate Cuba on a map. Then, using the map, have students explain why the United States would be concerned about communism in Cuba.

 role-play with a partner a scene between President Kennedy and Nikita Khrushchev in which they discuss the fate of Berlin.

 take turns assuming the role of President Kennedy announcing to Americans that Cuba is under quarantine.

Reteaching Activity

Have students list events leading to the building of the Berlin Wall. They then use their lists to write a short summary of the effect the building of the Berlin Wall had on the people of East and West Berlin as well as on relations between the United States and the Soviet Union.

Alternative Assessment

Students can list six facts about the Bay of Pigs invasion in 1961 on individual index cards. Then, ask students to use their cards to deliver a short oral report about the Bay of Pigs invasion to the class.

SECTION 3: President Johnson and the Great Society
Student Edition, pages 496–499

Section Objectives
* Describe President Johnson's actions regarding civil rights.
* Explain how Johnson decided to fight poverty in the United States.
* Describe health-care programs initiated by President Johnson.
* Describe Johnson's plan for the Great Society.

Words to Know
Great Society, Medicare, Medicaid

Cooperative Group Activity

"The Great Society" Biography
Materials: reference materials (Unit 8 Bibliography and Internet sites, pages 236–240)

Procedure: Remind students that, as President, Lyndon B. Johnson fought for civil rights and improvements in education and health care. Organize students into groups of three or four to make book jackets for a biography of Lyndon Johnson. Students may wish to do additional research on President Johnson and his policies for this activity.

- Group members research information about Lyndon Johnson and his policies.
- Some members use the research to write the book jacket copy for a biography about President Johnson titled *President Johnson and the Great Society.*
- Other group members create the book cover.
- Students incorporate information about President Johnson and his policies to write their synopsis about what might be in the book. Encourage students to use descriptive language to entice people to purchase the book.
- Group members choose a spokesperson to read their synopsis to the class. Display the book jackets.

Customizing the Activity for Individual Needs

ESL To help students reinforce the concept of the Great Society, have them work with English-proficient students to discuss their ideas of what a Great Society should be. Have them consider ideas from their native countries.

Learning Styles Students can:

 work in groups to create a chart that lists President Johnson's ideas, goals, and programs for the Great Society.

 organize all the book jackets in a display.

 work in pairs to take turns relating facts about Johnson's programs in health care, education, civil rights, and the war on poverty. One student chooses the topic while the other student relates a fact about the topic. Have students switch roles often.

Enrichment Activity

Have students create a plan for their own present-day Great Society including their ideas and goals for America's future, and ways to carry out their ideas. Students create a three-column chart, writing their ideas and goals in the first column, and the programs and organizations that will help carry out these ideas in the second column. In the third column, students list ways in which Americans will benefit.

Alternative Assessment

Students can list the programs that Lyndon Johnson initiated during his presidency on individual index cards. On the back of each card, students can list how each program related to Johnson's vision of the Great Society.

Closing the Chapter
Student Edition, pages 500–501

Chapter Vocabulary

Review with students the Words to Know on page 485 of the Student Edition. Then have them complete the Vocabulary Review on page 500 of the Student Edition, by determining if each statement is *true* or *false*. If the statement is false, have students change the underlined term to make it true.

For more vocabulary practice, have them complete the vocabulary exercise on page 173 in the Classroom Resource Binder.

Test Tip

Have students practice answering multiple-choice questions by having them review the chapter to write three questions using this format. Then, have pairs of students exchange questions and choose the correct answer for each question. Remind students to eliminate answers that they know are not correct.

Learning Objectives

Have students review their Chapter Goals and Self-Check worksheet found on page PA 6 of the Classroom Resource Binder. They can check off the goal they have reached. Note that each section of the quiz corresponds to a Learning Objective.

Group Activity

Summary: Students create posters about the space program, including famous astronauts, events that took place in space, and their ideas for future space exploration.

Materials: reference materials (Unit 8 Bibliography and Internet sites, pages 236–240); posterboard; markers

Procedure: You may wish to have students research information about the U.S. space program as well as the astronauts who have participated in it. Organize students into small groups and have them brainstorm ideas for creating a poster that can be used to teach other students about the space program. Encourage students to include pictures and words about the astronauts and events that occurred in space, as well as ideas about our future in space. Group members should assign themselves specific tasks for creating the poster. Have them give it a title. Groups choose a spokesperson to present and explain their posters to the class.

Assessment: Use the Group Activity Rubric found on page *xiii* of this guide. Fill in the rubric with the following additional information. For this activity, students should have

- created a poster that includes pictures and words based on the space program.
- titled the poster.

RELATED MATERIALS See the Unit Overview page for related Globe Fearon books that can be used to enrich and extend the materials in the chapter.

Assessing the Chapter

Traditional Assessment

Chapter Quiz
The Chapter Quiz on page 501 of the Student Edition can be used as an open-book test, a closed-book test, or a homework assignment. Use the quiz to identify concepts in the chapter that students need to review. Chapter Tests can be found in the Classroom Resource Binder on pages 177–178. Workbook pages 109–112 can be·used for additional practice.

Chapter Tests
Use Chapter Tests A and B on pages 177–178 in the Classroom Resource Binder to further assess mastery of chapter concepts.

Additional Resources
Use the Resource Planner on page 187 of this guide to assign additional exercises from the Classroom Resource Binder.

Alternative Assessment

Presentation
Have students present a scene to the class of the landing on the moon. Students role play the parts of Neil Armstrong, Buzz Aldrin, and Michael Collins. They should include the famous quote in their presentation and incorporate information about the landing as well as the expectations of the American people.

Journal
Have students write a journal entry that compares President Kennedy's vision of America as a New Frontier with President Johnson's vision of the nation as the Great Society.

Unit Assessment

This is the last chapter in Unit 8, *A Changing Society*. To assess cumulative knowledge and provide standardized-test practice, have students complete the Unit Review Test on page 502 of the Student Edition, and the Unit 8 Cumulative Test on pages 179–180 of the Classroom Resource Binder.

Unit 9 ▸ Years of Change

CHAPTER 27	PORTFOLIO PROJECT	BUILDING YOUR SKILLS	GROUP ACTIVITY	TIMELINE
Working for Change 1960–1975	A Flyer	Writing an Essay	Comparing and Contrasting	Challenges at Home

CHAPTER 28	PORTFOLIO PROJECT	VOICES FROM THE PAST	GROUP ACTIVITY	TIMELINE
The Vietnam War 1960–1973	A Survey	Protest Songs	Planning a Time Capsule	The United States in Vietnam

CHAPTER 29	PORTFOLIO PROJECT	CONNECTING HISTORY AND...	GROUP ACTIVITY	TIMELINE
Entering a New Decade 1970–1975	Bulletin Board Display	Economics: Inflation	Making a Chart	A Difficult Decade

RELATED MATERIALS

These are some of the Globe Fearon books that can be used to enrich and extend the material in this unit.

Content

Skills

Content

Fearon's Our Century 1960–1970
Explore the decade's history including the Kennedy years and the space race.

Active Learning in Social Studies
A high-interest worktext that reinforces basic skills.

Historical Case Studies: The Vietnam War
Provide an in-depth look at the Vietnam War.

Chapter 27 • **Working for Change** 1960–1975

Chapter at a Glance

SE page

504	*Opening the Chapter and Portfolio Project*
506	SECTION 1 African American Protests
511	*Building Your Skills: Writing an Essay*
512	SECTION 2 Women Demand Equality
516	SECTION 3 Rights for All Americans
520	Chapter *Review and Group Activity*

Learning Objectives

- Discuss the rise of the black power movement.
- Identify the causes and effects of riots in the cities during the mid–1960s.
- Discuss the steps women took to gain equal treatment.
- Describe the political and social gains of Latinos.
- Explain the struggle of Native Americans and Asian Americans to gain civil rights.

Social Studies Skills

- Use a timeline to identify events that occurred during the civil rights movement.
- Compare and contrast the goals of the different civil rights movements.

Writing Skills

- Create a protest sign describing reasons for engaging in a protest march.
- Write interview questions to ask Malcolm X.
- Write a paragraph explaining why the Equal Rights Amendment should be ratified.
- Write a brief essay describing how Latinos, Native Americans, and Asian Americans worked to gain their civil rights.

Map and Chart Skills

- Use a map to identify states that ratified the ERA.

Resource Planner

Chapter 27	Use the Program Resources below for reteaching, reinforcement, and
Working for Change	enrichment. Additional activities for customizing the lessons can be found in this guide.

Key
Reteaching = ⤺ Reinforcement = ⬇ Enrichment = ⤻

Sections	Program Resources		
	⬇ **Workbook Exercises**	**Teacher's Planning Guide**	**Classroom Resource Binder**
African American Protests	113	⤻ p. 196	⤻ Concept Builder 27 *Working For Change* ⤻ Geography and Economics 9 *Social Change* Outline Map 1 *United States: Political*
Building Your Skills: Writing an Essay		⤻ p. 197	⬇ Feature Practice 182, 183 *Writing an Essay* Writing and Test-Taking Tips 2 *Recognizing Key Words for an Essay Question* Graphic Organizer 5 *Main Idea and Supporting Details*
Women Demand Equality	114, 115	⬇ p. 198	⤻ Concept Builder 27 *Working For Change*
Rights for All Americans	116	⤺ p. 199	⤻ Concept Builder 27 *Working For Change*
Chapter 27 Review		p. 199	⬇ Words to Know 181 ⤻ Challenge ⬇ Chapter Tests A & B, 186,187

Opening the Chapter
Student Edition, pages 504–505

Photo Activity

Direct students' attention to the cover of *Ms.* magazine. Point out that the magazine was created to give women equal representation in the media. Then direct their attention to the photograph of the equality march. Mention that both women and men are marching for the same cause. Have students learn the cause by reading the banner displayed in the photo. Ask: *What does "women for racial and economic equality" mean?* List students' responses on the chalkboard. Ask students whether they think women have achieved these goals and how the students arrived at their answer.

Words to Know

Review the Words to Know on page 505 of the Student Edition. To help students remember the words, have them scan the chapter to find each bold faced word and the words or phrases that give clues about the word's meaning. Then, have students write what they believe to be the correct definition of each word. To check their answers, have them use the Glossary in the Student Edition.

The following words and definitions are covered in this chapter:

black power a movement among African Americans to gain political and economic power

Black Panther party a political party formed to work for the rights of African Americans

gender whether a person is male or female

feminism a political and social movement that favors equal rights for women

lobby to try to make lawmakers pass certain laws

bilingual able to speak two languages very well

life expectancy the number of years a person can expect to live

nisei second-generation Japanese Americans

Portfolio Project

Summary: Students create a protest sign that would be used in a march during the 1960s by writing a slogan or message that explains the reason for protesting.

Materials: posterboard; markers

Procedure: After students have read the chapter, have them choose a group that interests them.

Ask students to create a protest sign that they think members of the group might have carried at a protest march. Encourage them to make their message short and clear. You may wish to have students complete this project as a homework assignment.

Assessment: Use the Individual Activity Rubric on page *xii* of this guide. Fill in the rubric with the additional information below. For this project, students should have

- created a protest sign based on factual information.
- composed a clear and concise message.

Learning Objectives

Review the Learning Objectives on page 505 of the Student Edition before starting the chapter. Students can use the list as a learning guide. Suggest they write the objectives in a journal or use the Chapter Goals and Self-Check worksheet found on page PA 6 of the Classroom Resource Binder.

After reading each section of the chapter, have students write an example of what they learned under the appropriate objective. Suggest that students use these worksheets as a practice guide to help them study for the chapter test.

Timeline

Use the timeline to discuss the sequence of events in this chapter. Point out the timeline's title, its time span, and the intervals. After students have read the chapter, have them review the timeline and suggest additional entries.

SECTION 1: African American Protests
Student Edition, pages 506–510

Section Objectives

- Explain the concept of black power.
- Identify reasons why the Black Panther party was formed.
- Explain why riots broke out in cities during the 1960s.
- ∗ Explore the beliefs that many African Americans held about white society during the 1960s.
- ∗ Discuss the changes African Americans wanted to initiate.

Words to Know

black power, Black Panther party

Cooperative Group Activity

Differing Views on Civil Rights

Materials: reference materials (Unit 9 Bibliography and Internet sites, pages 236–240)

Procedure: Remind students that by 1964, many African Americans felt that changes in civil rights had progressed too slowly. Some leaders of the civil rights movement felt nonviolence was no longer the answer. Organize the students into seven groups to assume the role of newspaper journalists, reporting on the civil rights movement during the 1960s.

- Group members review information and conduct research to write a newspaper article about their topic.

- Each group will write a newspaper article on one of the following topics: *Dr. Martin Luther King, Jr., Malcolm X, James Meredith, Stokely Carmichael, black power, the Black Panther party,* or *riots.*

- Each group member writes a complete sentence to answer one of the following questions about the group's topic: *Who or what is the article about? What happened? When did it happen? Why did it happen?*

- Group members combine their sentences into a paragraph. They edit their articles.

- Group members think of a headline for their article, and choose a spokesperson to present the article to the class.

Customizing the Activity for Individual Needs

ESL To help students understand the concept of *black power,* ask them to think of ways people have power over their own lives. Examples might include having a good education, working at a job that you like, being able to voice your beliefs, and taking care of yourself and your family.

Learning Styles Students can:

 complete a Description Web (Classroom Resource Binder, page G0 3) using terms, phrases, and proper names from the civil rights movement of the 1960s.

 create an index card matching game by writing the names of civil rights leaders on one set of index cards and their achievements on a second set of index cards. Students can work in pairs to play their matching game.

 work with a partner to discuss the role of black power in the civil rights movement.

Enrichment Activity

Remind students that during the 1960s, the Black Panther party wanted more and better jobs for African Americans, better housing, better education, and an end to the unfair treatment by police. The Black Panthers said that black violence was the answer to white violence. Have students work in small groups to discuss how Dr. Martin Luther King, Jr. and Malcolm X might have responded to the beliefs and actions of the Black Panther party. Have students write a short speech from the perspective of both leaders. The speech should address their reactions to the Black Panthers' approach to gaining civil rights.

Alternative Assessment

Students can compose three questions about the fight for civil rights in the 1960s. Examples include: *What were the demands of the Black Panther party? Who was Malcolm X? What happened in Los Angeles in 1965?* Students exchange papers with a partner. They then answer the questions and work with their partners to verify answers.

BUILDING YOUR SKILLS:
Writing an Essay
Student Edition, page 511

Lesson Objectives

- Social Studies Skill: Write an essay about the civil rights movement that emphasizes the work of Dr. Martin Luther King, Jr. and his belief in achieving equality without violence.

- Social Studies Skill: Write an essay explaining why Malcolm X changed his views on separate societies for African Americans and white Americans.

- Social Studies Skill: Write an essay to be published in a newspaper that describes what remains to be accomplished in the area of civil rights.

Activities

Nonviolence Is the Way

Procedure: Invite students to write a one- to two-page essay that focuses on the work of Dr. Martin Luther King, Jr. Have students emphasize his beliefs about how to achieve civil rights through nonviolence.

Continued on Page 198

Chapter **27**

Continued from Page 197

Separate Societies

Procedure: Remind students that during the 1960s, some African Americans believed that they would be better off living separately from whites. Ask students to write an essay from the perspective of Malcolm X, explaining why he changed his views and realized people needed to live and work together.

Civil Rights Today

Procedure: Ask students to write a one-page essay that could be published on the editorial page of a newspaper about civil rights issues that remain to be addressed in today's society.

Practice

Have students complete Building Your Skills: Writing an Essay on page 183 of the Classroom Resource Binder.

SECTION 2: Women Demand Equality

Student Edition, pages 512–515

Section Objectives

- Compare how the Equal Pay Act of 1963 and the Civil Rights Act of 1964 helped women gain equal rights.
- Describe the Equal Rights Amendment and why it was dropped in 1982.
- Describe the goals of the National Organization for Women.

Words to Know

gender, feminism, lobby

Cooperative Group Activity

Support NOW... Now!

Materials: reference materials (Unit 9 Bibliography and Internet sites, pages 236–240); construction paper; markers

Procedure: Explain to students that the civil rights movement of the 1960s spread to other groups of people who felt that society treated them unfairly. American women began to demand equal treatment. Form small groups to create a pamphlet about the National Organization for Women (NOW) to engender support for women. Students may wish to conduct further research on this topic.

- Group members review information and conduct research on the National Organization for Women.
- Students create a pamphlet about NOW that includes the following information: *the beliefs and goals of NOW, how NOW will achieve its goal, explanation of the term* feminism, *and NOW's position on the Equal Pay Act of 1963, the Civil Rights Act of 1964, the Education Amendments Act of 1972, and the Equal Credit Opportunity Act.*
- Different group members write the text, draw illustrations for the pamphlet, and design the cover.
- Groups choose a spokesperson to present their pamphlet to the class.

Customizing the Activity for Individual Needs

ESL To help students understand acronyms such as NOW, point out that each letter represents a complete word. Review other acronyms they have studied, such as the NAACP and the ERA. Ask students to suggest new acronyms for groups they know.

Learning Styles Students can:

 make a chart that shows the goals of NOW.

 work in pairs to make banners that display slogans that might have been used by women who joined NOW.

 work with a partner to recite phrases that women could chant while picketing for equal rights. Examples include: *NOW will fight for every right! Respect our choices. Hear our voices!*

Reinforcement Activity

Review that the Equal Rights Amendment, which declared that men and women be treated equally by law, was ratified by only 35 of the required 38 states within 10 years. As a result, the ERA did not become law. Organize the students into pairs and have them write a short essay that summarizes women's fight for equal rights and possible reasons why the Equal Rights Amendment was not ratified by 38 states within 10 years.

Alternative Assessment

Students can prepare an oral summary on the topic of NOW by writing five key facts on index cards. Students can present their oral summary to a partner or to the class.

SECTION 3: Rights for All Americans
Student Edition, pages 516–519

Section Objectives

- Identify ways Latinos worked toward equal rights in the 1960s.
- Describe the Chicano movement.
- Explain how Native Americans and Asian Americans worked toward equal rights.
- * Describe the role of Latinos, Native Americans, and Asian Americans in the civil rights movements of the 1960s.

Words to Know

bilingual, life expectancy, nisei

Cooperative Group Activity

A Civil Rights Documentary

Materials: reference materials (Unit 9 Bibliography and Internet sites, pages 236–240); posterboard

Procedure: Remind students that the 1960s began a period of change for many groups in the United States. Latinos, Native Americans, and Asian Americans followed the example of African Americans as they fought for their civil rights. Organize the class into groups to assume the roles of documentary filmmakers who are planning to make a film about the struggle of Latinos, Native Americans, and Asian Americans in their fight for civil rights in the 1960s.

- Group members review and research information about Latinos, Native Americans, and Asian Americans who were fighting for civil rights in the 1960s.
- Students write an outline that reflects the information they will include in their documentary.
- Group members discuss a rationale for the film and why it should be made.
- Group members share their outlines and rationales with classmates.

Customizing the Activity for Individual Needs

ESL To help students understand the concept of civil rights, have them create a list of the civil rights all Americans are entitled to.

Learning Styles Students can:

 create a Comparison-Contrast chart (Classroom Resource Binder, page G0 4) with information about the civil rights movements of Latinos and Native Americans.

 design a poster that reflects support for the Chicano movement and farm workers' rights.

 work with a partner to think of questions they would have asked César Chávez if they had interviewed him. One student then uses the questions to interview the other student, who assumes the role of César Chávez. Students switch their roles.

Reteaching Activity

Have each student choose one of the groups they read about in the section. Students then write a brief essay that reflects the struggles of this group in gaining civil rights. Students should include factual information about the group's struggle for rights in their essays.

Alternative Assessment

Student pairs can write three cause and effect statements about the struggle for civil rights among, Latinos, Asian Americans, and Native Americans. Students can write their statements on chart paper and then share and discuss them with classmates.

Closing the Chapter
Student Edition, pages 520–521

Chapter Vocabulary

Review with students the Words to Know on page 505 of the Student Edition. Then have them complete the Vocabulary Review on page 520 of the Student Edition, by completing each sentence with a term from the list.

For more vocabulary practice, have them complete the vocabulary exercise on page 181 of the Classroom Resource Binder.

Test Tip

Have students choose three paragraphs from the chapter and write the main idea of each paragraph on an index card.

Learning Objectives

Have students review their Chapter Goals and Self-Check worksheet found on page PA 6 of the Classroom Resource Binder. They can check off

Chapter 27

the goal they have reached. Note that each section of the quiz corresponds to a Learning Objective.

Group Activity

Summary: Students compare and contrast the goals of groups seeking civil rights during the 1960s.

Materials: chart paper; markers

Procedure: Organize the class into small groups. Have each group choose several groups who fought for civil rights during the 1960s, such as Latinos, African Americans, Asian Americans, Native Americans, and women. Students then gather information and take notes about the methods each group used to achieve its goals. Have students compare and contrast the methods each group used to achieve their goals for civil rights.

Assessment: Use the Group Activity Rubric found on page *xiii* of this guide. Fill in the rubric with the following additional information. For this activity, students should have

- participated in a discussion comparing the groups' goals for achieving civil rights
- made a chart recording the group's methods.

RELATED MATERIALS See the Unit Overview page for related Globe Fearon books that can be used to enrich and extend the materials in the chapter.

Assessing the Chapter

Traditional Assessment

Chapter Quiz

The Chapter Quiz on page 521 of the Student Edition can be used as an open-book test, a closed-book test, or a homework assignment. Use the quiz to identify concepts in the chapter that students need to review. Chapter Tests can be found in the Classroom Resource Binder on pages 186–187. Workbook pages 113–116 can be used for additional practice.

Chapter Tests

Use Chapter Tests A and B on pages 186–187 in the Classroom Resource Binder to further assess mastery of chapter concepts.

Additional Resources

Use the Resource Planner on page 195 of this guide to assign additional exercises from the Classroom Resource Binder and Workbook.

Alternative Assessment

Real-Life Connection

- Students make a two-column chart about modern-day civil rights movements.
- Students list the names of groups and organizations that are fighting for civil rights in the first column.
- In the second column, students write how each group or organization hopes to achieve its goals.

Presentation

- Students choose a group of people who fought for civil rights during the 1960s and 1970s.
- Students then create a storyboard, using illustrations and captions or labels, that describes the struggle of this group in gaining civil rights.
- Students present their storyboards to the class.

Chapter 28 · The Vietnam War 1960–1973

Chapter at a Glance

SE page

522   *Opening the Chapter and Portfolio Project*

524   SECTION 1   A Distant War Divides a Nation

530   *Voices From the Past: Protest Songs*

531   SECTION 2   The Conflict Grows

537   SECTION 3   The War Ends

540   *Chapter Review and Group Activity*

Learning Objectives

- Explain the political situation in Vietnam during the 1960s.
- Discuss how the United States became involved in Vietnam.
- Identify the reasons why many Americans were against the war.
- Discuss President Richard Nixon's actions during the war.
- Identify the events that led to the end of the Vietnam War.

Social Studies Skills

- Explore the rise of protest music during the Vietnam years.
- Use a timeline to identify national and world events related to the Vietnam War.
- Plan a time capsule of memorabilia from the Vietnam War years.

Writing Skills

- Prepare a survey to determine people's feelings about the Vietnam War.
- Writing a paragraph in reply to President Johnson's decision to send American troops to Vietnam.
- Write a paragraph describing the problems U.S. soldiers faced in guerrilla warfare.
- Write a paragraph explaining your decision to either print or not print the Pentagon Papers in the newspaper.

Map and Chart Skills

- Use a map to identify countries that might fall to communism according to the domino theory.
- Use a chart to compare and contrast the different types of warfare used by U.S. soldiers and the Viet Cong.

Chapter 28 The Vietnam War	Use the Program Resources below for reteaching, reinforcement, and enrichment. Additional activities for customizing the lessons can be found in this guide.

Key

Reteaching = ⌒□   Reinforcement = ⇩□   Enrichment = ⌒

Sections	Program Resources		
	⇩ Workbook Exercises	Teacher's Planning Guide	Classroom Resource Binder
A Distant War Divides a Nation	117, 118	⇩ p. 203	⌒ Transparency 10 *The Vietnam War, 1964–1975*
Voices From the Past: Protest Songs		⌒□ p. 204	⌒ Feature Practice 190 *Voices From the Past: Women in Vietnam*
The Conflict Grows	119	⇩ p. 204	
The War Ends	120	⇩ p. 205	
Chapter 28 Review		p. 206	⇩ Words to Know 188 ⌒ Challenge 191 ⇩ Chapter Tests A & B, 192, 193

Customizing the Chapter

Opening the Chapter
Student Edition, pages 522–523

Photo Activity

Direct students' attention to the photograph of U.S. troops headed into battle. Explain that during the Vietnam War, the United States relied heavily on the use of helicopters. Helicopters were used in moving supplies and soldiers in and out of Vietnam, and to help in fighting battles. Then, point out the peace symbol in the right corner of the photo. Ask students to identify the background behind the peace symbol (the U.S. flag). Ask students why they think people who were against the war wore this symbol. Have students speculate how public opinion can affect a government's actions.

Words to Know

Review the Words to Know on page 523 of the Student Edition. To help students remember the words, have them work in pairs to create a chart that lists the word and the meaning of each vocabulary word.

The following words and definitions are covered in this chapter:

domino theory belief that if one country falls to communism, others nearby will fall, one after the other

Viet Cong Communist Vietnamese in South Vietnam

guerrilla warfare fighting by troops who are not members of a regular army using surprise attacks

depose to remove from office

napalm a sticky gasoline jelly used in bombs

Agent Orange a powerful chemical that kills all plant life where it is sprayed

conscientious objector a person whose beliefs do not let him or her take an active part in war

deferment putting off, or delaying, having to serve in the armed forces

Vietnamization President Nixon's plan for turning over the fighting of the Vietnam War to the South Vietnamese

censor to make changes in or to take parts out

Portfolio Project

Summary: Students prepare a survey to examine people's feelings about the Vietnam War, and then write a report based on their findings.

Procedure: As students read information about the Vietnam War from each section of the chapter, have them prepare questions to ask how Americans felt, and still feel, about the Vietnam War. When students have prepared questions, have them conduct a survey, asking six people they know to answer their questions. Students then compile the results of their survey into a written report about the topic. You may wish to have students complete this project as a homework assignment.

Assessment: Use the Individual Activity Rubric on page *xii* of this guide. Fill in the rubric with the additional information below. For this project, students should have

- prepared a list of questions and conducted a survey.
- written a report based on the results of the survey.

Learning Objectives

Review the Learning Objectives on page 523 of the Student Edition before starting the chapter. Students can use the list as a learning guide. Suggest they write the objectives in a journal or use the Chapter Goals and Self-Check worksheet found on page PA 6 of the Classroom Resource Binder.

After reading each section of the chapter, have students write an example of what they learned under the appropriate objective. Suggest that students use these worksheets as a practice guide to help them study for the chapter test.

Timeline

Use the timeline to discuss the sequence of events in this chapter. Point out the timeline's title, its time span, and the intervals. After students have read the chapter, have them review the timeline and suggest additional entries.

SECTION 1: A Distant War Divides a Nation
Student Edition, pages 524–529

Section Objectives

- Describe the war between Vietnam and France, and the results of the war.
- Describe the fighting between North and South Vietnam.
- Explain the Gulf of Tonkin incident and what occurred as a result of the incident.
- Explain President Johnson's promise to the American people concerning Vietnam.
- * Discuss how U.S. involvement in the Vietnam War divided the nation.

Words to Know

domino theory, Viet Cong, guerrilla warfare, depose

Cooperative Group Activity

Debate Over War

Materials: reference materials (Unit 9 Bibliography and Internet sites, pages 236–240)

Procedure: Remind students that the United States did not want to become too involved in the problems of Vietnam. Yet, U.S. leaders wanted to stop the spread of communism. The country faced a dilemma that would have sweeping consequences for all involved. Organize students into two groups. Have one group prepare a debate supporting U.S. involvement in Vietnam. The second group will oppose U.S. involvement. You may wish to have students conduct further research for this activity.

- Group members brainstorm a list of at least five ideas that support their point of view about U.S. involvement in Vietnam.
- They write a list of facts that support their ideas.
- Students select a spokesperson to lead the debate and rehearse what that student will say.
- Groups conduct a debate that explores both sides of the issue.

Customizing the Activity for Individual Needs

ESL To help students understand how a debate is conducted, review the rules and format that will be used.

Learning Styles Students can:

 use a Main Idea and Details chart (Classroom Resource Binder, page GO 5) to prepare their notes for the debate.

 create and organize note cards listing reasons for their opinions.

 work with a partner to sum up the main ideas presented in the debate.

Reinforcement Activity

Have students make a chart of at least three "Pro" and three "Con" statements regarding U.S. involvement in Vietnam.

Alternative Assessment

Students can review information about the promises and actions of President Eisenhower, President Kennedy, and President Johnson in relation to Vietnam. Students then write key facts on note cards to use in an oral presentation about the topic.

VOICES FROM THE PAST:
Protest Songs
Student Edition, page 530

Objectives
- Social Studies Skill: Write the lyrics to a protest song.
- Social Studies Skill: Write protest slogans or simple messages on signs.
- Social Studies Skill: Create symbols or logos that represent peace.

Activities

Songs for Changing Times
Materials: cassette tape player or compact disc player; recordings of protest music

Procedure: Have students listen to protest songs and discuss and analyze the lyrics. Invite groups of students to write their own lyrics to protest songs they know or to other familiar melodies. Encourage them to incorporate contemporary issues.

The Message is Simple
Materials: posterboard; colored markers

Procedure: Remind students that many Americans chanted slogans or sang simple songs during protest rallies against the Vietnam War. Invite students to think of simple slogans or messages that protest war. Using posterboard and markers, have them create protest signs.

Let There Be Peace
Materials: markers

Procedure: Explain to students that many people used peace symbols to protest the war. Then ask students to create their own peace symbol. Mention that a dove is a bird that often is used to represent peace.

Practice

Have students complete Voices From the Past: Women in Vietnam on page 190 of the Classroom Resource Binder.

SECTION 2: The Conflict Grows
Student Edition, pages 531–536

Section Objectives
- Explain why U.S. soldiers had a difficult time fighting against the Viet Cong.
- Describe the Tet offensive and its effect on the United States.
- Explain why some Americans protested the draft.
- Describe the events of the presidential election of 1968.

Words to Know

napalm, Agent Orange, conscientious objector, deferment

Cooperative Group Activity

Reporting the News
Materials: reference (Unit 9 Bibliography and Internet sites, pages 236–240)

Procedure: Remind students that by 1966, U.S. troops were fighting hard in Vietnam. Each day Americans were killed or wounded, and the country was being pulled deeper and deeper into an unpopular war. Organize the class into four groups to write a TV news segment about one of the following issues: *the Viet Cong, the Tet offensive, Americans protesting the war,* or *the election of 1968.*

You may wish to have students conduct further research to complete this activity or watch actual TV news segments for ideas.

- Groups assign the tasks of writing different segments to individual members. They discuss how long each segment will be. Students supplement their reports with maps, photos, and graphs.
- Group members practice delivering their news reports.
- Students deliver their news reports to the class in the order in which they occurred.

Customizing the Activity for Individual Needs

ESL To help students understand the vocabulary word *conscientious objector,* ask them what issues they believe in strongly. What would they do if they were forced to act against their beliefs? Tell students that some conscientious objectors left their homes in the United States, or went to jail, to avoid fighting in a war they did not believe in.

Learning Styles Students can:

 complete a Description Web (Classroom Resource Binder, page G0 3) with terms and phrases that describe an anti-war protest.

 create banners that protest the war with pictures and slogans.

 tape-record their summaries of the TV segments.

Reinforcement Activity

Remind students that many Americans felt that the Vietnam War was a mistake. Have students make a protest minibook that lists on each page reasons why the United States should not be involved in the Vietnam War. Students should include the following information in their minibooks: *the use of napalm; Agent Orange; other weapons used in fighting the war; the Tet offensive; protest against the draft;* and *the number of soldiers wounded and killed in the war.*

Alternative Assessment

Students can make an outline of the growing conflict in Vietnam using the following topics: *A Difficult Fight; The Tet Offensive; Voices Against the War;* and *The Election of 1968.*

Section Objectives

- Identify President Nixon's Vietnamization plan.
- Explain President Nixon's two plans to end American involvement in Vietnam.
* Describe the feelings of many veterans when they returned from the Vietnam War.

Words to Know

Vietnamization, censor

Cooperative Group Activity

A Vietnam Veterans Memorial

Materials: markers; construction paper

Procedure: Remind students that many Vietnam veterans felt they were treated poorly when they returned from the war. The Vietnam Veterans Memorial was built to honor the veterans. Organize the students into three groups to design Vietnam Veterans Memorials that will honor the veterans and educate young people about the war and its effects on the United States.

- Group members discuss what the effects of the Vietnam War were on the United States and which is the best way to represent it.
- Groups decide where the memorial should be built and what materials should be used.
- Group members then draw a detailed illustration of the monument and write a speech for the dedication ceremony.
- Each group presents its idea to the class.

Customizing the Activity for Individual Needs

ESL To help students understand the concept of a war memorial, ask partners to discuss someone who meant a great deal to them. What made that person special? What could they do to honor that person? Explain that the United States wanted to show the veterans that they honored them by building a memorial. Point out that many countries have war memorials to those who died in battle.

Learning Styles Students can:

 look at pictures of the Vietnam Veterans Memorial and other war memorials, such as the Korean War Memorial and the Iwo Jima Memorial in Washington, D.C., to help them design their memorials.

build a clay model of their memorial.

 work with a partner to rehearse the speech for the dedication ceremony.

Enrichment Activity

Tell students that another way the government honors people is to have the postal service issue a stamp commemorating them. Ask students to design a stamp commemorating the Vietnam veterans. Students should then write a brief paragraph explaining why it is important to honor Vietnam veterans.

Alternative Assessment

Students can assume the role of a veteran whose tour of duty has just ended. They write a letter about how things are at home to a friend who is still serving in Vietnam.

Closing the Chapter
Student Edition, pages 540–541

Chapter Vocabulary

Review with students the Words to Know on page 523 of the Student Edition. Then have them complete the Vocabulary Review on page 540 of the Student Edition, by answering each statement as *true* or *false*. If the sentence is false, have them change the underlined word to make it true.

For more vocabulary practice, have them complete the vocabulary exercise on page 188 of the Classroom Resource Binder.

Test Tip

Encourage students to review all their answers before handing in their test papers. Remind them that it is a good idea to review their answers in order to catch any careless errors or missed questions.

Learning Objectives

Have the students review their Chapter Goals and Self-Check worksheet found on page PA 6 of the Classroom Resource Binder. They can check off the goal they have reached. Note that each section of the quiz corresponds to a Learning Objective.

Group Activity

Summary: Students plan a time capsule that describes to future generations the anti-war protests of the Vietnam War years.

Procedure: Organize students into groups of three or four to create a plan for a time capsule that describes anti-war protests of the Vietnam War years. Group members decide on items they will place in their capsule, such as anti-war songs and poems, posters, news headlines, letters, and memorabilia from U.S. soldiers. Students work cooperatively to write their plan and list items. Students should make their plan as detailed and as inclusive as possible.

Assessment: Use the Group Activity Rubric found on page *xiii* of this guide. Fill in the rubric with the following additional information. For this activity, students should have

- participated in selecting items to include in their time capsule.
- written a detailed plan of what they will include in their time capsule.

RELATED MATERIALS See the Unit Overview page for related Globe Fearon books that can be used to enrich and extend the materials in the chapter.

Traditional Assessment

Chapter Quiz

The Chapter Quiz on page 541 of the Student Edition can be used as an open-book test, a closed-book test, or a homework assignment. Use the quiz to identify concepts in the chapter that students need to review. Chapter Tests can be found in the Classroom Resource Binder on pages 192–193. Workbook pages 117–120 can be used for additional practice.

Chapter Tests

Use Chapter Tests A and B on pages 192–193 in the Classroom Resource Binder to further assess mastery of chapter concepts.

Additional Information

Use the Resource Planner on page 202 of this guide to assign additional exercises from the Classroom Resource Binder and Workbook.

Alternative Assessment

Presentation

- Students prepare to have a radio talk-show about the presence of the United States in Vietnam.
- Students should include the following headings in their discussion: *Background Information, President Kennedy's Policies, President Johnson's Policies, President Nixon's Policies,* and *Public Reaction to the War.*
- Students form into groups of four and choose members to represent a talk show host, President Kennedy, President Johnson, and President Nixon.
- Students present their shows to the class.

Open-Ended

- Students have a round-table discussion that compares warfare techniques of the Vietnam War to those used in the Civil War, World War I and World War II.
- Students gather background information.
- Students choose a person who will lead the discussion.
- Students include as many facts and details as possible. They may wish to refer to the Student Edition.

Chapter 29 • **Entering a New Decade** 1970–1975

Chapter at a Glance

SE page

542   *Opening the Chapter and Portfolio Project*

544   SECTION 1   Ending the Cold War

547   SECTION 2   Changes at Home

551   *Connecting History and Economics: Inflation*

552   SECTION 3   Watergate

556   *Chapter Review and Group Activity*

Learning Objectives

- Explain how President Nixon improved relations with China.
- Discuss how President Nixon handled the social and economic problems of the 1970s.
- Describe the steps that led to the Watergate scandal and the resignation of President Nixon.

Social Studies Skills

- Explore how inflation affects the economy.
- Use a timeline to identify both domestic and foreign affairs during the Nixon administration.
- Outline the steps taken in the Watergate investigation by making a chart.

Writing Skills

- Write a paragraph describing ten events of the 1970s, and identify those that greatly changed peoples' daily lives.
- Write an article for a farm journal describing Nixon's meeting with Brezhnev.
- Prepare a chart explaining how the Vietnam War and the 1973 war in the Middle East changed the lives of Americans.
- Write a paragraph describing an effective leader.

Resource Planner

Chapter 29 Entering a New Decade	Use the correlating Program Resources for reinforcement, reteaching, or enrichment. Additional activities for customizing the lessons can be found in this guide.

Key
Reteaching = ⌒   Reinforcement = ⇓   Enrichment = ⌒

Sections	Program Resources		
	⇓ Workbook Exercises	Teacher's Planning Guide	Classroom Resource Binder
Ending the Cold War	121	⇓ p. 210	⌒ Outline Map 4 *The World* ⌒ Transparency 16 *Regions of the United States*
Changes at Home	122	⌒ p. 211	
Connecting History and Economics: Inflation		⌒ p. 212	⌒ Feature Practice 196 *Connecting History and Economics: The Consumer Price Index*
Watergate	123, 124	p. 212	
Chapter 29 Review		p. 213	⇓ Words to Know 194 ⌒ Challenge 197 ⇓ Chapter Tests A & B, 198, 199 ⇓ Unit Test Parts I & II, 200, 201

Customizing the Chapter

Opening the Chapter
Student Edition, pages 542–543

Photo Activity

Invite students to look at the photograph and newspaper headlines. Discuss the importance of Nixon's visit to Communist China and how it might affect future dealings between the two countries. Then, direct students' attention to the photograph of Chou En-lai escorting President and Mrs. Nixon on their visit to China. Mention that the President was invited to China to discuss relations between the two countries. Have students predict the topics that might be covered in the meeting between Chou En-lai and Nixon.

Words to Know

Review the Words to Know on page 543 of the Student Edition. To help students remember the words, have them scan the text for the boldfaced vocabulary words. Then, ask them to find and record each word's definition.

The following words and definitions are covered in this chapter:

normalize to continue normal dealings with a country, or begin again

détente an easing of tension between nations

revenue sharing a program in which the federal government shares its income from taxes with state and local governments

affirmative action a program for correcting the effects of discrimination

stagflation a rise in prices together with a drop in business activity and more unemployment

executive privilege the right of a President to withhold important information from other branches of the government

perjury lying in court while under oath

Portfolio Project

Summary: Students prepare ten statements describing events that occurred in the 1970s to be used in a bulletin-board display.

Materials: colored markers

Procedure: As students read the chapter, ask them to write ten short statements describing events that occurred during the 1970s. Remind them to date each event. Students should use a colored marker to underline the statements which describe events that greatly changed peoples' daily lives. Students arrange their statements in the order in which they occurred and create a bulletin-board display using their statements.

Assessment: Use the Individual Activity Rubric on page *xii* of this guide. Fill in the rubric with the additional information below. For this project, students should have

- prepared ten statements describing events of the 1970s.
- placed the statements in chronological order.

Learning Objectives

Review the Learning Objectives on page 543 of the Student Edition before starting the chapter. Students can use the list as a learning guide. Suggest they write the objectives in a journal or use the Chapter Goals and Self-Check worksheet found on page PA 6 of the Classroom Resource Binder.

After reading each section of the chapter, have students write an example of what they learned under the appropriate objective. Suggest that students use these worksheets as a practice guide to help them study for the chapter test.

Timeline

Use the timeline to discuss the sequence of events in this chapter. Point out the timeline's title, its time span, and the intervals. After students have read the chapter, have them review the timeline and suggest additional entries.

SECTION 1: Ending the Cold War
Student Edition, pages 544–546

Section Objectives

- Describe relations between the United States and other countries, such as Chile, Vietnam, and Cambodia.
- Explain why Soviet leaders worried about the changing relationship between the United States and China.
- ∗ Explain why President Nixon agreed to reopen relations between the United States and China.

Words to Know

normalize, détente

Cooperative Group Activity

The Cold War Begins to Thaw

Materials: reference materials (Unit 9 Bibliography and Internet sites, pages 236–240)

Procedure: Remind students that as the Vietnam War came to an end, President Nixon turned his attention to enhancing relations with China, the Soviet Union, and other countries. Organize the class into pairs. Have one partner investigate Nixon's plan to normalize relations between the United States and China. Have the second partner investigate Nixon's goal to build détente between the United States and the Soviet Union. You may wish to have students conduct further research on these topics.

- One partner assumes the role of President Nixon and writes a letter to the leader of China explaining U.S. reasons for wanting to change relations.
- The other partner assumes the role of President Nixon and writes a letter to the leader of the Soviet Union to discuss détente.
- Students should include as much factual information in their letters as they can.

Customizing the Activity for Individual Needs

ESL To help students understand the concept of *détente,* ask them if they have ever had the experience of breaking off a friendship with someone. Have student volunteers describe their feelings after breaking off a friendship, such as loneliness, tension, or rivalry. Then, ask students to describe how they might go about repairing, or starting up, that same friendship. List their responses on the chalkboard. Explain how *détente* is similar to repairing a friendship, except that it involves countries such as the United States and the Soviet Union.

Learning Styles Students can:

 complete a Sequence of Events chart (Classroom Resource Binder, page G0 1) with information about President Nixon's foreign policy.

 sort index cards with words, phrases, and proper names into categories. Example: *Soviet Union (country)* or *Leonid Brezhnev (leader).*

 work with a partner to assume the roles of an interviewer and President Nixon. Have the interviewer ask questions about the President's personal views on changing relations with China and the Soviet Union. President Nixon responds with answers.

Reinforcement Activity ⬇

Have partners take turns relating a conflict with a classmate, friend, or sibling, and how they resolved this conflict. Then, have students list the problems the United States faced with the Soviet Union and with China. Next to each problem, have students list possible solutions, such as resolution through compromise or negotiation. Students should compile their information into chart form.

Alternative Assessment

Partners can review information about U.S. relations with China and the Soviet Union. Students then write questions about the information, beginning with the words *who, what, when, where,* and *why.* Partners take turns asking each other the questions and reviewing the answers.

SECTION 2: Changes at Home
Student Edition, pages 547–550

Section Objectives

- Describe Nixon's revenue sharing plan for the United States.
- Describe the civil rights programs that Nixon initiated during his presidency.
- Identify the major economic problems that the United States faced in the early 1970s.
* Explain President Nixon's domestic policy.

Words to Know

revenue sharing, affirmative action, stagflation

Cooperative Group Activity

Reporting the News

Materials: reference materials (Unit 9 Bibliography and Internet sites, pages 236–240)

Procedure: Remind students that in addition to repairing relations with Communist countries around the world, President Nixon was also concerned about economic and social problems in the United States. Divide the class into four groups. You may wish to have students conduct further research on U.S. domestic problems during the Nixon years.

- Group members brainstorm and make a list of possible television news stories about domestic problems, both economic and social, that the nation faced during the 1970s.
- Students choose one story and write a brief news report that conveys important facts and details about the topic.
- Group members choose a spokesperson to read their news report to the class.
- Students decide which news stories are the most informative and why.

Customizing the Activity for Individual Needs

ESL To help students understand new vocabulary terms, have them write the terms *revenue sharing, inflation,* and *stagflation* and their definitions in their notebooks. Students then work with an English-proficient partner to use each term in a sentence.

Learning Styles Students can:

 complete a Cause and Effect chart (Classroom Resource Binder, page G0 2) showing how the problems the economy faced during the Nixon administration and their effects.

 create a poster depicting how the oil shortage affected Americans.

 assume the role of President Nixon addressing the nation about his plans for solving the country's economic and social problems.

Enrichment Activity

Divide the class into groups to make a list of economic and social problems that the United States faces today. You may wish to have students read current news articles in newspapers or magazines to gather information. Then, have students brainstorm ways to solve some of these problems. Invite students to share their problems and solutions with the class.

Alternative Assessment

Students can write four cause and effect statements about domestic problems, including statements addressing inflation, revenue sharing, stagflation, and affirmative action.

CONNECTING HISTORY AND ECONOMICS: Inflation
Student Edition, page 551

Objectives
- Social Studies Skill: Compare and contrast the cost of particular items and whether they have inflated over a five-year period.
- Social Studies Skill: Use a chart to identify possible ways to control inflation.
- Social Studies Skill: Identify the effects on the basic necessities if a sharp price rise occurs.

Activities
Rising Costs
Procedure: Ask students to make a list of items that would be considered basic needs, such as a carton of milk, toothpaste, housing, and shoes. Then have them ask family members how much the items cost five years ago. Have students compare and contrast these costs with today's

prices to determine whether the prices have risen, dropped, or stayed the same. Students can make a bar graph to show the change in prices.

Controlling Inflation
Materials: newspapers; chart paper; markers

Procedure: Have students scan the business section of at least two newspapers to find articles about inflation and possible ways in which inflation can be controlled. Ask them to use this information to summarize ways to control inflation.

Basic Needs
Procedure: Ask students to assume the role of consumers living in an inflated economy. Mention that the cost of living has risen by fifty percent. Assuming that their wages have not increased, have students make a list of basic necessities they cannot do without as well as items that they would no longer be able to afford. Students can write a journal entry reflecting the affects of inflation.

Practice
Have students complete Connecting History and Economics: Consumer Price Index on page 196 of the Classroom Resource Binder.

SECTION 3: Watergate
Student Edition, pages 552–555

Section Objectives
- Describe the Senate investigation into the Watergate break-in and its connection to President Nixon.
- Describe the events of the Watergate incident.

Words to Know
executive privilege, perjury

Cooperative Group Activity

A Three-Act Play
Materials: reference materials (Unit 9 Bibliography and Internet sites, pages 236–240)

Procedure: Remind students that the events of the Watergate break-in and subsequent cover-up caused Richard Nixon to become the first President to resign from office. Organize students into three groups to write a three-act play about Watergate. You may wish to have students conduct further research on this topic.

- Group members review information and conduct additional research about the Watergate scandal.
- The first group writes the first act and includes information about the break-in at the Watergate building, the headquarters for the Democratic National Committee.
- Students in the second group write the second act. They read the first act and focus on the actions of *Washington Post* reporters Bob Woodward and Carl Bernstein.
- Students in the third group write the third act. They read the first and second acts and focus on information about the Senate investigation of the Oval Office audiotapes, executive privilege, Nixon's resignation, and President Ford's pardon of Nixon.
- Groups edit their play, assign roles, and rehearse all three acts.
- Group members perform their play for the class.

Customizing the Activity for Individual Needs

ESL To help students understand the concept of leadership, have them create a list of the qualities that make a good leader.

Learning Styles Students can:

 complete a Sequence of Events chart (Classroom Resource Binder, G0 1) about the Watergate scandal.

 write important events of the Watergate scandal on index cards, and have a partner order the cards according to when each event occurred.

 take the role of moderator of the play and explain to the audience what it will be about.

Enrichment Activity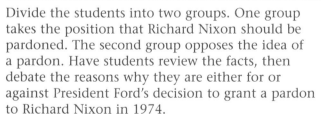

Divide the students into two groups. One group takes the position that Richard Nixon should be pardoned. The second group opposes the idea of a pardon. Have students review the facts, then debate the reasons why they are either for or against President Ford's decision to grant a pardon to Richard Nixon in 1974.

Alternative Assessment

Students can create a timeline that covers significant events during the Watergate scandal.

Closing the Chapter
Student Edition, pages 556–557

Chapter Vocabulary

Review with students the Words to Know on page 543 of the Student Edition. Then have them complete the Vocabulary Review on page 556 of the Student Edition, by completing each sentence with a term from the list.

For more vocabulary practice, have them complete the vocabulary exercise on page 194 of the Classroom Resource Binder.

Test Tip

Have students review the information in the chapter and write key ideas on index cards. Then, students can work with a partner to compare key ideas. Encourage students to review their index cards before taking a test on the information.

Learning Objectives

Have students review their Chapter Goals and Self-Check worksheet found on page PA 6 of the Classroom Resource Binder. They can check off the goal they have reached. Note that each section of the quiz corresponds to a Learning Objective.

Group Activity

Summary: Students make a chart that traces the steps in the Watergate incident and the investigation.

Materials: chart paper; marker

Procedure: Organize the class into small groups to review information and take notes on the events that occurred during the Watergate incident. Then, have them make a list of the events that occurred during the investigation. Group members use their findings to create a chart showing this information. Have group members present their chart to the class.

Assessment: Use the Group Activity Rubric found on page *xiii* of this guide. Fill in the rubric with the following additional information. For this activity, students should have

- traced the steps in the Watergate incident and the investigation.
- created a chart of their findings.

RELATED MATERIALS See the Unit Overview page for related Globe Fearon books that can be used to enrich and extend the materials in the chapter.

Traditional Assessment

Chapter Quiz
The Chapter Quiz on page 557 of the Student Edition can be used as an open-book test, a closed-book test, or a homework assignment. Use the quiz to identify concepts in the chapter that students need to review. Chapter Tests can be found in the Classroom Resource Binder on pages 198–199. Workbook pages 121–124 can be used for additional practice.

Chapter Tests
Use Chapter Tests A and B on pages 198–199 in the Classroom Resource Binder to further assess mastery of chapter concepts.

Additional Resources
Use the Resource Planner on page 209 of this guide to assign additional exercises from the Classroom Resource Binder and Workbook.

Alternative Assessment

Performance
- Students review the information and take notes about President Nixon's accomplishments and problems.
- Students write part of a memoir from the perspective of Richard Nixon after he resigned from office.
- Students then assume the role of Richard Nixon and act out the scene they have written.

Student Interview
Write the following events on separate slips of paper: *reopening relations with China, U.S. bombing in Cambodia, the desegregation of all schools,* and *the Watergate incident.* Distribute one slip of paper to each student. Ask:
- What was significant about this act or event?
- How did this event or act affect Americans during the 1970s?
- Who were some key figures in this event or act?
- What were the consequences or effects of this event or act?

Unit Assessment
This is the last chapter in Unit 9, *Years of Change.* To assess cumulative knowledge and provide standardized-test practice, administer the Unit Review Test on page 558 of the Student Edition and the Unit 9 Cumulative Test on pages 200–201 of the Classroom Resource Binder. These tests are in multiple-choice format.

Unit 10 ▷ Forward to the Future

CHAPTER 30	PORTFOLIO PROJECT	BUILDING YOUR SKILLS	GROUP ACTIVITY	TIMELINE
Changes at Home and Abroad 1976–1988	An Interview	Taking a Test	Brainstorming a List	Changes at Home and Far Away

CHAPTER 31	PORTFOLIO PROJECT	VOICES FROM THE PAST	GROUP ACTIVITY	TIMELINE
Progress and Problems 1988–2000	Making a Chart	Maya Angelou	Writing a Poem	New Role for America

CHAPTER 32	PORTFOLIO PROJECT	A CLOSER LOOK...	GROUP ACTIVITY	TIMELINE
A New Century 1990–the future	Story Setting	The Heroes of September 11, 2001	Writing a News Report	Challenges for Today and the Future

RELATED MATERIALS

These are some of the Globe Fearon books that can be used to enrich and extend the material in this unit.

Content ▷

Fearon's Our Century 1980–1990
Explore the decade's history including the Reagan era, the Cold War, and the years following the Cold War.

Skills ▷

Survival Guide for Students
This resource provides a complete study skills curriculum for getting organized in school and in life.

Cultural Diversity ▷

Historical Case Studies: Voices of America
Focuses on past and present immigration issues.

Chapter 30 · Changes at Home and Abroad 1976–1988

Chapter at a Glance

SE page

560   *Opening the Chapter and Portfolio Project*

562   SECTION 1   A New Kind of Leader

567   *Building Your Skills: Taking a Test*

568   SECTION 2   Turning Toward Conservatism

572   SECTION 3   Acting in a Changing World

576   *Chapter Review and Group Activity*

Learning Objectives

- Identify the successes and problems President Carter faced at home.
- Explain how President Carter helped bring peace between Egypt and Israel.
- Describe the Iran hostage crisis.
- Discuss President Reagan's social and economic policies.
- Describe President Reagan's foreign policy.

Social Studies Skills

- Identify tips for taking a test.
- Use a timeline to describe foreign affairs that took place during the Carter and Reagan administrations.

Writing Skills

- Write questions for an interview with an older person about recent events.
- Write a letter to President Carter about how you believe the United States should treat Soviet dissidents.
- Write a paragraph explaining why it is important to balance the federal budget.
- List steps to describe the domino theory by showing how it might work in Central America.
- Write a paragraph to identify reasons why people vote for presidential candidates.

Map and Chart Skills

- Use a chart to identify trouble spots around the world between 1982 and 1987.

Resource Planner

Chapter 30 Changes at Home and Abroad	Use the Program Resources below for reteaching, reinforcement, and enrichment. Additional activities for customizing the lessons can be found in this guide. Key Reteaching = ⤺ Reinforcement = ⬇ Enrichment = ⤻

Sections	Program Resources		
	⬇ Workbook Exercises	Teacher's Planning Guide	Classroom Resource Binder
A New Kind of Leader	125	⤺ p. 218	⤺ Outline Map 4 *The World* Transparency 16 *Regions of the United States*
Building Skills: Taking a Test		⬇ p. 219	⬇ Feature Practice 204, 205 *Taking a Test* Writing and Test-Taking Tip 7 *Short Answer Test Questions* Graphic Organizer 6 *KWL Chart*
Turning Toward Conservatism	126	⤻ p. 220	
Acting in a Changing World	127, 128	⤻ p. 221	⤺ Outline Map 4 *The World* Transparency 16 *Regions of the United States*
Chapter 30 Review		p. 221	⬇ Words to Know 202 ⤺ Challenge 206 ⬇ Chapter Tests A & B, 207, 208

Customizing the Chapter

Opening the Chapter
Student Edition, pages 560–561

Photo Activity

Direct students' attention to the photograph of Anwar Sadat, leader of Egypt, Menachem Begin, leader of Israel, and U.S. President Jimmy Carter, and the *Time* magazine cover. Explain that the three leaders met to agree on peaceful relations between the countries of Israel and Egypt. Have students brainstorm a list of ground rules that would need to be followed during a meeting between peace-seeking representatives of two countries in conflict.

Words to Know

Review the Words to Know on page 561 of the Student Edition. To help students remember the words, have them refer to a dictionary to create a semantic map for each vocabulary word. Ask them to include the definition, part of speech, and list of related words or topics that relate to the word. Invite students to take turns sharing and discussing their maps with classmates.

The following words and definitions are covered in this chapter:

human rights the basic freedoms that all people should have

dissident a person who strongly disagrees with government policies or its rule

hostage a person who is held captive until certain demands are met

federal deficit the difference between the amount of money the government spends and what it collects

national debt the amount of money the federal government owes

contra a rebel fighting the Sandinista government in Nicaragua

special prosecutor an investigator who looks into the actions of the President and other high officials

glasnost a policy that allows open discussion about Soviet life and politics

Portfolio Project

Summary: Students develop questions to ask an older person about a significant U.S. or world event that occurred between 1976 and 1988.

Materials: notepad; pen; tape recorder

Procedure: After students have read about significant world events of the 1970s and 1980s, have them choose one event that interests them. Ask students to reread information about this event and take notes on the subject. Students use their notes to develop a list of questions to ask an older person about this event. During the interview, students take detailed notes about the responses. Additionally, they may wish to use a tape recorder to record a transcript of the conversation. Students should ask permission of the person they are interviewing before using a tape recorder. Students then use the information they obtained from the interview to record answers later. If appropriate, have students read their notes to the class.

Assessment: Use the Individual Activity Rubric on page *xii* of this guide. Fill in the rubric with the additional information below. For this project, students should have

- developed a list of questions about one event.
- taken accurate notes during the interview and recorded answers later.

Learning Objectives

Review the Learning Objectives on page 561 of the Student Edition before starting the chapter. Students can use the list as a learning guide. Suggest they write the objectives in a journal or use the Chapter Goals and Self-Check worksheet found on page PA 6 of the Classroom Resource Binder.

After reading each section of the chapter, have students write an example of what they learned about under the appropriate objective. Suggest that students use these worksheets as a practice guide to help them study for the chapter test.

Timeline

Use the timeline to discuss the sequence of events in this chapter. Point out the timeline's title, its time span, and the intervals. After students have read the chapter, have them review the timeline and suggest additional activities.

SECTION 1: A New Kind of Leader
Student Edition, pages 562–566

Section Objectives

- Describe the changes that took place between the Soviet Union and the United States during the Carter presidency.
- Describe the Camp David Accords.
- Explain what happened during the Iran hostage crisis.
- Identify successes and problems of the Carter administration.

Words to Know

human rights, dissident, hostage

Cooperative Group Activity

The Carter Presidency

Materials: reference materials (Unit 10 Bibliography and Internet sites, pages 236–240)

Procedure: Remind students that Jimmy Carter defeated Gerald Ford in the presidential election of 1976. With a background in farming and politics, Carter was known for his business sense, his concern for human rights, and his strong ethics. Organize students into three groups to create a bulletin-board display. You may wish to have students conduct further research on Jimmy Carter as President.

- Students review information and conduct research about Jimmy Carter's term as U.S. President.
- Each group member plans and designs a different part of a bulletin-board display that provides information and highlights significant issues and events of Carter's presidency.
- One group draws illustrations. A second group writes newspaper headlines describing Carter's presidency, and a third group constructs banners and posters to hang on the board.
- Students from each group make a presentation to the class about the display.

Customizing the Activity for Individual Needs

ESL To help students understand the meaning of human rights, have partners discuss the human rights' records of other countries around the world. They may wish to include their native countries in the discussion.

Learning Styles Students can:

 design a button that promotes human rights. Explain that human rights are the basic freedoms that all people should have, such as the right to life, liberty, and equality. Remind students that Carter believed that all nations should give human rights to their citizens.

 work in small groups to cast votes about President Carter's decisions on certain topics that are written on sheets of paper. Example: *Do you agree with Carter's decision to pardon men who avoided the draft during the Vietnam War?* Students write *agree* or *disagree* on an index card to cast their vote on each question.

work in pairs to discuss Carter's foreign policy and human rights record.

Reteaching Activity

Have students work in small groups and assume the role of presidential aides to Jimmy Carter. Ask them to write a schedule that shows the President's agenda for one day during the Iran hostage crisis. Have students include factual information to support their agendas. Example:
9:00 AM   Carter meets with advisers to discuss the hostage crisis.
11:00 AM   Carter makes a public announcement that innocent Americans have been taken as hostages by Iranian revolutionaries.

Reconvene the class and have students share their schedules.

Alternative Assessment

Students can complete a Description Web (Classroom Resource Binder, page GO 3) by writing information about the Carter administration. Encourage students to include information about the following topics in their webs: *the U.S. economy, foreign relations, the Camp David Accords,* and *the Iran hostage crisis.*

Chapter
30

BUILDING YOUR SKILLS:
Taking a Test
Student Edition, page 567

Objectives

- Social Studies Skill: Identify strategies for answering comprehension questions on a test.
- Social Studies Skill: Identify ways to answer multiple-choice questions on a test.
- Social Studies Skill: Use a variety of formats to answer questions on a test.

Activities

Writing and Answering Essay Questions

Procedure: Invite students to write an essay question about two of the following four topics: *U.S. economy under President Carter, foreign relations in the 1970s, the Camp David Accords,* or *the Iran hostage crisis.* Tell students to begin each essay question with one of the following words: *compare, contrast, define, describe, explain, evaluate,*

Continued on page 220

Continued from page 219

or *review*. After writing their questions, students exchange papers with a partner and choose one essay question to answer.

What's the Right Choice?

Procedure: On separate index cards, have students write five multiple-choice questions based on the information found in the section they just read. Have students exchange index cards with a partner and answer the questions. Remind students that they should read all of the choices first, then decide which answers to eliminate before determining the correct one.

A Short Question Test

Procedure: Have students create a test on the subject of the Carter presidency that includes questions of different formats, such as true/false questions, fill-in-the-blank questions, and match-up questions. Then, organize students into small groups to exchange tests and answer the questions.

Practice

Have students complete Building Your Skills: Taking a Test page 204 of the Classroom Resource Binder.

SECTION 2: Turning Toward Conservatism
Student Edition, pages 568–571

Section Objectives

- Identify reasons why Ronald Reagan was a popular President.
- Explain President Reagan's idea about the role of the federal government.
- Describe how President Reagan planned to grow the U.S. economy.

Words to Know

federal deficit, national debt

Cooperative Group Activity

The President's Agenda

Materials: reference materials (Unit 10 Bibliography list and Internet sites, pages 236–240)

Procedure: Remind students that the United States faced high inflation, recession, and joblessness when Ronald Reagan became President. Reagan had new ideas about government, society, and the economy. Divide the class into groups to assume the role of three groups of Reagan's advisers. Each group of advisers will write a presidential memo on inflation, recession, and joblessness.

- Group members review information about their topic and conduct research about the Reagan presidency.
- Students assume the role of Reagan and his advisers and plan to hold a meeting in the Oval Office to discuss the problems of the country, possible solutions, and Ronald Reagan's new ideas about the government, society, and the economy.
- Group members compose a memo to the President that describes actions to help the country get back on track.

Customizing the Activity for Individual Needs

ESL To help students understand what the Oval Office is, explain the origin of the term and the significance of the room.

Learning Styles Students can:

 use markers to highlight key action words in their memos to the President.

 draw a picture of President Reagan sitting in the Oval Office with a thought bubble over his head. Have students fill in the bubble with a word or brief statement that addresses how he will solve one of the problems that the country is facing.

 work with a partner to read aloud their memos to the President.

Enrichment Activity

Remind students that in 1981, Reagan said, "Government is not the solution to our problem; government is the problem." Organize students into groups to discuss the meaning of Reagan's words. Then ask students to write a summary explaining why they think that many Americans agreed with Reagan's ideas about the government.

Alternative Assessment

Students can write a journal entry, from the perspective of Ronald Reagan, reflecting his ideas about how the country should be run. Ask students to address the following topics in their entries: *Reagan's ideas about U.S. government and society* and *Reagan's ideas about improving the U.S. economy.*

SECTION 3: Acting in a Changing World *Student Edition, pages 572–575*

Section Objectives
- Explain why Reagan sent U.S. troops to Nicaragua.
- Describe the Iran-Contra affair.
- Describe the changes that occurred in the Soviet Union during the 1980s.
- * Discuss whether President Reagan's policies were good for the United States.

Words to Know
contra, special prosecutor, glasnost

Cooperative Group Activity

Debating the Presidency
Procedure: Remind students that President Reagan believed the United States should play an active role in world affairs, especially by fighting communism and by keeping peace in the Middle East. Some Americans agreed with Reagan's policies, while others protested against them. Organize students into two groups.

- Students in one group assume the role of Reagan supporters and discuss why they feel he is doing an effective job in office. Group members make a list of reasons that support their beliefs.
- Students in the second group assume the role of Americans who do not feel that Reagan is doing an effective job in office. Group members make a list of reasons that support their beliefs.
- Groups then hold a debate based on their pro-Reagan or anti-Reagan stances.

Customizing the Activity for Individual Needs
ESL To help students understand new vocabulary, have them write the terms *contra, special prosecutor,* and *glasnost* and their definitions on a sheet of paper. Have ESL students work with English-proficient students to write a sentence using each term.

Learning Styles Students can:

 fill in a Main Idea and Supporting Details chart (Classroom Resource Binder, page GO 5) with information about President Reagan's foreign policy.

 create a chart that combines reasons people supported or did not support Reagan's policies.

 tape-record the debates and replay them for the class.

Enrichment Activity
Have students write a short essay on the following topic: *Qualities and Traits of an Effective President.* In their essays, students should include their opinion about Ronald Reagan as an effective or ineffective President and cite examples that support this opinion.

Alternative Assessment
Students can work with a partner to review information about the sending of U.S. troops to Nicaragua, the Iran-Contra affair, and changes in the Soviet Union. Have students take turns asking each other questions about people, issues, and events relating to these topics. Some examples include: *Why did Reagan call the Soviet Union an "evil empire"? What was the significance of the Iran-Contra affair? Who were the contras?*

Closing the Chapter
Student Edition, pages 576–577

Chapter Vocabulary
Review with students the Words to Know on page 561 of the Student Edition. Then have them complete the Vocabulary Review on page 576 of the Student Edition, by matching each term on the list with its definition.

For more vocabulary practice, have them complete the vocabulary exercise on page 202 of the Classroom Resource Binder.

Test Tip
Have students review each section of the chapter and list the main ideas and important details. Then, have students work with a partner to compare their lists.

Learning Objectives
Have students review their Chapter Goals and Self-Check worksheet found on page PA 6 of the Classroom Resource Binder. They can check off the goal they have reached. Note that each section of the quiz corresponds to a Learning Objective.

Group Activity
Summary: Students compare and contrast why Americans voted for Jimmy Carter and Ronald

Reagan, then brainstorm a list of reasons why Americans vote for a presidential candidate today.

Materials: chart paper; markers

Procedure: Organize students into groups of three or four. Group members discuss the reasons why people voted for Jimmy Carter and the reasons why Americans voted for Ronald Reagan. Students create a list of reasons why people vote for a presidential candidate today. Students decide on the reasons they believe are most pertinent and draw a star next to each one.

Assessment: Use the Group Activity Rubric found on page *xiii* of this guide. Fill in the rubric with the following additional information. For this activity, students should have

- brainstormed a list of reasons why Americans vote for presidential candidates today.
- identified reasons they believe to be most pertinent.

RELATED MATERIALS   See the Unit Overview page for related Globe Fearon books that can be used to enrich and extend the materials in the chapter.

Assessing the Chapter

Traditional Assessment

Chapter Quiz
The Chapter Quiz on page 577 of the Student Edition can be used as an open-book test, a closed-book test, or a homework assignment. Use the quiz to identify concepts in the chapter that students need to review. Chapter Tests can be found in the Classroom Resource Binder on pages 207–208. Workbook pages 125–128 can be used for additional practice.

Chapter Tests
Use Chapter Tests A and B on pages 207–208 in the Classroom Resource Binder to further assess mastery of chapter concepts.

Additional Resources
Use the Resource Planner on page 217 of this guide to assign additional exercises from the Classroom Resource Binder and Workbook.

Alternative Assessment

Presentation
- Students review information about the Carter and Reagan presidencies.
- Students compare and contrast the Carter and Reagan presidencies by completing a Comparison-Contrast chart (Classroom Resource Binder, page GO 4).
- Students present their charts to the class.

Performance
- Students write a scene between Ronald Reagan and one of his advisers discussing how they will improve U.S. economy.
- Students act out the scene for the class.

Chapter 31 · **Progress and Problems** 1988–2000

Chapter at a Glance

SE page

578		*Opening the Chapter and Portfolio Project*
580	SECTION 1	Politics and Presidents
584	SECTION 2	A New Role in the World
591	SECTION 3	New Rights and Opportunities
595		*Voices From the Past:* Maya Angelou
596		*Chapter Review and Group Activity*

Chapter
31

Learning Objectives

- Describe the elections of 1988, 1992, and 1996.
- Discuss the economy during the Bush and Clinton presidencies.
- Explain the importance of the end of the cold war and the Persian Gulf War.
- Identify the areas where U. S. troops helped keep the peace during the 1990s.
- Describe new opportunities for minorities and women.

Social Studies Skills

- Explore Maya Angelou's message.
- Use a timeline to identify events that occurred as the twentieth century ended.
- Identify changes that occurred in the United States and the world during the 1990s.

Writing Skills

- Create a chart that identifies the changes that occurred in the United States during the 1990s.
- Write a news article describing the 1988 or 1992 election.
- Create a poster that either supports or protests U.S. sanctions against U.S. companies in South Africa.
- Write an editorial describing the pros and cons of a national health-care program for all Americans.
- Write a poem that discusses ways to end violence.

Map and Chart Skills

- Use a map to identify the countries that make up the Middle East.
- Use a chart to identify countries in which the United States was involved in peacekeeping efforts.

Resource Planner

Chapter 31 Progress and Problems	Use the Program Resources below for reteaching, reinforcement, and enrichment. Additional activities for customizing the lessons can be found in this guide.

Key
Reteaching = ⌢   Reinforcement = ⇩   Enrichment = ⌢

Sections	Program Resources		
	⇩ Workbook Exercises	Teacher's Planning Guide	Classroom Resource Binder
Politics and Presidents	129	⌢ p. 225	
A New Role in the World	130, 131	⇩ p. 226	⌢ Outline Map 4 *The World* ⌢ Transparency 16 *Regions of the United States* ⌢ Geography and Economics 10 *The Cold War Ends*
New Rights and Opportunities	132	⌢ p. 227	
Voices From the Past: Maya Angelou		⌢ p. 228	⌢ Feature Practice 211 *Voices From the Past: Making Predictions*
Chapter 31 Review		p. 228	⇩ Words to Know 209 ⌢ Challenge 212 ⇩ Chapter Tests A & B, 213, 214

Customizing the Chapter

Opening the Chapter
Student Edition, pages 578–579

Photo Activity

Explain to students that the photograph shows people celebrating the fall of the Berlin Wall in 1989. Point out the sign in the lower right corner that marked the border between East and West Berlin. Have students speculate how people felt when the wall came down and why.

Words to Know

Review the Words to Know on page 579 of the Student Edition. To help students remember the words, have them create a Description Web for each word (Classroom Resource Binder, page GO 3). Ask them to write their ideas of what the word means in the outer circles. Afterwards, encourage them to refer to the Glossary in the Student Edition to check their definitions.

The following words and definitions are covered in this chapter:

primary an early election that helps a political party choose its candidate

downsize to make smaller, to reduce the size of the work force

budget surplus the amount of money that is left over after spending

grand jury a jury that decides if charges against a person are strong enough to go to trial

ethnic cleansing the removal of one group of people by another group in the same region

coalition a temporary alliance of countries for a special action

underclass a group of people with few job skills and little education

workfare a government program in which people have to work to receive aid

Portfolio Project

Summary: Students list changes in the United States and around the world during the 1990s. They then create a chart with the headings *Progress* and *Problems* in which they write their list of items.

Materials: chart paper; pen

Procedure: As students read, have them make a list of changes that occurred in the United States and around the world during the 1990s. Students then sort their list of changes according to those that show progress and those that are problems. Students make a chart with the headings *Progress* and *Problems,* and list their changes under the appropriate heading. For example, students would write *improvements in the economy* under the heading *Progress.*

Assessment: Use the Individual Activity Rubric on page *xii* of this guide. Fill in the rubric with the additional information listed below. For this project, students should have

• made a list of changes that occurred in the United States and around the world.

• made a chart listing the progress and problems.

Learning Objectives

Review the Learning Objectives on page 579 of the Student Edition before starting the chapter. Students can use the list as a learning guide. Suggest they write the objectives in a journal or use the Chapter Goals and Self-Check worksheet found on page PA 6 of the Classroom Resource Binder.

After reading each section of the chapter, have students write an example of what they learned about under the appropriate objective. Suggest

that students use these worksheets as a practice guide to help them study for the chapter test.

Timeline

Use the timeline to discuss the sequence of events in this chapter. Point out the timeline's title, its time span, and the intervals. After students have read the chapter, have them review the timeline and suggest additional entries.

SECTION 1: Politics and Presidents
Student Edition, pages 580–583

Section Objectives
• Describe the state of the U.S. economy under President Bush and explain why taxes were raised.
• Identify significant domestic and foreign events that occurred during the Clinton years.
* Describe the 1988 and 1992 presidential elections and their outcomes.

Words to Know
primary, downsize, budget surplus, grand jury

Cooperative Group Activity

Two Presidents, Two Approaches
Materials: reference materials (Unit 10 Bibliography and Internet sites, pages 236–240)

Procedure: Remind students that in 1992, there were three Presidential candidates: Republican George Bush, Democrat Bill Clinton, and third-party candidate H. Ross Perot. Divide the class into three groups and assign each group a candidate from the 1992 election.

• Group members research their candidate's 1992 campaign platform.
• Students then prepare campaign literature and speeches promoting their candidate's point of view.
• A spokesperson from each group presents its materials to the class.

Customizing the Activity for Individual Needs
ESL To help students understand the concept of a *primary*, write the term *primary* and its definition on the chalkboard. Then, select three students to assume the role of presidential candidates for the ABC political party. Explain to students that only one of the three people can be chosen as the official

presidential candidate from the ABC political party. Have students write their choice for candidate on a slip of paper. Tally the votes and announce the candidate. Explain to students that they have just conducted a primary election. Have them discuss why primary elections are needed. Also mention that primary elections are held for offices other than that of President.

Learning Styles Students can:

 complete a Comparison-and-Contrast chart (Classroom Resource Binder, page GO 4) with information about the presidential candidates.

 draw and label a political cartoon that represents the three presidential candidates.

 work in groups of three to hold a debate between Bush, Clinton, and Perot.

Enrichment Activity

Organize students into small groups to discuss how they would run the country if they were President. Encourage them to talk about the policies they would implement, the issues they would address, and their goals while in office. Have group members list their discussion points on chart paper under the heading: *If I Were President . . .* Ask students to name a past President who they most identify with and who they would support. Have students write a paragraph explaining their choice and reasons.

Alternative Assessment

Pair students to review information from the section and write questions about the section that begin with the words *who, what, when, where, why,* and *how.* Partners can trade papers and answer each other's questions.

SECTION 2: A New Role in the World *Student Edition, pages 584–590*

Section Objectives

• Explain events in Yugoslavia after the cold war.

• Explain why Saddam Hussein invaded Kuwait.

• Describe Operation Desert Storm and identify the results of the Gulf War.

• Describe how the United States tried to bring about change in South Africa.

∗ Discuss the United States' role as a superpower.

Words to Know

ethnic cleansing, coalition

Cooperative Group Activity

Reporting World News

Materials: reference materials (Unit 10 Bibliography and Internet sites, pages 236–240)

Procedure: Remind students that while George Bush was President, the republics of the Soviet Union broke free of central rule. As the cold war ended, conflicts in many other countries broke out, as well. The United States was the only superpower remaining in the world. No other country had enough power and money to try to end conflicts around the globe. Organize students into six groups to assume the roles of newspaper journalists reporting on world events. You may wish to have students conduct further research on world conflicts during the 1980s and 1990s.

• Each group reviews information and conducts research to write newspaper articles on one of the following events: *the end of the cold war, ethnic cleansing in Yugoslavia after the cold war, the Persian Gulf War, Operations Desert Shield and Desert Storm, results of the Gulf War,* or *victory for human rights in South Africa.*

• Members of each group write ideas on their topics and share them with the group. The members then write a group article.

• All group members combine their articles in a newspaper format, and name their newspaper.

Customizing the Activity for Individual Needs

ESL To help students understand the concept of a superpower nation, have partners discuss U.S. involvement in other countries. Invite students to discuss the ways other nations might perceive the United States. Students should then discuss their opinion of U.S. involvement in conflicts around the world.

Learning Styles Students can:

 create a timeline (Classroom Resource Binder, page GO 8) of 1980s–1990s world events.

 sort index cards of 1980s–1990s world events into the order in which the events occurred.

 read their newspaper articles to the class.

Reinforcement Activity

Organize students into small groups to write a proposal for a documentary film about the conflicts and changes occurring around the world as the cold war ended. Have students include the following information in their proposals: *the significance of making the documentary* and *information that they will be covering in the documentary.* Have group members share their proposals with the class.

Alternative Assessment

Students can write an essay that describes how the United States was involved in peacekeeping efforts around the world after the end of the cold war. Remind students to state whether the efforts were successful or unsuccessful.

SECTION 3: New Rights and Opportunities
Student Edition, pages 591–594

Section Objectives
- Describe the efforts made to fight violence and crime in the 1990s.
- Identify gains in equality during the 1980s.
- * Describe new programs and laws that were initiated in the United States during the 1990s.

Words to Know
underclass, workfare

Cooperative Group Activity

Gains and Losses

Procedure: Remind students that during the 1980s and 1990s the gap between rich and poor people in the United States widened, with more homeless people than ever before. During this same time, however, many groups gained rights and opportunities. Divide the class into groups.

- Students brainstorm and write a list of questions that they can ask family members, teachers, or other adults about the gains and losses that took place in the 1980s and 1990s. Examples include: *Do you feel that women gained rights and had more opportunities during this time? How do you feel about states setting up workfare instead of welfare?*

- Groups present their list of questions to the class.
- Students vote on the top five questions to ask family members, teachers, and other adults.
- One group member uses the top five questions to conduct a poll by interviewing the other members of the group. Students record the responses on paper.
- Group members analyze the data and make a chart that compares and contrasts the results.
- Groups share their charts with the class.

Customizing the Activity for Individual Needs

ESL To help students understand the concept of government reforms, have them share if and how the governments in their native countries responded to the needs of their citizens.

Learning Styles Students can:

 make a Description Web (Classroom Resource Binder, page GO 3) describing the gains and losses occurring in American society during the 1980s and 1990s.

 write the names of Americans who made a difference during the 1980s and 1990s on one side of the index cards and write a sentence describing his or her contributions on the other side.

 work with a partner to take turns calling out events of the 1980s and 1990s while their partner describes the event. Have students switch roles often.

Enrichment Activity

Remind students that today, millions of Americans do not have health insurance. Have students develop a health care proposal that would allow all Americans to have health coverage. Have students share their plans with the class, and then vote on the plans that would be most effective.

Alternative Assessment

Assign students one of the following topics: *equal rights, disabilities, welfare reform, health care reform,* or *fighting violence and crime.* Students can design a newspaper advertisement relating to their topic, using slogans and pictures to convey their message.

VOICES FROM THE PAST:
Maya Angelou
Student Edition, page 595

Objectives
- Social Studies Skill: Write an illustrated book jacket to describe Maya Angelou's life and work.
- Social Studies Skill: Write a poem or song that could be presented at the next presidential inauguration.
- Social Studies Skill: Design a mural to identify inspirational messages that could be raised at the next presidential inauguration.

Activities
About Maya Angelou
Procedure: Have students conduct research on the poet Maya Angelou to create a book jacket biography about her life and work. After students write the text of the biography, encourage them to read it aloud. Have students draw illustrations to supplement the text of their biographies about Angelou.

New Beginnings
Procedure: Have students assume the role of a poet or songwriter who has been chosen to share his or her work at the next presidential inauguration. Encourage students to write about new beginnings, and what the American people should hope and strive for in the next four years.

A Picture Is Worth a Thousand Words
Materials: mural paper; markers; newspapers; magazines; scissors

Procedure: Ask students to create a mural that could be displayed at the next presidential inauguration. Have them write simple words, phrases, or messages that are inspirational. Encourage them to draw pictures as well as cut out photos from magazines and newspapers that convey a positive message to the American people.

Practice
Have students complete Voices From the Past: Making Predictions page 211 of the Classroom Resource Binder.

Closing the Chapter
Student Edition, pages 596–597

Chapter Vocabulary
Review with students the Words to Know on page 579 of the Student Edition. Then have them complete the Vocabulary Review on page 596 of the Student Edition, by determining whether each statement is true or false. If the sentence is false, have them change the underlined term it to make it true.

For more vocabulary practice, have them complete the vocabulary exercise on page 209 in the Classroom Resource Binder.

Test Tip
Have students choose a partner with whom they can review each section of the chapter. Students should read each section to review the vocabulary terms and significant information presented. Have students quiz each other by answering the section review questions.

Learning Objectives
Have students review their Chapter Goals and Self-Check worksheet found on page PA 6 of the Classroom Resource Binder. They can check off the goal they have reached. Note that each section of the quiz corresponds to a Learning Objective.

Group Activity
Summary: Students write a poem about the ways in which violence and crime could be curtailed in the United States.

Procedure: Organize students into groups of three or four. Each group thinks of ways to stop violence in the United States and around the world. Students make a list of their ideas. Then, students compose poems that reflect their group's ideas. Students should practice reading their poems aloud and revise them if necessary. Group members read their poems aloud to the class.

Assessment: Use the Group Activity Rubric found on page *xiii* of this guide. Fill in the rubric with the following additional information. For this activity, students should have

- brainstormed a list of ways to stop violence.
- participated in writing and presenting a poem that reflects their thoughts and feelings.

RELATED MATERIALS   See the Unit Overview page for related Globe Fearon books that can be used to enrich and extend the materials in the chapter.

Traditional Assessment

Chapter Quiz

The Chapter Quiz on page 597 of the Student Edition can be used as an open-book test, a closed-book test, or a homework assignment. Use the quiz to identify concepts in the chapter that students need to review. Chapter Tests can be found in the Classroom Resource Binder on pages 213–214. Workbook pages 129–132 can be used for additional practice.

Chapter Tests

Use Chapter Tests A and B on pages 213–214 in the Classroom Resource Binder to further assess mastery of chapter concepts.

Additional Resources

Use the Resource Planner on page 224 of this guide to assign additional exercises from the Classroom Resource Binder and Workbook.

Alternative Assessment

Presentation

- Small groups of students review information about the Persian Gulf War.
- Students create a circle graph to show the total number of Americans who fought in the war and the number of women who served in the war.
- Students create a second circle graph to show the total number of Americans who returned after fighting the Persian Gulf War and the number of Americans who were killed in the war.
- Students present their graphs to the class.

Real-Life Connection

Students review information about the gains and losses to American society during the 1980s and 1990s. Then, students think about ways to improve society today by creating new opportunities for the future. Students write entries in their journals about their ideas.

Chapter
31

Chapter 32 · A New Century 1990–the future

Chapter at a Glance

SE page

598		*Opening the Chapter and Portfolio Project*
600	SECTION 1	Challenges for a New President
606	SECTION 2	Challenges for All Americans
610		*Chapter Review and Group Activity*

Learning Objectives

- Discuss the 2000 presidential election and how it was decided.
- Describe the terrorist attacks of September 11, 2001, and the U.S. response to the attacks.
- Discuss the environmental issues that challenge Americans in the twenty-first century.
- Explore how technology has improved space exploration and health care.

Social Studies Skills

- Use a timeline to describe events that occurred in the last decade of the twentieth century and the beginning of the twenty-first century.
- Understand the role of the U.S. Supreme Court in deciding the 2000 presidential election.

- Explain the difference between the popular vote and the electoral vote in a presidential election.
- Analyze the response of American citizens to the terrorist attacks of September 11, 2001.
- Explore how technology has improved health care and space research.

Writing Skills

- Write the setting of a story that takes place in the year 2050 in the United States.
- Write an article about U.S. military action in Iraq.
- Write a list that identifies ways to save energy and money.
- Write a television news report about an event in the chapter.

**Chapter 32
A New Century**

Use the Program Resources below for reteaching, reinforcement, and enrichment. Additional activities for customizing the lessons can be found in this guide.

Key
Reteaching = ⤺   Reinforcement = ⬇   Enrichment = ⤴

Sections	Program Resources		
	⬇ Workbook Exercises	Teacher's Planning Guide	Classroom Resource Binder
Challenges for a New President	133	⬇ p. 232	⤺ Concept Builder 32 *A New Century*
Challenges for All Americans	134, 135	⬇ p. 234	⤺ Document-Based Questions 8 *It's the Computer Age!* Transparency 11 *Estimated United States Population by the Year 2005 by States*
Chapter 32 Review		p. 234	⬇ Words to Know 215 ⤺ Challenge 218 ⬇ Chapter Tests A & B, 219, 220 ⬇ Unit Tests Parts I & II, 221, 222

**Chapter
32**

Customizing the Chapter

Opening the Chapter
Student Edition, pages 598–599

Photo Activity
Direct students' attention to the photo of the millennium celebration. Mention that people all over the world celebrated the beginning of the new millennium on January 1, 2000. Have students develop a list of reasons why people regard a new millennium as a historical event. Encourage students to discuss the hopes and concerns that they have for the twenty-first century.

Words to Know
Review the Words to Know on page 599 of the Student Edition. To help students remember

the words, pair students and distribute 14 index cards to each pair. Have students write the seven vocabulary words and their definitions on separate index cards. Have pairs mix up the cards and take turns matching a word to its definition. After students have matched up the cards, have them check their answers by looking up each word in the Glossary in the Student Edition.

The following words and definitions are covered in this chapter:

millennium a period of 1,000 years

popular vote a vote cast by a citizen in a presidential election

electoral vote a vote cast by a chosen elector in a presidential election

resolution an official statement of opinion

acid rain rain that is polluted by harmful chemicals

global warming the theory, or idea, that Earth's temperature is slowly rising

recycling using a product more than once

Portfolio Project

Summary: Students write a plan for the setting of a story that takes place in the year 2050, describing what they would like the future of the United States to be.

Procedure: As students read the chapter, have them think about what they would like the future of the United States to be. Encourage them to think about technology, the environment, and challenges Americans face. Students write about a futuristic setting for a story that takes place in the year 2050. Students describe the outdoors and the places where the characters live, work, and play. Students draw pictures of their settings, label objects, and describe how each object will be used. If appropriate, students can share their futuristic settings with the class.

Assessment: Use the Individual Activity Rubric on page *xii* of this guide. Fill in the rubric with the additional information below. For this project, students should have:

- written about a futuristic setting for a story in the year 2050.
- drawn and labeled a picture of the setting.

Learning Objectives

Review the Learning Objectives on page 599 of the Student Edition before starting the chapter. Students can use the list as a learning guide. Suggest they write the objectives in a journal or use the Chapter Goals and Self-Check worksheet found on page PA 6 of the Classroom Resource Binder.

After reading each section of the chapter, have students write an example of what they learned about under the appropriate objective. Suggest that students use these worksheets as a practice guide to help them study for the chapter test.

Timeline

Use the timeline to discuss the sequence of events in this chapter. Point out the timeline's title, its time span, and the intervals. After students have read the chapter, have them review the timeline and suggest additional entries.

SECTION 1: Challenges for a New President
Student Edition, pages 600–605

Section Objectives

* Describe the presidential election of 2000 and how it differed from other elections.
- Discuss the terrorist attacks of September 11, 2001.
- Identify how the U.S. government responded to the terrorist attacks of September 11, 2001.
- Discuss Operation Enduring Freedom and Operation Iraqi Freedom.

Words to Know

millennium, popular vote, electoral vote, resolution

Cooperative Group Activity

The Presidential Election of 2000

Materials: reference materials (Unit 10 Bibliography and Internet sites, pages 236–240); chart paper; markers

Procedure: Remind students that the 2000 presidential election was a historical event. The nation did not know who the President-elect was for five weeks after election day. Have students conduct research on the presidential election of 2000. Divide the class into four or five small groups to create an illustrated timeline of the 35-day event.

- Students review information and research the events of the 2000 presidential election.

- Group members divide the timeline into six one-week intervals, beginning with the week of Monday, November 6, 2000 (Election Day was Tuesday, November 7) and ending with the week of Monday, December 18, 2000 (the Supreme Court decision to stop the Florida recount was made on Tuesday, December 12).
- Each group member fills in important events for one week of the timeline.
- Students illustrate the timeline events with drawings, newspaper headlines, and magazine photographs.

Customizing the Activity for Individual Needs

ESL To help students understand some of the vocabulary used during the 2000 election, define the following terms: *chad ballot, recount, concession speech.* Encourage students to use these terms in an oral summary of the election.

Learning Styles Students can:

 design a poster about the events of the 2000 presidential election.

 cut out articles and photos of the election from newspapers and magazines.

 conduct a mock interview in which one student interviews "voters" after George W. Bush is announced as the new President-elect of the United States.

Reinforcement Activity

Distribute to groups of students several articles about the election, the recount in Florida, and the Supreme Court decision to stop the recount. Then have a roundtable discussion about the election. Elicit from students their opinion about the way the election was decided. Discuss the implications of this election: Albert Gore, Jr., received the majority of popular votes, but George W. Bush received the majority of electoral votes. Ask: *How do you think the voters felt about the new President-elect? What challenges do you think he faced as he entered office?*

Alternative Assessment

Students can write cause-and-effect statements about topics such as *the 2000 presidential election; events of September 11, 2001; the creation of the position of Director of Homeland Security; U.S. military action in Afghanistan; U.S. military action in Iraq.*

SECTION 2: Challenges for All Americans
Student Edition, pages 606–609

Objectives
- Identify ways in which Americans have helped to protect the environment and reduce pollution.
- Describe some of the energy problems that the United States faces today.
- Identify advancements in space technology.
- Describe improvements in health care.
* Discuss problems the United States faces in the twenty-first century and how Americans can work together.

Words to Know
acid rain, global warming, recycling

Cooperative Group Activity

Protecting the Environment
Materials: reference materials (Unit 10 Bibliography and Internet sites, pages 236–240)

Procedure: Remind students that the future holds exciting changes and challenges as well as the need to face existing problems, such as pollution and other threats to the environment. It is through cooperation that Americans will meet the challenges of the future. Divide the class into small groups to write speeches. You may wish to have students conduct further research on topics such as pollution and energy problems.

- Group members make a list of environmental problems that they believe the country is facing today and possible solutions to these problems.
- Group members use their list to write a five-minute speech motivating Americans to work together and solve the problems.
- Group members choose a spokesperson to read their speech to the class.

Customizing the Activity for Individual Needs

ESL To help students understand the concept of energy problems, have them work with English-proficient students to match index cards that list energy problems with cards that list possible solutions for conserving energy.

Learning Styles Students can:

 complete a Cause and Effect chart (Classroom Resource Binder, page GO 2) about pollution.

 draw and label a picture that shows one kind of pollution or energy problem today.

 work with a partner to compose slogans that will motivate Americans to work together to solve problems, such as: *Let's solve our problems of today. We'll work together and find a way.*

Reinforcement Activity

Students create ideas for a national organization that helps solve particular problems that the country is facing today. Students name the organization and identify and list its goals. They then design a pamphlet that promotes their organization.

Alternative Assessment

Students can develop a list of eight questions about pollution control and energy challenges that Americans face today. Have pairs of students exchange papers and answer each other's questions. Ask both pairs of students to review their answers.

Closing the Chapter
Student Edition, pages 610–611

Chapter Vocabulary

Review with students the Words to Know on page 599 of the Student Edition. Then have them complete the Vocabulary Review on page 610 of the Student Edition by matching each definition with a term from the list.

For more vocabulary practice, have them complete the vocabulary exercise on page 215 of the Classroom Resource Binder.

Test Tip

Have students take the Chapter Quiz on page 611 of the Student Edition. Encourage students to read through their answers to check that they have answered each question thoroughly. After students have received their corrected quiz, have them look up the correct answer to each question they answered incorrectly on the quiz.

Learning Objectives

Have students review their Chapter Goals and Self-Check worksheet found on page PA 6 of the Classroom Resource Binder. They can check off the goal they have reached. Note that each section of the quiz corresponds to a Learning Objective.

Group Activity

Summary: Students prepare a TV news report on one event from the chapter.

Materials: reference materials (Unit 10 Bibliography and Internet sites, pages 236–240); note cards; video camera (optional)

Procedure: Have groups of four or five students select one topic from the chapter: the 2000 presidential election; the terrorist attacks of September 11, 2001; the U.S. response to the terrorist attacks; environmental concerns; advances in space technology; or improvements in health care. Group members then research the topic, using resources such as newspapers, magazines, and the Internet. Each group collects notes and prepares a brief TV news report that includes the five *W*s: who, what, where, when, and why. One or two members of the group may be selected to present the report. Students may decide to videotape the report or simply present it to the class orally.

Assessment: Use the Group Activity Rubric found on page *xiii* of this guide. Fill in the rubric with the following additional information. For this activity, students should have

- researched and summarized one topic in the chapter.
- helped to create a TV news report of the topic and presented it to the class.

RELATED MATERIALS See the Unit Overview page for related Globe Fearon books that can be used to enrich and extend the materials in the chapter.

Traditional Assessment

Chapter Quiz

The Chapter Quiz on page 611 of the Student Edition can be used as an open-book test, a closed-book test, or a homework assignment. Use the quiz to identify concepts in the chapter that students need to review. Chapter Tests can be found in the Classroom Resource Binder on pages 219–220. Workbook pages 133–135 can be used for additional practice.

Chapter Tests

Use Chapter Tests A and B on pages 219–220 in the Classroom Resource Binder to further assess mastery of chapter concepts.

Additional Resources

Use the Resource Planner on page 231 of this guide to assign additional exercises from the Classroom Resource Binder and Workbook.

Alternative Assessment

Presentation

- Students write 20 questions about American life in the late twentieth century and early twenty-first century. They may include information about advances in pollution control, space technology, health care, and energy consumption.
- Students work in groups of five to present a quiz show. One student is the host. Panel members work in pairs to answer the questions.

Student Interview

Have individual students answer the following questions about the topic of the U.S. response to the terrorist attacks of September 11, 2001.

- What does the Director of Homeland Security do?
- What was Operation Enduring Freedom?
- How was the UN involved in Iraq?
- What was Operation Iraqi Freedom?

Unit Assessment

This is the last chapter in Unit 10: *Forward to the Future*. To review and assess cumulative understanding and provide standardized-test practice, have students complete the Unit Review Test of page 612 of the Student Edition, and the Unit 10 Cumulative Test on pages 221–222 of the Classroom Resource Binder.

Chapter
32

Bibliography

UNIT 1

The Aztec Empire, **Conrad Stein** Traces the Aztec Empire from its beginnings to its conquest by Hernán Cortés. (Marshall Cavendish, 1995)

Who Really Discovered America, **Stephen Krensky** Discusses the various groups of people who may have landed in North America before Columbus. (Hastings House Book Publishers, 1991)

Indians of the Northeast Woodlands, **Beatrice Siegel** Examines American Indian culture in a question and answer format. It covers the periods before and after the arrival of Europeans, as well as the present. (Walker, 1992)

Seeds of Change: The Story of Cultural Change After 1492, **Sharryl Hawke** Traces the impact of the Columbian exchange using artwork, maps, and photographs. (Addison-Wesley, 1992)

A Multicultural Portrait of Colonial Life, **Carolyn Kott Washburne** Describes the lives of Native Americans and European settlers in colonial America. (Marshall Cavendish, 1993)

Growing Up in Colonial America, **Tracy Barrett** Explores what life was like for a child in colonial America. (The Millbrook Press, 1995)

The Colonies in Revolt, **Alden Carter** Describes the period between the 1760s and 1770s when the relationship between the colonies and Great Britain fell apart. This time period started the beginnings of a revolution. (Watts, 1988)

Marco Polo, **Zachary Kent** A biography of the explorer and his adventures in the Far East. It traces the path Marco Polo followed through Asian lands and the discoveries he made along the way. (Children's Press, 1992)

Morning Girl, **Michael Dorris** The story takes place in 1492, just before the arrival of Columbus. A brother and sister in the Bahamas describe what happens when explorers enter their islands and their lives. (Hyperion Books for Children, 1992)

The Sign of the Beaver, **Elizabeth George Speare** A novel about life in the wilderness and the relationship between white settlers and Indians in the 1700s. (Dell Publishing, 1983)

Websites

www.afroam.org/history/slavery
www.nationalgeographic.com/lewisclark/exped.html
www.rrangers.org
www.ushistory.org
www1.minn.net/~keithp

UNIT 2

A Convention of Delegates: The Creation of the Constitution, **Dennis Hauptly** In this story students can see how famous men worked together to solve problems concerning the way the country was run. (Simon & Schuster, 1987)

George Washington and the Birth of Our Nation, **Milton Meltzer** The life of our first President, beginning with his childhood in Virginia and ending with his retirement in Mount Vernon. (Franklin Watts, 1986)

The Louisiana Purchase, **Gail Sakurai** Provides information about the Louisiana Purchase, from the time Spanish explorers reached the Mississippi River to the U.S. acquisition of East and West Florida from Spain. (Children's Press, 1998)

Samuel Slater's Mill and the Industrial Revolution, **Christopher Simonds** Describes the arrival of Samuel Slater to the United States. Slater built a successful cotton mill in Rhode Island. This mill is one step in the change of the United States from a farming to an industrial nation. (Silver Burdett Press, 1990)

Battle of the Alamo, **Andrew Santella** Chronicles the time period during which the Mission San Antonio de Valero was established and Texas joined the Union as the twentieth eighth state. (Children's Press, 1997)

The Oregon Trail, **Leonard Everett Fisher** Students can learn what the 2,000 mile route that stretched from the Missouri River to the Columbia River was like, and the role it played in the western expansion of America. (Holiday House, 1990)

Cowboys of the Wild West, **Russell Freedman** A description of the cowboys of the 1890s, who drove herds across the wild prairies. (Scholastic, 1985)

Remember the Ladies: The First Women's Rights Convention, **Norma Johnston** The convention in 1848 brings women from all backgrounds together to discuss their rights (Scholastic, 1995)

The Story of Sacajawea, Guide to Lewis and Clark, **Della Rowland** A biography of the young woman who helped guide the explorers, Lewis and Clark, on their journey through the western United States. (Dell Publishing, 1989)

A Gathering of Days, **Joan W. Blos** Historical fiction—the journal of a nineteenth century New England girl. (Scribner, 1979)

Websites

www.cherokee.org
www.eliwhitney.org/ew.htm
www.historychannel.com
www.nara.gov/exhall/charters/constitution/confath.html
www.ukans.edu/kansas/seneca/oregon/gold.html

UNIT 3

Bull Run, **Paul Fleischman** Historical fiction—a story about the first major battle of the Civil War told from 16 points of view. (Harper Collins, 1995)

Emancipation Proclamation: Why Lincoln Really Freed the Slaves, **Robert Young** An account of Lincoln and his role in the Emancipation Proclamation. It explains how political leaders at the time felt about the slavery issue. (Silver Burdett Press, 1994)

Those Courageous Women of the Civil War, **Karen Zeinert** Describes the different roles women had during the Civil War. (Millbrook Press, 1998)

Civil War Soldiers, **Catherine Reef** An account of the African American soldiers who took part in over 400 Civil War battles. (Twenty-First Century Books, 1993)

Battle of the Ironclads, **Alden Carter** Describes two battleships of the Civil War and the impact they had on the war. (Franklin Watts, 1993)

The Day Fort Sumter Was Fired On: A Photo History of the Civil War, **Jim Haskins** A history of the Civil War and the Reconstruction period featuring photographs, sketches, paintings, and posters. (Scholastic, 1995)

Lincoln: A Photobiography, **Russell Freedman** A biography of Lincoln's life focusing on his presidential years. A sampling of his writings is included. (Houghton Mifflin Co., 1987)

Who Comes with Cannons? **Patricia Beatty** Truth Hopkins is a young Quaker who opposes slavery and the Civil War. In this novel, she accompanies a runaway slave who seeks refugee on her family's farm. (William Morrow, 1992)

Steal Away Home, **Lois Ruby** In this novel, a young girl discovers her house was once a station on the Underground Railroad. (Macmillan, 1994)

Websites

www.bchm.org/wrr
www.civil-war.net
www.cr.nps.gov/csd/exhibits/douglass
www.historychannel.com
www.impeach-andrewjohnson.com

UNIT 4

The Iron Horse: How Railroads Changed America, **Richard Wormser** Describes how the greatest development of the nineteenth century changed American society. (Walker and Co., 1993)

The Immigrant Experience, **David Reimers** Discusses immigration in North America, from the Spanish explorers in the sixteenth century to the diverse "melting pot" of the United States in the twentieth century. (Chelsea House, 1988)

Immigrant Kids, **Russell Freedman** The life of an immigrant child in the late 1800s and early 1900s is presented through text and photographs. (Dutton, 1980)

Ellis Island, **Catherine Reef** Reviews the history of this immigration center, where more than 12 million immigrants entered the United States over a 60 year period. (Dillon Press, 1991)

The Great Ancestor Hunt, **Lila Perl** Students can learn to trace their ancestors and find out about their family's past. (Clarion Books, 1989)

Turn of the Century, Our Nation One Hundred Years Ago, **Nancy Levinson** Portrays life in the United States one hundred years ago. It shows how past events made our country what it is today. (Lodestar Books, 1994)

Kids at Work: Lewis Hine and the Crusade Against Child Labor, **Russell Freedman** An account of the hardships that children endured working in mines, fields, mills and factories across the United States, and the man who worked to change it. (Clarion Books, 1994)

Andrew Carnegie, **John Bowman** A biography of the hardworking businessman who became the richest man in the world. (Silver Burdett Press, 1989)

Thomas Edison and Electricity, **Steve Parker** A biography of Thomas Edison, "the greatest inventor of his age." (Harper Collins, 1992)

The Great Wheel, **Robert Lawson** In this work of historical fiction, a young man is chosen to help build the world's first Ferris wheel for the 1893 Chicago World's Fair. (Walker & Co., 1993)

Websites

www.cprr.org
www.ellisisland.com/indexHistory.html
www.history.Ohio-state.edu/projects/uscartoons/GAPEC
www.naacp.org
www.pbs.org/weta/the west
www.pbs.org/wgbh/amex/carnegie
www.pbs.org/wgbh/amex/technology/forgotteninv.html
www.tomedison.org

UNIT 5

The Spanish-American War, **Deborah Bachrach**
Details the events leading up to the Spanish-American War and its significance for the United States. (Simon & Schuster, 1991)

The Spanish-American War: Imperial Ambitions, **Alden R. Carter** Provides an overview of the events behind this sixteen week war between the United States and Spain. It discusses the outcome of the war and the impact it had on the United States. (Franklin Watts, 1992)

World War I, **Tom McGowen** Provides an overview of World War I, including the military battles and political changes that took place. (Lucent Books, 1991)

Panama Canal, Gateway to the World, **Judith St. George** Presents a history of the canal which connected the Atlantic and Pacific oceans. (G.P. Putnam's Sons, 1989)

The Great Migration: An American Story, **Jacob Lawrence** The story of the African Americans who left their homes in the South to move to northern industrial cities. It is told through a series of paintings and poetry. (Harper Collins, 1993)

First World War, **John D. Clare** Describes World War I through storytelling, personal accounts, and photographs. (Harcourt Brace, 1995)

Bully for You Teddy Roosevelt, **Jean Fritz** A biography of Teddy Roosevelt. Students can learn about his family, his politics, and his love for the outdoors. (G.P. Putnam's Sons, 1991)

Edith Bolling Galt Wilson, **Alice K. Flanagan** A biography of the wife of President Woodrow Wilson. (Children's Press, 1998)

Good-bye, Billy Radish, **Gloria Skurzynski** Historical fiction set in America during World War I. It describes the fate of two young men facing the war. (Bradbury Press, 1992)

Summer Soldiers, **Susan Hart Lindquist** The story of a young man's struggles at home once his father goes off to war in 1918. (Delacorte Press, 1999)

Websites

www.cmstory.org/history/timeline/ww1.htm
www.cr.nps.gov/history/1spamwar.htm
www.pancanal.com/history
www.uss-salem.org/features/gwf

UNIT 6

1920's, **Margaret Sharman** Examines the 10 year period following the end of World War I. The events are shown in chronological order and illustrated with photographs, maps, and charts. (Raintree Steck-Vaughn, 1993)

The Dust Bowl, **John Farris** Discusses the Dust Bowl and the hardships it caused farmers in the Great Plains. (Lucent Books, 1989)

The Dust Bowl, Disaster on the Plains, **Tricia Andryszewski** An account of life in the Great Plains during the 1930s. Describes the storms and how the nation and people worked together to return life to normal. (Millbrook Press, 1993)

Crash of 1929, **Ronald Migneco** Provides an in-depth look at the stock market crash of 1929. (Lucent Books, 1989)

A Multicultural Portrait of the Great Depression, **Susan Rensberger** Examines the period between World War I and World War II when Americans fought to find work, food, and clothes. (Benchmark Books, 1996)

The New Deal, **Gail Stewart** Discusses the events leading up to the Great Depression and progresses through Roosevelt's plans for changes in the governing policies of the United States. (Macmillan, 1993)

Eleanor Roosevelt, A Life of Discovery, **Russell Freedman** A biography of Eleanor Roosevelt. It shows how she represented her husband and became an advocate for people in need. (Clarion Books, 1993)

Mother Jones, One Woman's Fight for Labor, **Betsy Harvey Kraft** A biography of a famous American Union organizer who became a labor leader when she was in her sixties. Her causes included miners, railroad workers, and children. (Clarion Books, 1995)

Out of the Dust, **Karen Hesse** Describes what life was like for a family living in Oklahoma during the dust bowl. (Scholastic, 1997)

Roll of Thunder, Hear My Cry, **Mildred Taylor** A novel about an African American family living in the South in the 1930s and the problems they faced. (Puffin Books, 1991)

Websites

www.bergen.org/AAST/Projects/depression
www.discovery.com/area/history/dustbowl/dustbowlopener.html
www.hfmgv.org/histories/hf/henry.html
www.nara.gov/exhall/exhibits.html
www.whitehouse.gov/WH/glimpse/presidents/html/fr32.thm

UNIT 7

The Holocaust, A History of Courage and Resistance, **Bea Stadler** Describes the experiences of Jews in Germany and in other European nations. (Behrman House, 1995)

The 761st Tank Battalion, African American Soldiers, **Kathryn Pfeifer** Also known as the Black Panthers, this battalion served during World War II and played an important role in helping bring about Germany's surrender. (Twenty-First Century Books, 1994)

World War II, **Tom McGowen** A book to help students follow the events of the war. (Franklin Watts, 1993)

Rosie the Riveter: Women Working on the Home Front in World War II, **Penny Colman** Describes how women's careers changed once World War II began and men left for the armed forces. (Random House, 1995)

The Korean War: America's Wars, **Deborah Bachrach** Examines the involvement of America in the Korean War. (Lucent Books, 1991)

The Fifties, **Tom Stacy** Discusses the culture and historical events of the 1950s, including the Korean War, civil rights, and the polio vaccine. (Steck-Vaughn, 1990)

I Am a Star: Child of the Holocaust, **Inge Auerbacher** An account of a child survivor of a concentration camp. (Penguin USA, 1993)

Journey to Topaz, **Yoshiko Uchida** A novel about the Japanese American evacuation that took place when war broke out between the U.S. and Japan in 1941. It is the story of one Japanese family and what they went through as a result of the evacuation orders. (Creative Arts Book Co., 1985)

Jacob's Rescue: A Holocaust Story, **Malka Drucker** A young boy in Poland who learns that it is not safe to be Jewish anymore is hidden with a Christian family. The novel is based on a true story. (Yearling/Dell, 1993)

Stepping on the Cracks, **Mary Hahn** A novel set in World War II America which describes what life was like on the home front during the war. (Clarion Books, 1991)

Websites

www.euronet.nl/users/wilfried/ww2/second.htm

www.koreanwar.org

www.nationalgeographic.com/midway/index.html

www.ushmm.org

UNIT 8

1950's, **Jane Duden** Photographs and articles are used to portray life in the U.S. between 1950 and 1959. (Silver Burdett Press, 1989)

Dwight D. Eisenhower: War Hero and President, **Marian G. Cannon** A biography of the commander general of the Allied Forces in Europe during World War II who became the 34th President of the United States. (Franklin Watts, 1990)

Harry S. Truman, **Barbara Silberdick Feinberg** Analyzes the 33rd President of the United States and his achievements while in office. (Frankin Watts, 1994)

Montgomery: Launching of the Civil Rights Movement, **Linda Wade** Describes the events of the 1960s and how they changed the idea of freedom in the United States. (Rourke Enterprises, 1991)

The Day Martin Luther King, Jr. Was Shot, **Jim Haskins** Provides a history of the civil rights movement through photographs, illustrations, and newspaper headlines. (Scholastic, 1992)

The Year They Walked, **Beatrice Siegel** Examines the life of Rosa Parks, who refused to give up her seat on a Montgomery bus. (Macmillan, 1992)

Jackie Robinson Breaks the Color Line, **Andrew Santella** A biography of the man who became the first African American baseball player in the major leagues. (Children's Press, 1996)

Flying to the Moon, An Astronaut's Story, **Michael Collins** Describes the life of Collins and his role in the Apollo 11 Moon Landing mission of 1969. (Farrar, Straus, and Giroux, 1994)

John Glenn, Astronaut and Senator, **Michael Cole** A biography of John Glenn, an astronaut who first went to space in 1962 and returned to space again in 1998. (Enslow Publishers, 1993)

John F. Kennedy: Portrait of a President, **Martin S. Goldman** A biography of John F. Kennedy who became the 35th President of the United States. (Facts on File, 1995)

And One for All, **Theresa Nelson** This novel, which takes place in the 1960s, describes how the events of the era affected the lives of three friends. (Orchard Books, 1989)

Websites

www.mlking.org

www.nps.gov/vive

www.pbs.org/kcet/johnglenn

www.trumanlibrary.org

www.historychannel.com

UNIT 9

The Vietnam War, **John Devaney** An account of this controversial war and the events that surrounded it, ending with the fall of Saigon in 1975. (Franklin Watts, 1992)

An Album of the Vietnam War, **Don Lawson** An illustrated history of the American involvement in the Vietnam War. (Franklin Watts, 1986)

A Nation in Turmoil, Civil Rights and the Vietnam War, **Gene Brown** Uses primary sources to discuss the social and political events of the 1960s and 1970s. (Twenty-First Century Books, 1994)

Always to Remember: The Story of the Vietnam Veterans Memorial, **Brent Ashabranner** A discussion of the Vietnam Veterans Memorial, including its construction and some of the controversies surrounding it. (Dodd Mead, 1988)

Lyndon Baines Johnson, **Dennis Eskow** A biography of the 36th President of the United States. (Franklin Watts, 1993)

1960's, **Jane Duden** A view, through articles and photographs, of what life was like between 1960 and 1969. (Crestwood House, 1989)

Richard Nixon, **Dee Lillegard** A biography of the 37th President of the United States, who was the first President to resign from office. (Children's Press, 1988)

The Story of Watergate, **Jim Hargrove** Describes the biggest political scandal in United States history. (Children's Press, 1988)

The Seventies, **Michael Garrett** Deals with events in the 1970s, including Watergate, the fall of Saigon, and skateboards. (Steck-Vaughn, 1990)

Charlie Pippin, **Candy Dawson Boyd** A student struggles to understand her father by finding out all she can about the Vietnam War and how fighting in it changed his life. (Puffin Books, 1988)

A Place Called Heartbreak: A Story of Vietnam, **Walter Dean Myers** A novel about a young Air Force pilot who is shot down over North Vietnam in 1965. (Raintree/Steck-Vaughn Publishers, 1992)

Websites

www.nixonlibrary.org

www.vietvet.org

www.vvmf.org

www.washingtonpost.com/wp-srv/national/longterm/watergate

www.womeninworldhistory.com

UNIT 10

The Eighties, **Edward Grey** Focuses on youth culture and political events of the 1980s. (Raintree/Steck-Vaughn Publishers, 1990)

Ronald Reagan, **Karen Judson** The life of the 40th President, from his birth in Illinois, to his days as an actor, through his activities in public office. (Enslow Publishers, 1997)

Album of Spaceflight, **Tom McGowen** Discusses the history of spaceflight, from the first rockets and satellites to projections for the future. (Rand McNally, 1983)

Seeing Earth from Space, **Patricia Luber** Demonstrates the way space photography has changed the way we view Earth. There are pictures of mountains, rivers, and land formations taken from space. (Orchard Books, 1990)

To Space and Back, **Sally Ride** Written to help answer some of the questions students have about astronauts on a space shuttle and the conditions astronauts face in space. (Lothrop, Lee & Shepard, 1986)

Adventures in Your National Parks, **edited by Donald J. Crump** Shows people taking part in park activities, such as exploring in Yosemite and biking along Cape Cod. It also explains how national parks help preserve the country's natural beauty. (National Geographic Society, 1988)

Bill Clinton: United States President, **Michael Dole** Looks at the life and times of Bill Clinton, from his boyhood in Arkansas to his inauguration as President of the United States. (Enslow Publishers, 1994)

The Gulf War, **Dr. John King** Describes the war and how the United States became involved. (Macmillan Publishing Company, 1991)

The Clinton Years: The Photographs of Robert McNeely, **Robert McNeely** The official White House photographer from 1993 to 1998, McNeely offers 200 of his best candid photographs with brief captions. (Callaway Editions, Inc., 2000)

Celebrate America in Poetry and Art, **Nora Panzer** A celebration of American life and history through American poetry, with corresponding illustrations from the collection of the National Museum of American Art. (Hyperion Books for Children, 1994)

L5: Behind the Moon, **Steve Tracy** The story of a group of people residing in the year 2060 in a huge satellite colony that orbits the earth and the moon. (Silver Burdett Press, 1995)

Contemporary Issues in the Environment, **Patricia D. Netzley** Examines government policies dealing with the environment. (Lucent Books, 1998)

The Day That Was Different: September 11, 2001: When Terrorists Attacked America, **Carole Marsh** Factual, sensitive information written for students about the events of September 11, 2001. (Gallopade Publishing Group, 2001)

Websites

www.pbs.org/wgbh/pages/frontline/gulf

www.reaganfoundation.org

www.sierraclub.org/global-warming

www.whitehouse.gov

www.worldgame.org/recall/energy.html

www.clintonpresidentialcenter.com

www.cnn.com

www.census.gov

www.georgebushfoundation.org

Activity Index

Use the index to find individual and group activities.

INDIVIDUAL ACTIVITIES

Booklets/Displays
Advertisements 85, 227
Booklet 174
Bulletin-board display 210
Designing a stamp 206
Museum display 84
Poster 108
Protest sign 196
Time capsules 53, 158

Charts/Outlines
Creating a chart 26, 100, 120, 175, 182, 191, 225
Creating an outline 161, 205
Creating a timeline 64, 68, 87, 169, 213

Presentations
Dialogue 151
Interviews 61, 218, 235
News broadcast 166
Reports 18, 198, 204
Speeches 91, 101
Television documentary 136

Writing
Articles
  magazine 99
  news 11, 24, 168
Biography 190
Cause-and-effect statements 199, 212, 233
Comparing and contrasting 188
Crossword puzzle 167
Diary entries 17, 40
Editorials 20, 107
Essay 106
Facts 13, 152
Journal entries 5, 10, 12, 25, 26, 32, 35, 54, 56, 69, 78, 98, 132, 176
Letters 3, 34, 54, 63, 70, 100, 159, 206
Lists 129, 181, 191
Newspaper headline 113
Paragraphs 4, 11, 18, 19, 33, 41, 70, 77, 92, 109
Poems 78, 116, 137
Proposal 227
Songs 46, 143
Statement 114
Stories 76, 232
Survey 203
True/false questions 6, 13, 62, 153, 177

GROUP ACTIVITIES

Booklets/Displays
Advertisements 129, 177
Bulletin-board display 218
Designing a memorial 205
Documentary films 42, 176, 198
Inventions 41
Map making 48, 158
Pamphlets 18, 68, 124, 198
Posters 54, 132, 191
Storyboards 56, 131, 143, 153, 160, 162
Time capsule 206

Charts/Outlines
Creating a chart 32, 43, 106, 213
Creating an outline 174
Creating a timeline 232

Presentations
Broadcasts 124, 145, 159
Campaigns 108, 139, 225
Closing argument 182
Debates 34, 72, 94, 117, 144, 154, 168, 203, 220
Panel discussions 27, 61, 76, 190
Presentations 4, 25, 41, 98, 137
Quiz games 151, 168, 235
Role-plays 10, 20, 26, 27, 64, 91, 93, 100
Skits 6, 19, 77, 136
TV news segments 184, 204, 211, 234

Writing
Articles
  magazines 84, 121, 131, 166
  news 11, 46, 114, 183, 196, 226
Biographies 12, 63, 181, 190
Comparing and contrasting 199, 221
Diary entry 78
Editorial 113
Help-wanted ad 87
Journal entries 63, 71
Laws 13, 101
Letters 5, 70, 92, 210
Lists 109, 139, 227
Newspaper headline 188
Play 212
Poems 3, 228
Position statements 79, 146
Presidential memo 220
Questionnaires 169, 176
Short papers 100, 116
Speeches 108, 233
Story 86
Travel plans 49